SALT WATER TAFFY

THE SEASIDE

JACK

∾ IN ∾

CALDERA'S REVENGE

PART 1

Oni Press, Inc.
publisher, Joe Nozemack
editor in chief, James Lucas Jones
marketing director, Cory Casoni
art director, Keith Wood
operations director, George Rohac
editor, Jill Beaton
editor, Charlie Chu
production assistant, Douglas E. Sherwood

1305 SE Martin Luther King Jr. Blvd.
Suite A
Portland, OR 97214

www.onipress.com

First Edition: April 2011
978-1-934964-62-0

1 3 5 7 9 10 8 6 4 2

Printed in U.S.A.

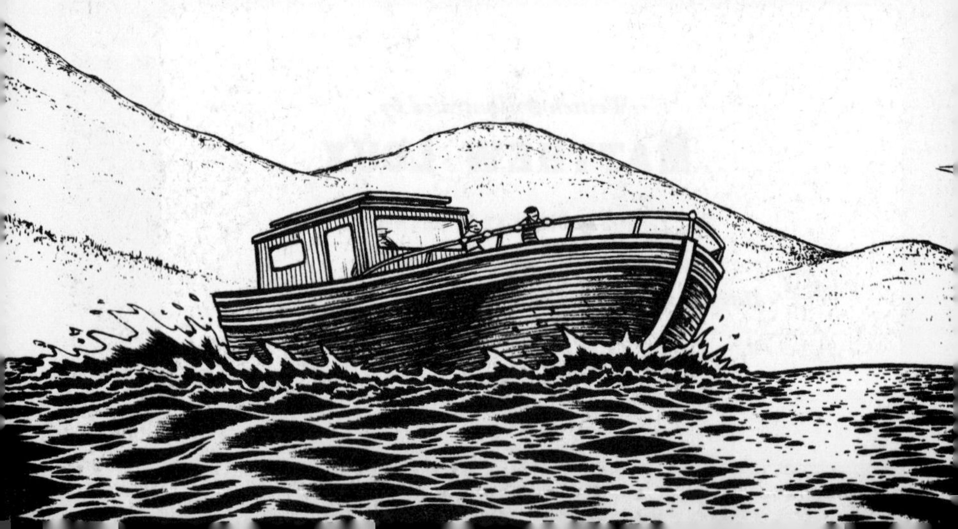

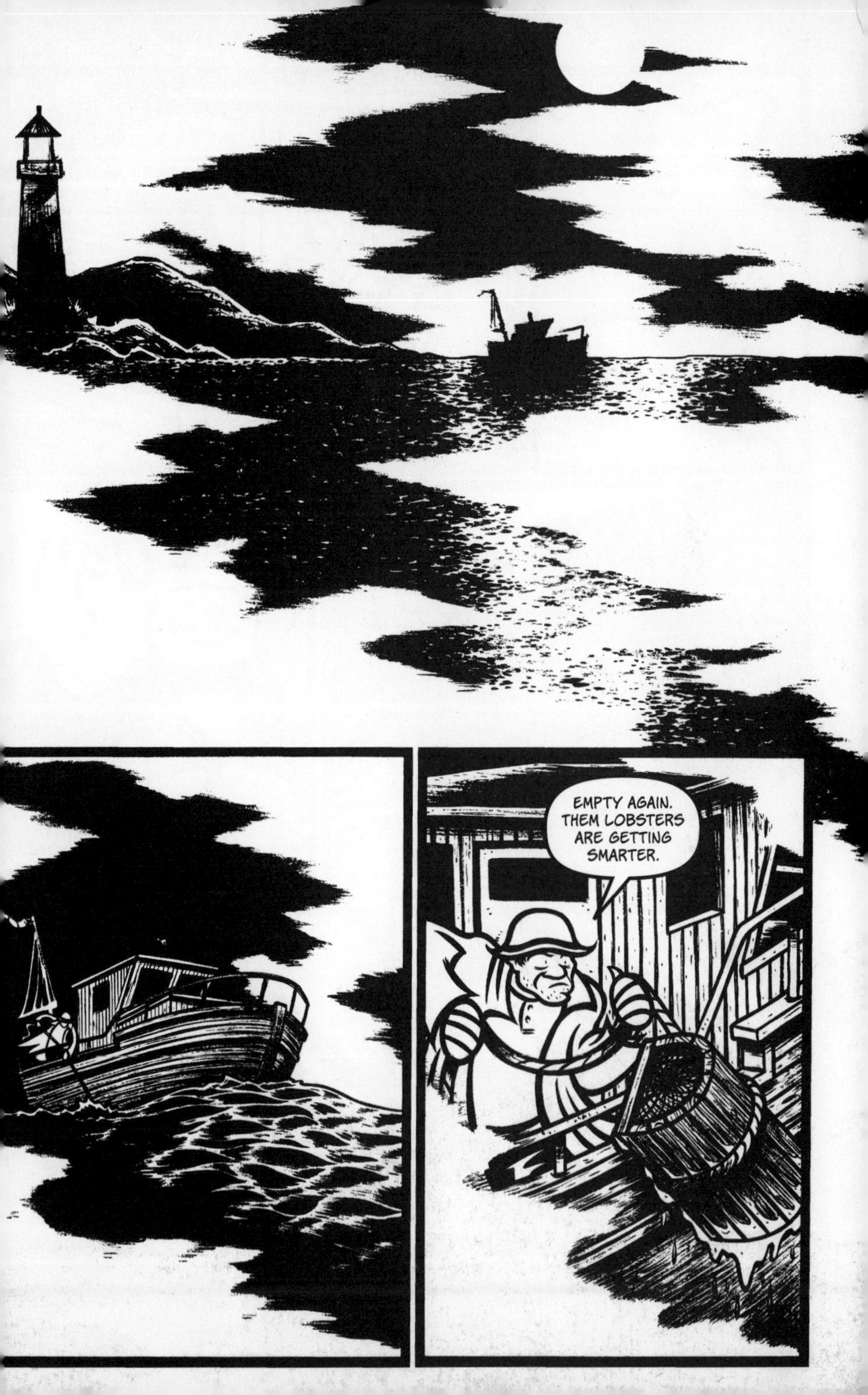
EMPTY AGAIN. THEM LOBSTERS ARE GETTING SMARTER.

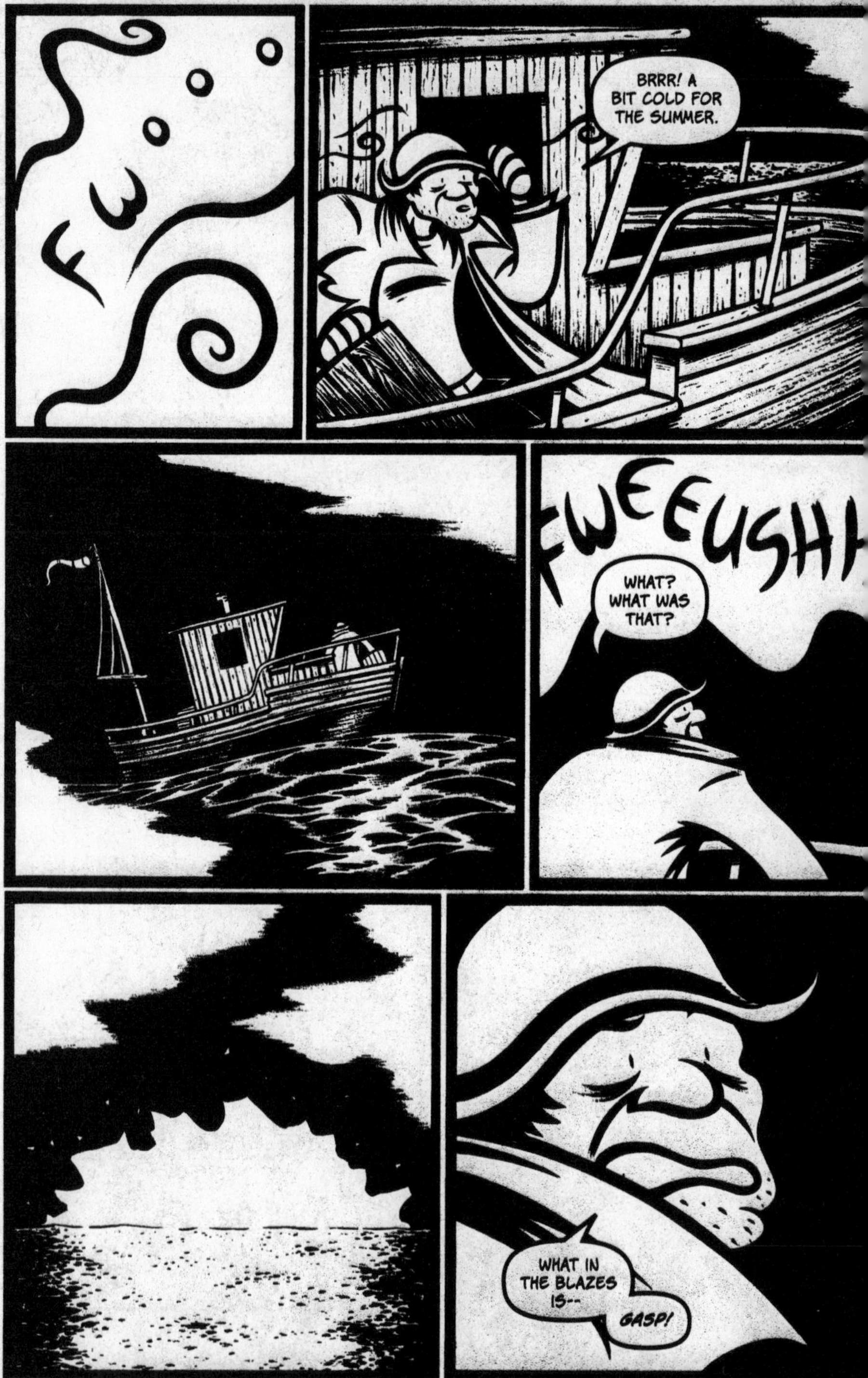
FWOOO
BRRR! A BIT COLD FOR THE SUMMER.
FWEEUSH
WHAT? WHAT WAS THAT?
WHAT IN THE BLAZES IS--
GASP!

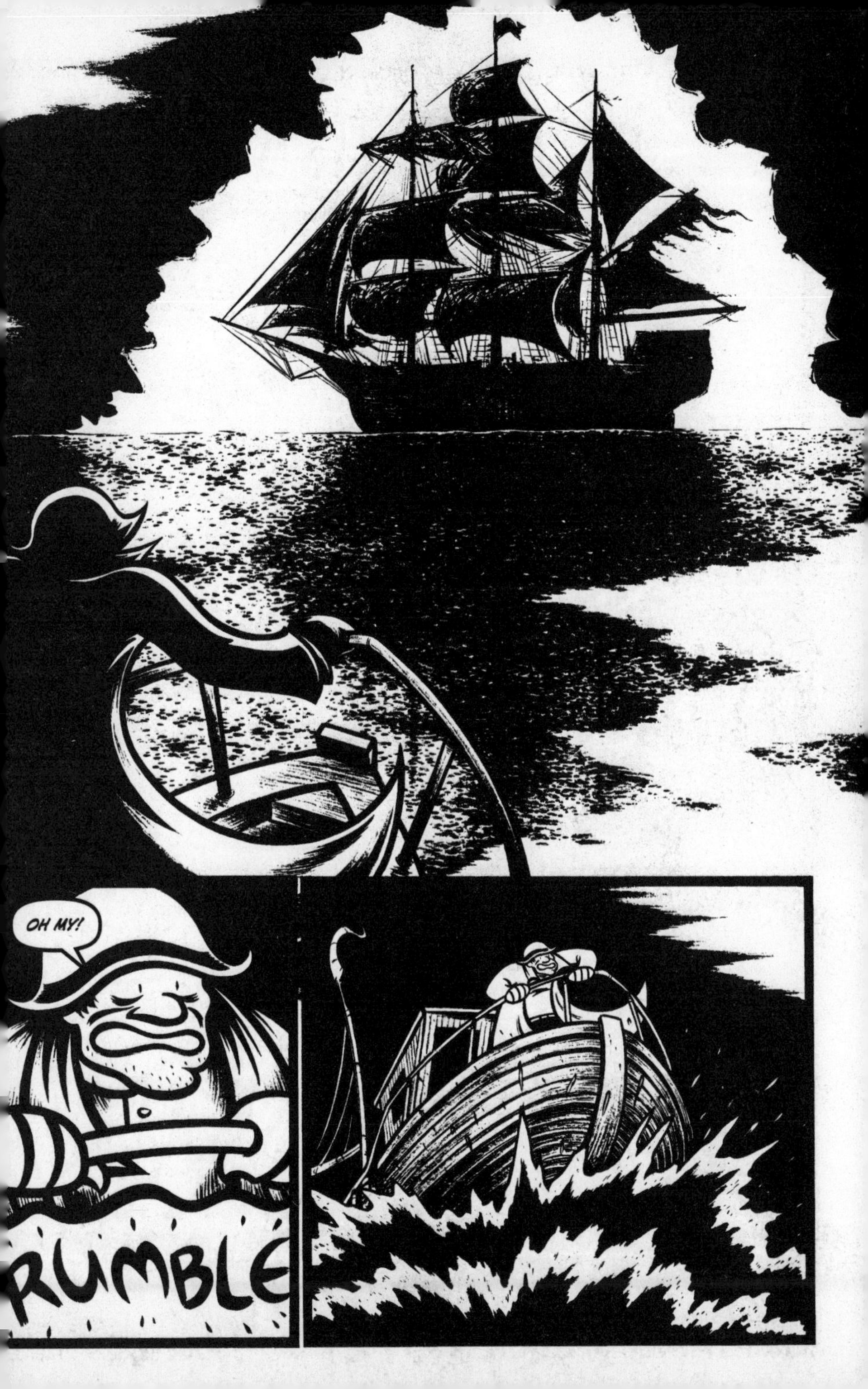
OH MY!
RUMBLE

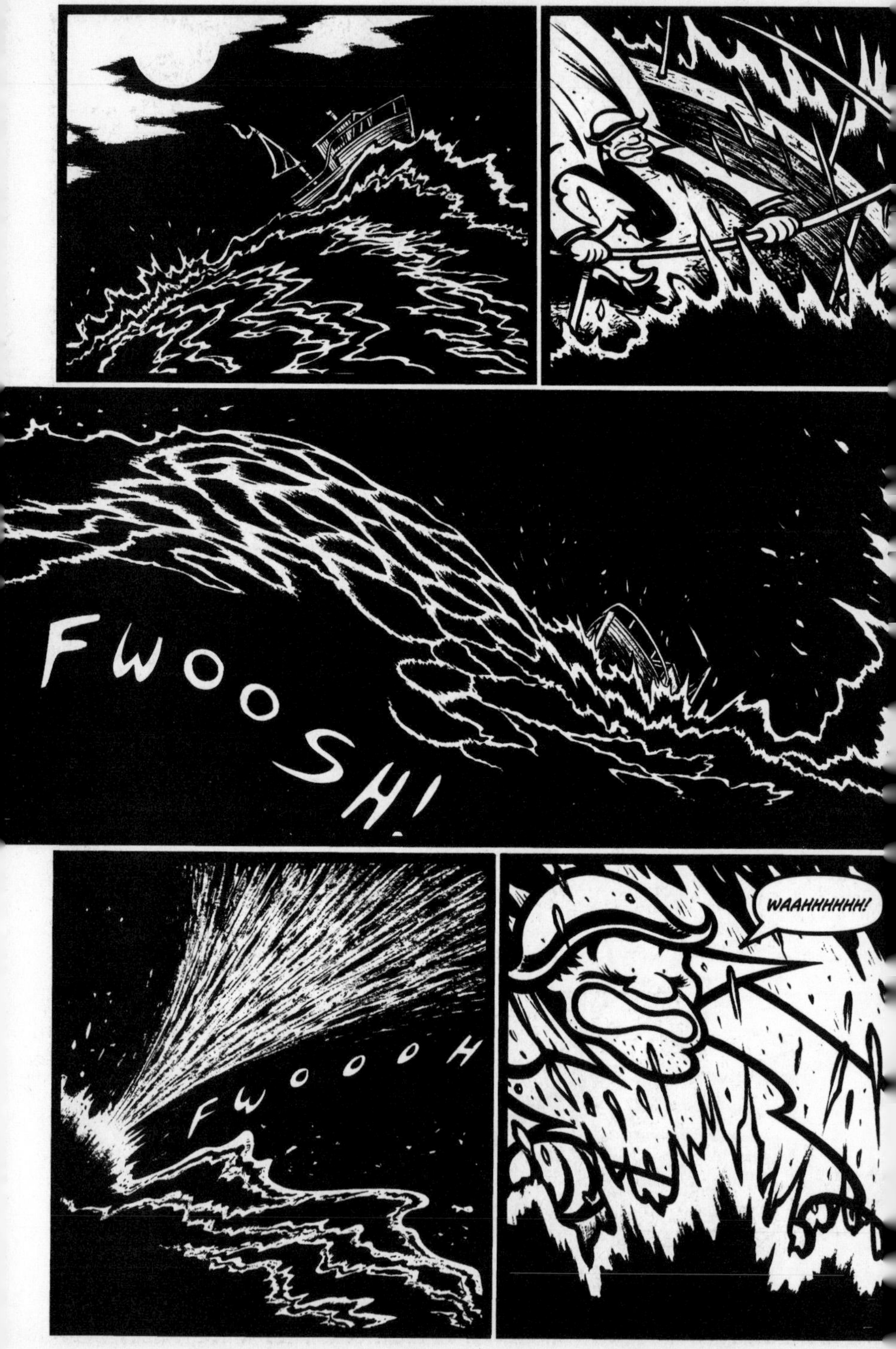
FWOOSH!
FWOOOOH
WAAHHHHHH!

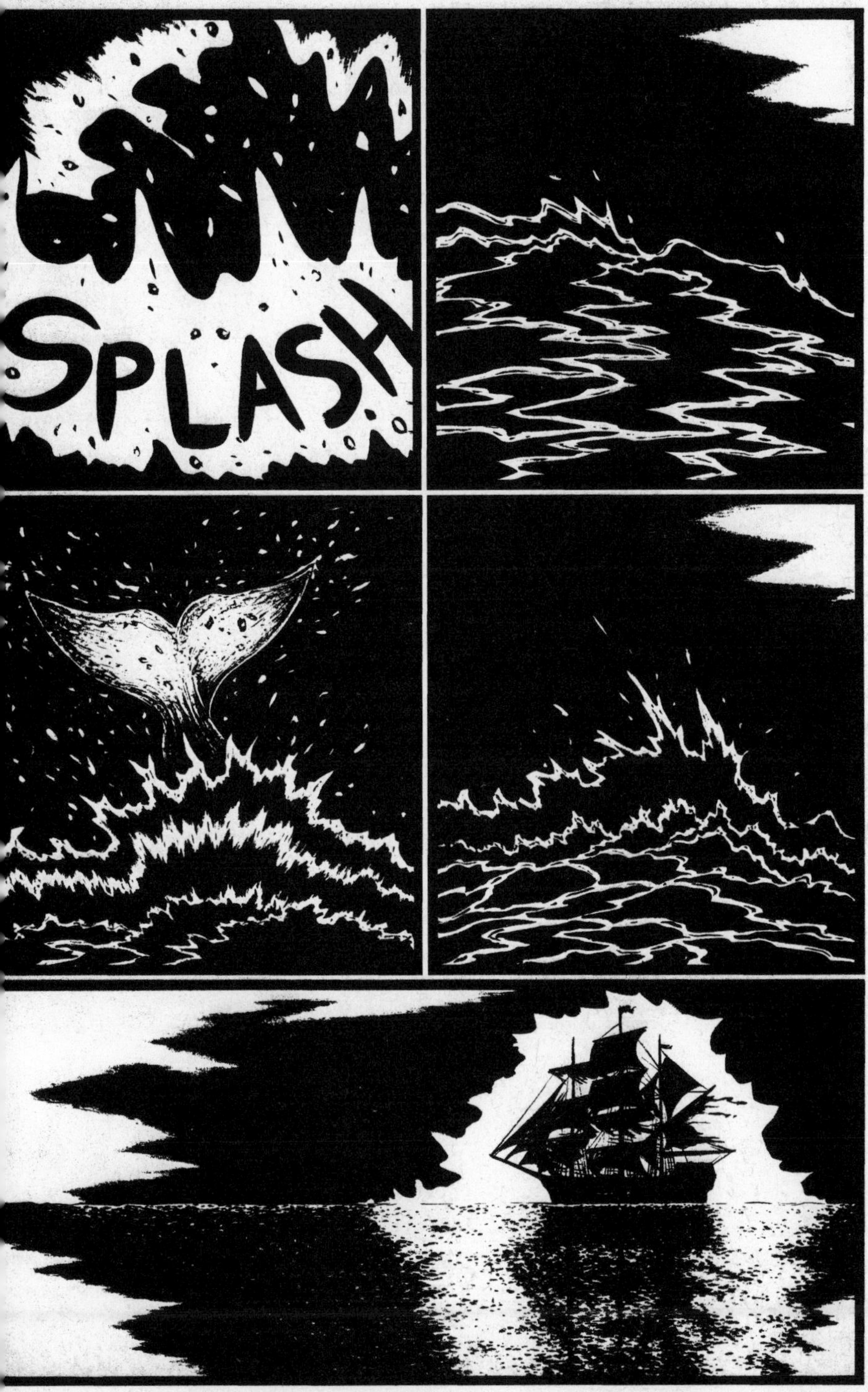
SPLASH

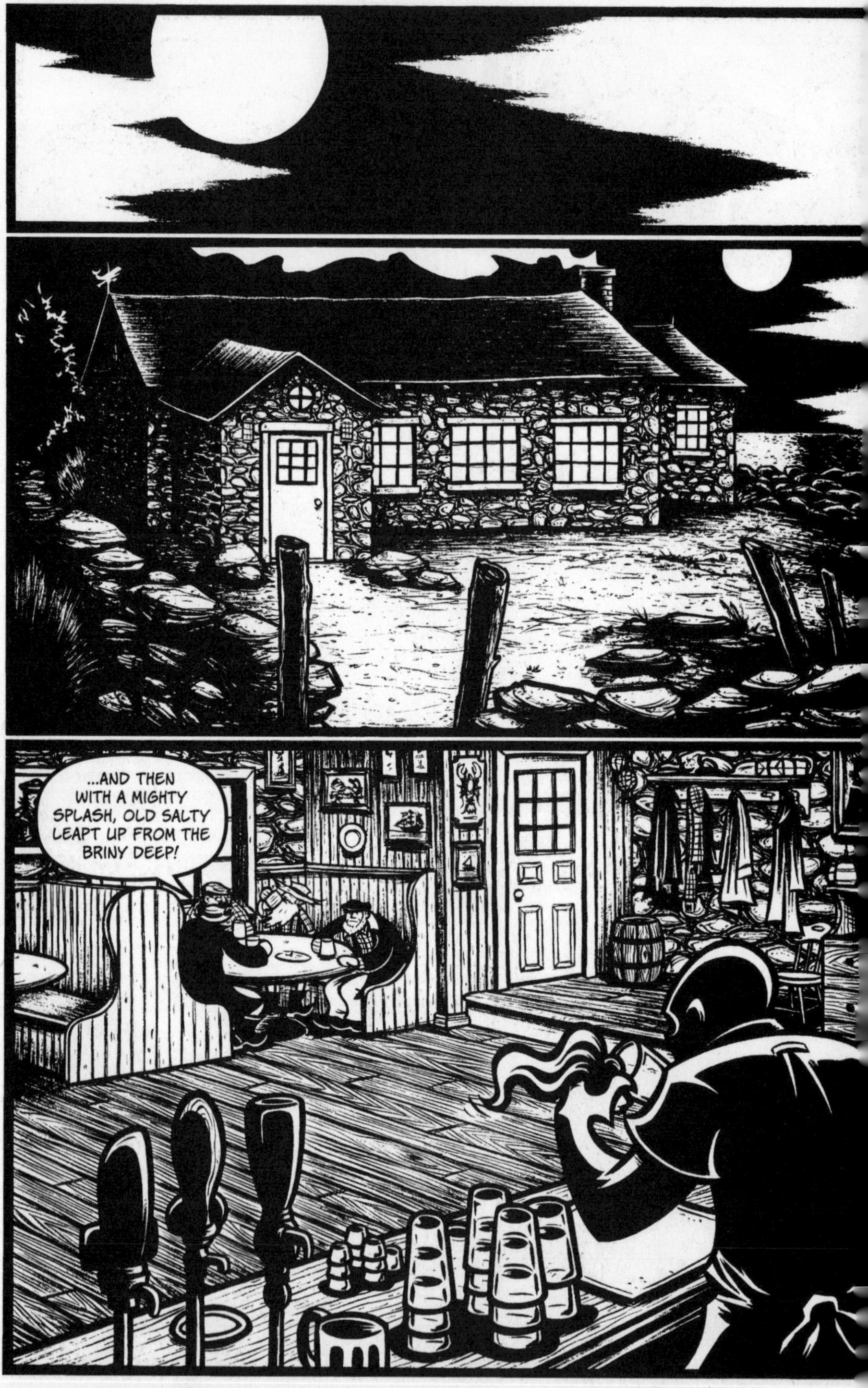
...AND THEN WITH A MIGHTY SPLASH, OLD SALTY LEAPT UP FROM THE BRINY DEEP!

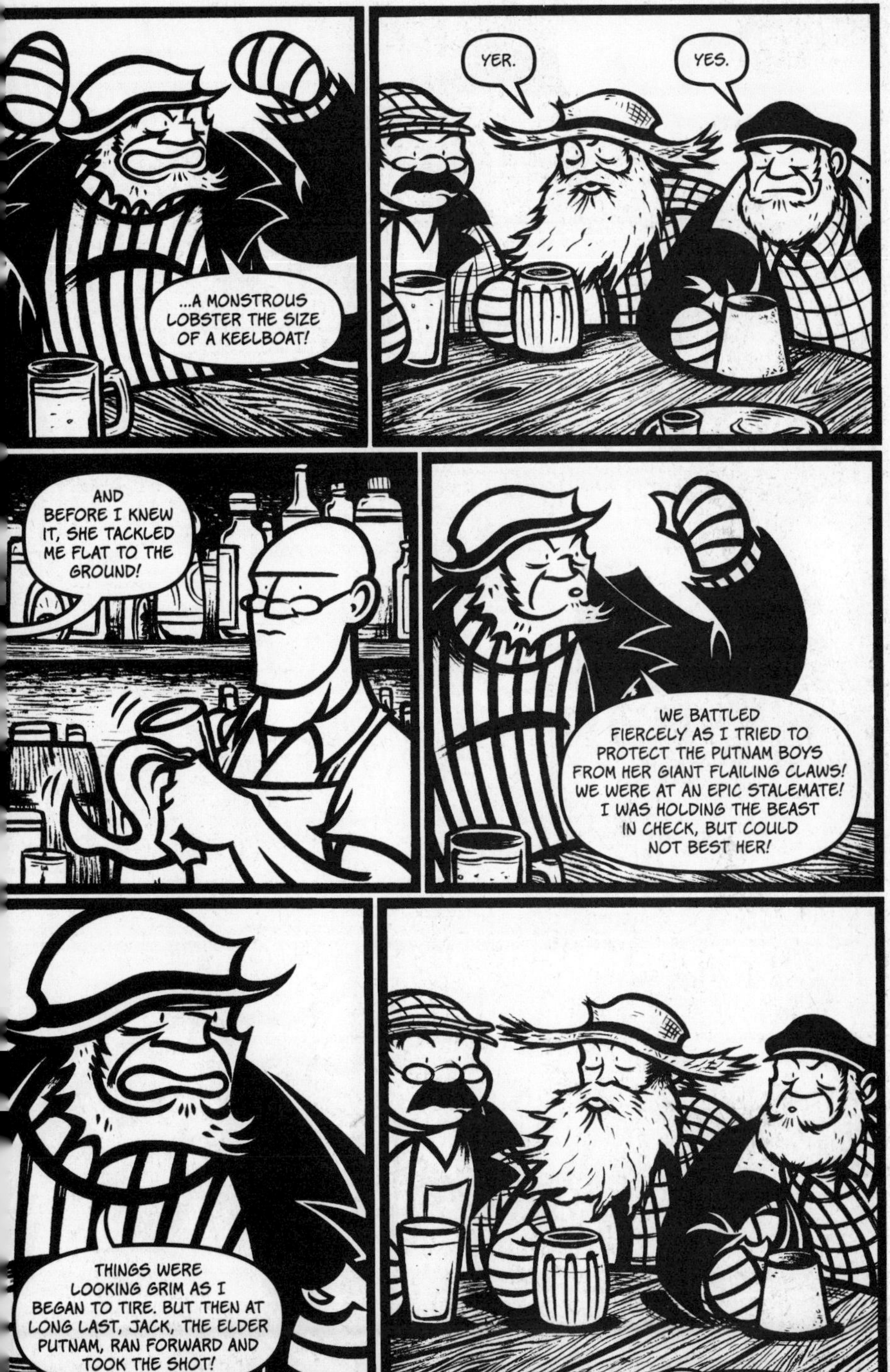
...A MONSTROUS LOBSTER THE SIZE OF A KEELBOAT!
YER.
YES.
AND BEFORE I KNEW IT, SHE TACKLED ME FLAT TO THE GROUND!
WE BATTLED FIERCELY AS I TRIED TO PROTECT THE PUTNAM BOYS FROM HER GIANT FLAILING CLAWS! WE WERE AT AN EPIC STALEMATE! I WAS HOLDING THE BEAST IN CHECK, BUT COULD NOT BEST HER!
THINGS WERE LOOKING GRIM AS I BEGAN TO TIRE. BUT THEN AT LONG LAST, JACK, THE ELDER PUTNAM, RAN FORWARD AND TOOK THE SHOT!

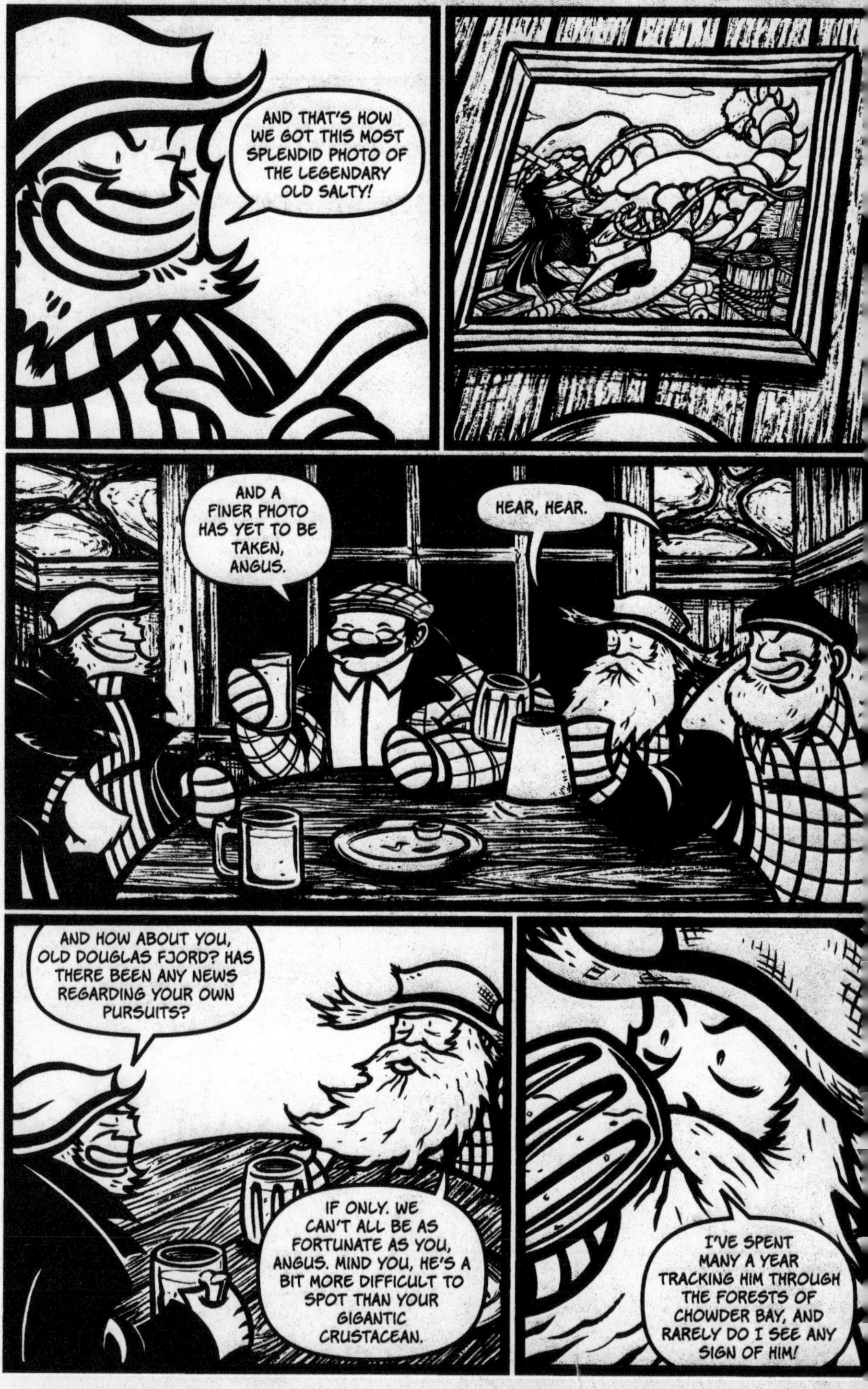
AND THAT'S HOW WE GOT THIS MOST SPLENDID PHOTO OF THE LEGENDARY OLD SALTY!
AND A FINER PHOTO HAS YET TO BE TAKEN, ANGUS.
HEAR, HEAR.
AND HOW ABOUT YOU, OLD DOUGLAS FJORD? HAS THERE BEEN ANY NEWS REGARDING YOUR OWN PURSUITS?
IF ONLY. WE CAN'T ALL BE AS FORTUNATE AS YOU, ANGUS. MIND YOU, HE'S A BIT MORE DIFFICULT TO SPOT THAN YOUR GIGANTIC CRUSTACEAN.
I'VE SPENT MANY A YEAR TRACKING HIM THROUGH THE FORESTS OF CHOWDER BAY, AND RARELY DO I SEE ANY SIGN OF HIM!

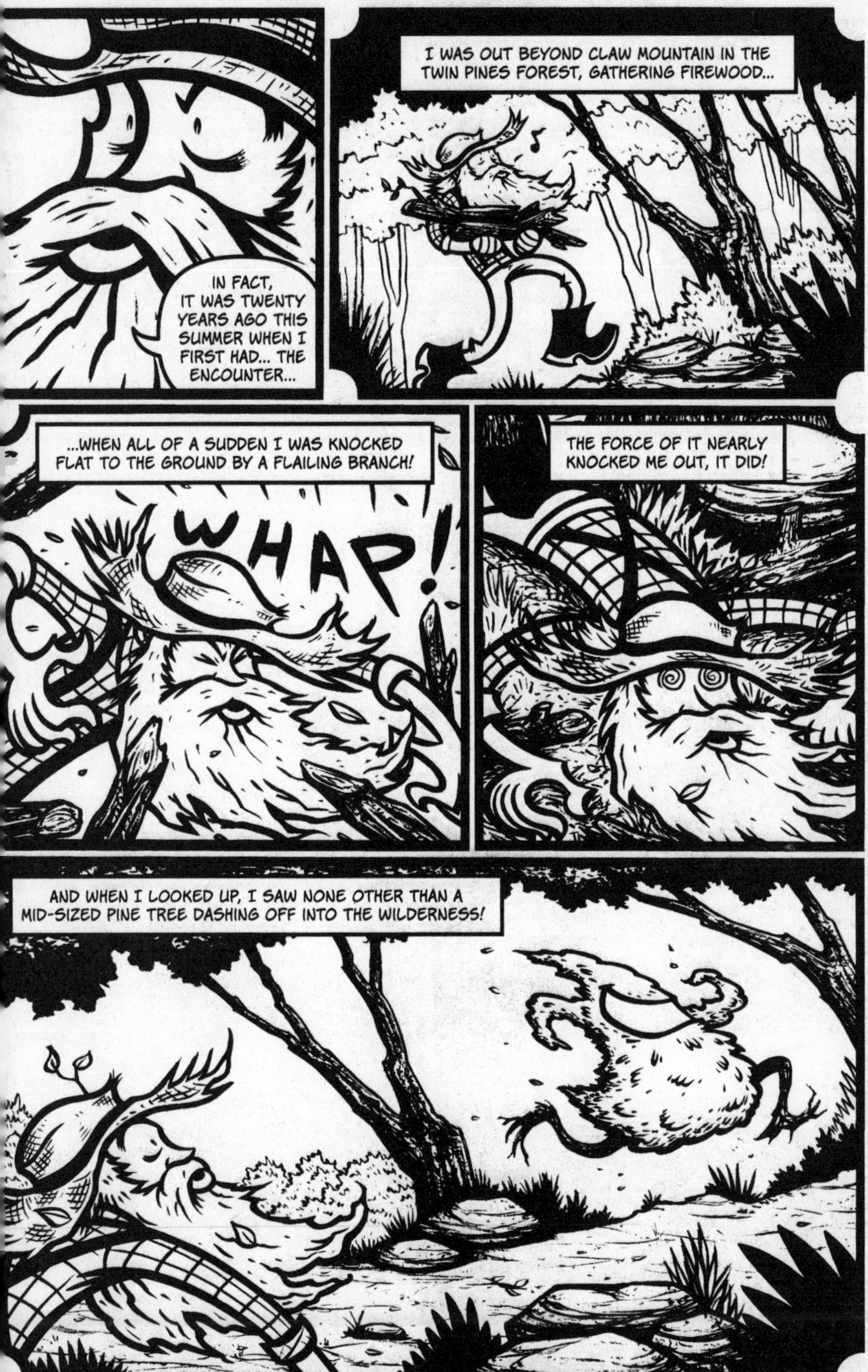
IN FACT, IT WAS TWENTY YEARS AGO THIS SUMMER WHEN I FIRST HAD... THE ENCOUNTER...
I WAS OUT BEYOND CLAW MOUNTAIN IN THE TWIN PINES FOREST, GATHERING FIREWOOD...
...WHEN ALL OF A SUDDEN I WAS KNOCKED FLAT TO THE GROUND BY A FLAILING BRANCH!
WHAP!
THE FORCE OF IT NEARLY KNOCKED ME OUT, IT DID!
AND WHEN I LOOKED UP, I SAW NONE OTHER THAN A MID-SIZED PINE TREE DASHING OFF INTO THE WILDERNESS!

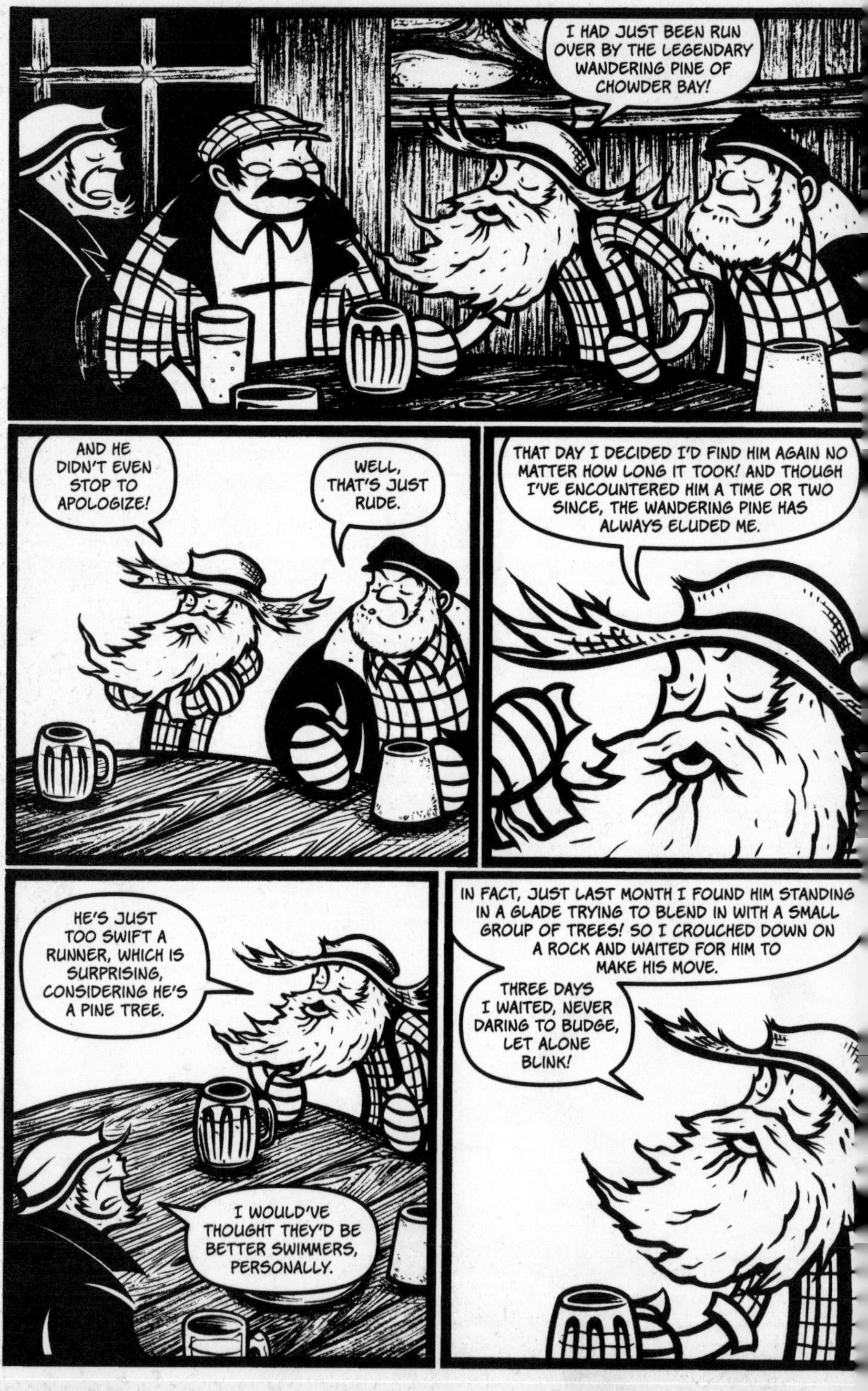
I HAD JUST BEEN RUN OVER BY THE LEGENDARY WANDERING PINE OF CHOWDER BAY!
AND HE DIDN'T EVEN STOP TO APOLOGIZE!
WELL, THAT'S JUST RUDE.
THAT DAY I DECIDED I'D FIND HIM AGAIN NO MATTER HOW LONG IT TOOK! AND THOUGH I'VE ENCOUNTERED HIM A TIME OR TWO SINCE, THE WANDERING PINE HAS ALWAYS ELUDED ME.
HE'S JUST TOO SWIFT A RUNNER, WHICH IS SURPRISING, CONSIDERING HE'S A PINE TREE.
I WOULD'VE THOUGHT THEY'D BE BETTER SWIMMERS, PERSONALLY.
IN FACT, JUST LAST MONTH I FOUND HIM STANDING IN A GLADE TRYING TO BLEND IN WITH A SMALL GROUP OF TREES! SO I CROUCHED DOWN ON A ROCK AND WAITED FOR HIM TO MAKE HIS MOVE.
THREE DAYS I WAITED, NEVER DARING TO BUDGE, LET ALONE BLINK!

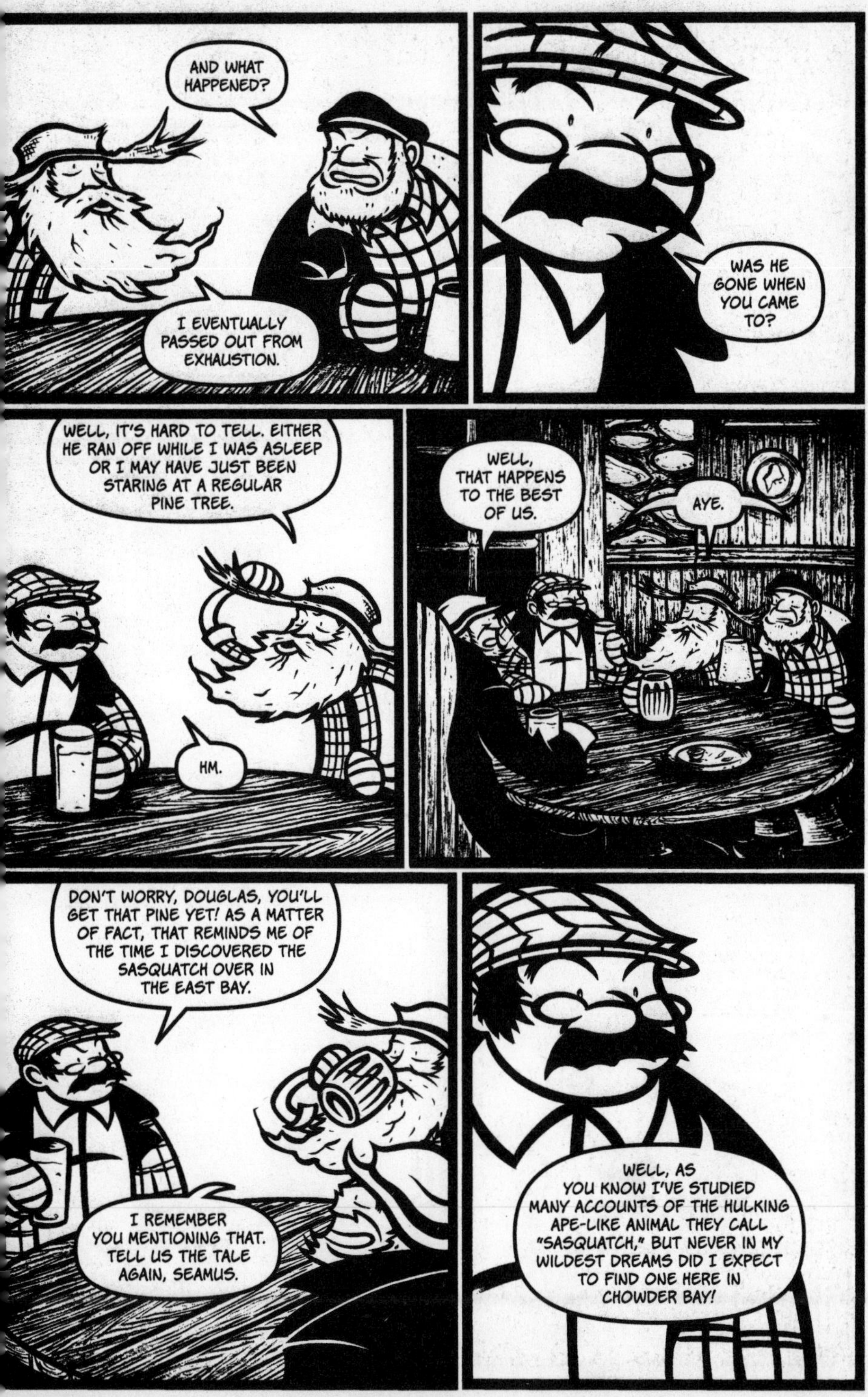
AND WHAT HAPPENED?
I EVENTUALLY PASSED OUT FROM EXHAUSTION.
WAS HE GONE WHEN YOU CAME TO?
WELL, IT'S HARD TO TELL. EITHER HE RAN OFF WHILE I WAS ASLEEP OR I MAY HAVE JUST BEEN STARING AT A REGULAR PINE TREE.
HM.
WELL, THAT HAPPENS TO THE BEST OF US.
AYE.
DON'T WORRY, DOUGLAS, YOU'LL GET THAT PINE YET! AS A MATTER OF FACT, THAT REMINDS ME OF THE TIME I DISCOVERED THE SASQUATCH OVER IN THE EAST BAY.
I REMEMBER YOU MENTIONING THAT. TELL US THE TALE AGAIN, SEAMUS.
WELL, AS YOU KNOW I'VE STUDIED MANY ACCOUNTS OF THE HULKING APE-LIKE ANIMAL THEY CALL "SASQUATCH," BUT NEVER IN MY WILDEST DREAMS DID I EXPECT TO FIND ONE HERE IN CHOWDER BAY!

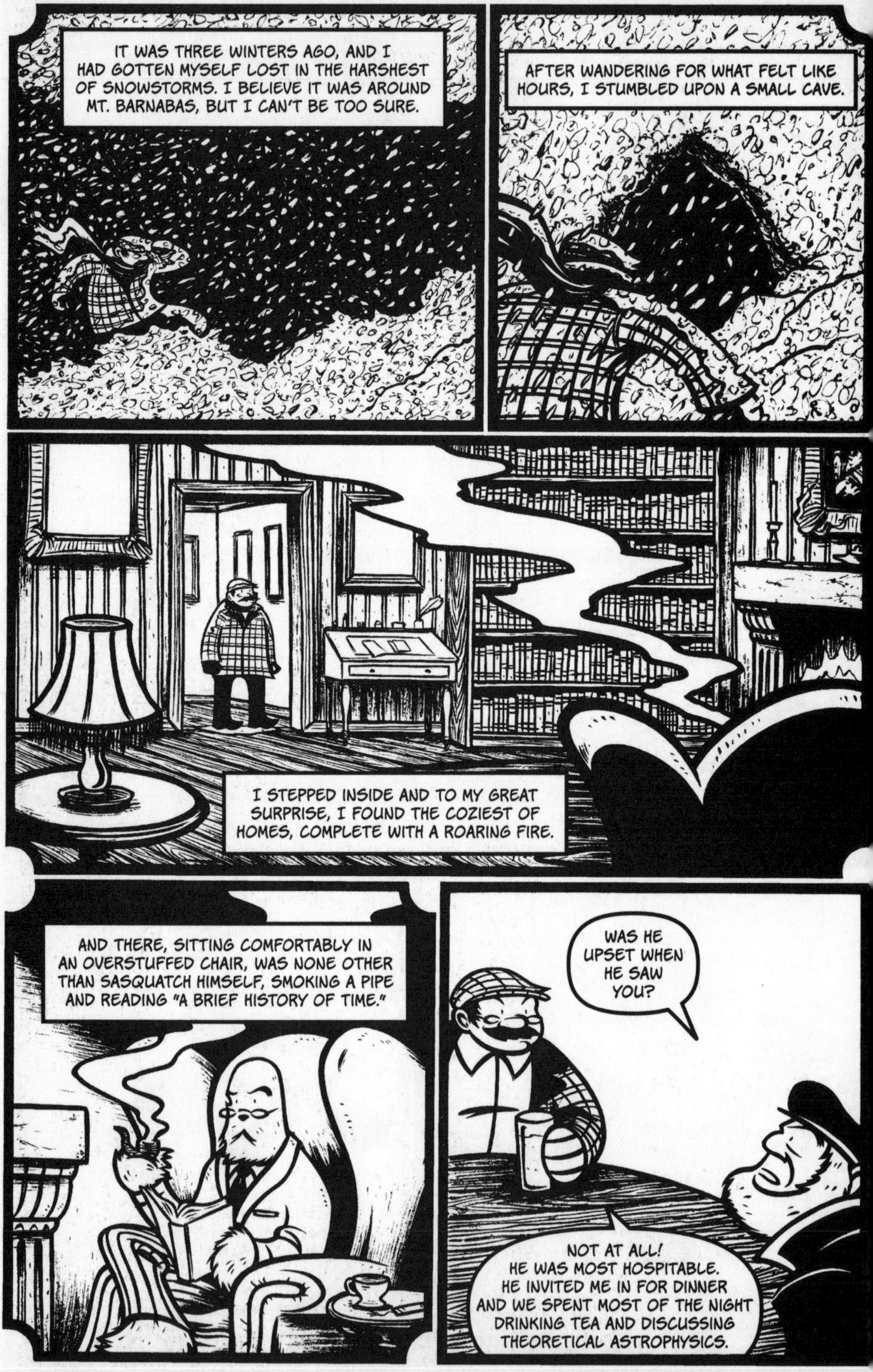
IT WAS THREE WINTERS AGO, AND I HAD GOTTEN MYSELF LOST IN THE HARSHEST OF SNOWSTORMS. I BELIEVE IT WAS AROUND MT. BARNABAS, BUT I CAN'T BE TOO SURE.
AFTER WANDERING FOR WHAT FELT LIKE HOURS, I STUMBLED UPON A SMALL CAVE.
I STEPPED INSIDE AND TO MY GREAT SURPRISE, I FOUND THE COZIEST OF HOMES, COMPLETE WITH A ROARING FIRE.
AND THERE, SITTING COMFORTABLY IN AN OVERSTUFFED CHAIR, WAS NONE OTHER THAN SASQUATCH HIMSELF, SMOKING A PIPE AND READING "A BRIEF HISTORY OF TIME."
WAS HE UPSET WHEN HE SAW YOU?
NOT AT ALL! HE WAS MOST HOSPITABLE. HE INVITED ME IN FOR DINNER AND WE SPENT MOST OF THE NIGHT DRINKING TEA AND DISCUSSING THEORETICAL ASTROPHYSICS.

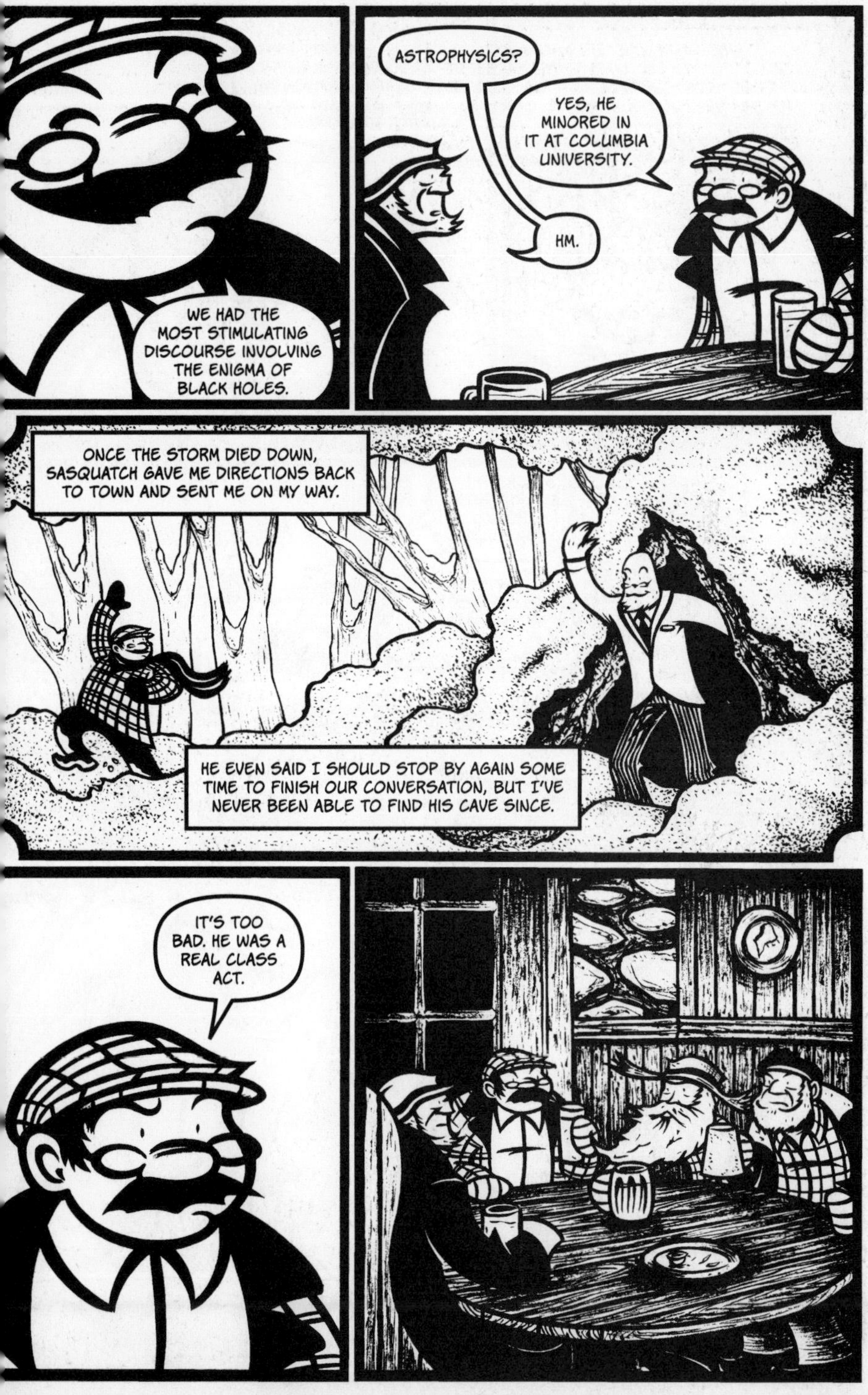
WE HAD THE MOST STIMULATING DISCOURSE INVOLVING THE ENIGMA OF BLACK HOLES.
ASTROPHYSICS?
YES, HE MINORED IN IT AT COLUMBIA UNIVERSITY.
HM.
ONCE THE STORM DIED DOWN, SASQUATCH GAVE ME DIRECTIONS BACK TO TOWN AND SENT ME ON MY WAY.
HE EVEN SAID I SHOULD STOP BY AGAIN SOME TIME TO FINISH OUR CONVERSATION, BUT I'VE NEVER BEEN ABLE TO FIND HIS CAVE SINCE.
IT'S TOO BAD. HE WAS A REAL CLASS ACT.

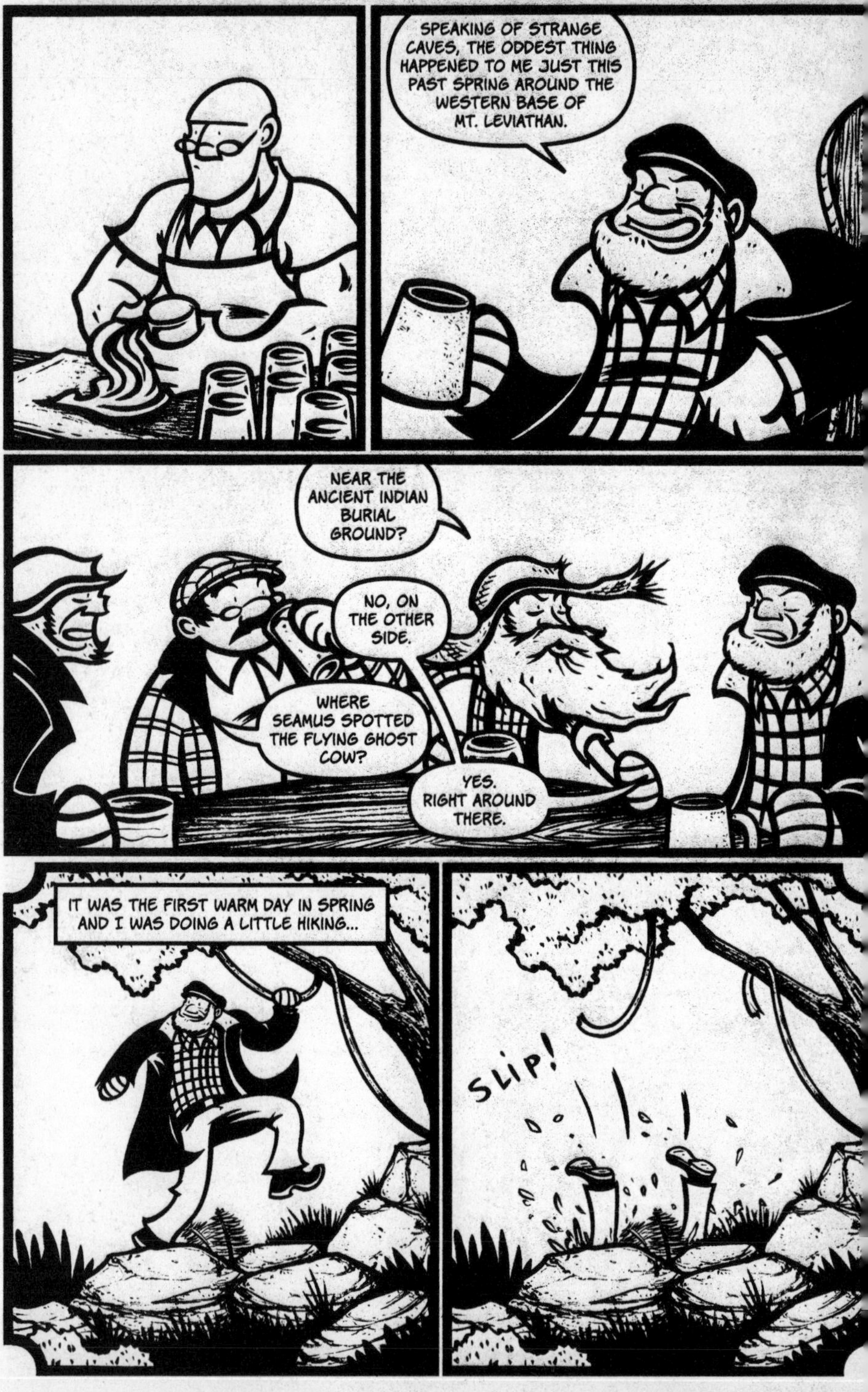
SPEAKING OF STRANGE CAVES, THE ODDEST THING HAPPENED TO ME JUST THIS PAST SPRING AROUND THE WESTERN BASE OF MT. LEVIATHAN.
NEAR THE ANCIENT INDIAN BURIAL GROUND?
NO, ON THE OTHER SIDE.
WHERE SEAMUS SPOTTED THE FLYING GHOST COW?
YES. RIGHT AROUND THERE.
IT WAS THE FIRST WARM DAY IN SPRING AND I WAS DOING A LITTLE HIKING...
SLIP!

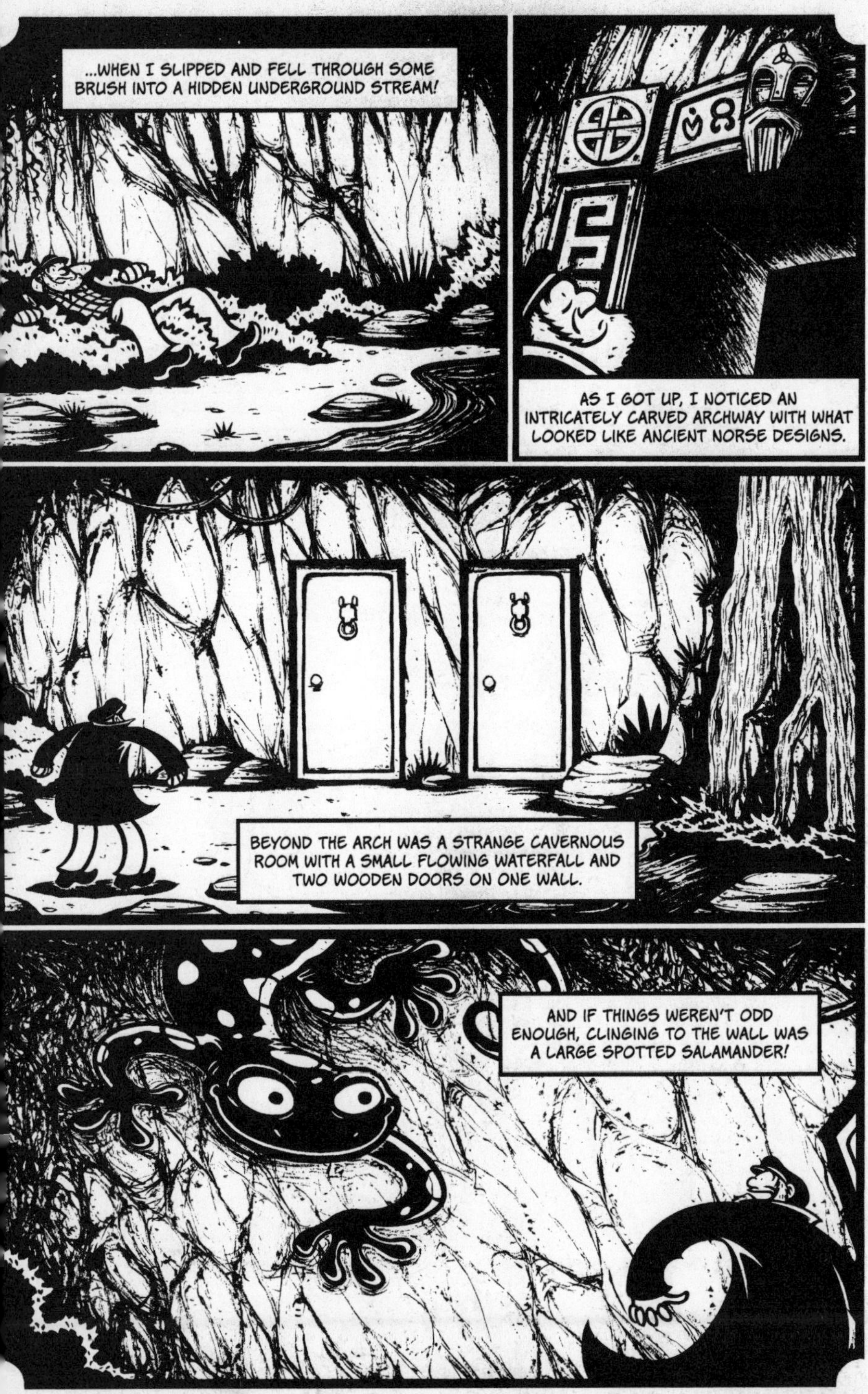
...WHEN I SLIPPED AND FELL THROUGH SOME BRUSH INTO A HIDDEN UNDERGROUND STREAM!
AS I GOT UP, I NOTICED AN INTRICATELY CARVED ARCHWAY WITH WHAT LOOKED LIKE ANCIENT NORSE DESIGNS.
BEYOND THE ARCH WAS A STRANGE CAVERNOUS ROOM WITH A SMALL FLOWING WATERFALL AND TWO WOODEN DOORS ON ONE WALL.
AND IF THINGS WEREN'T ODD ENOUGH, CLINGING TO THE WALL WAS A LARGE SPOTTED SALAMANDER!

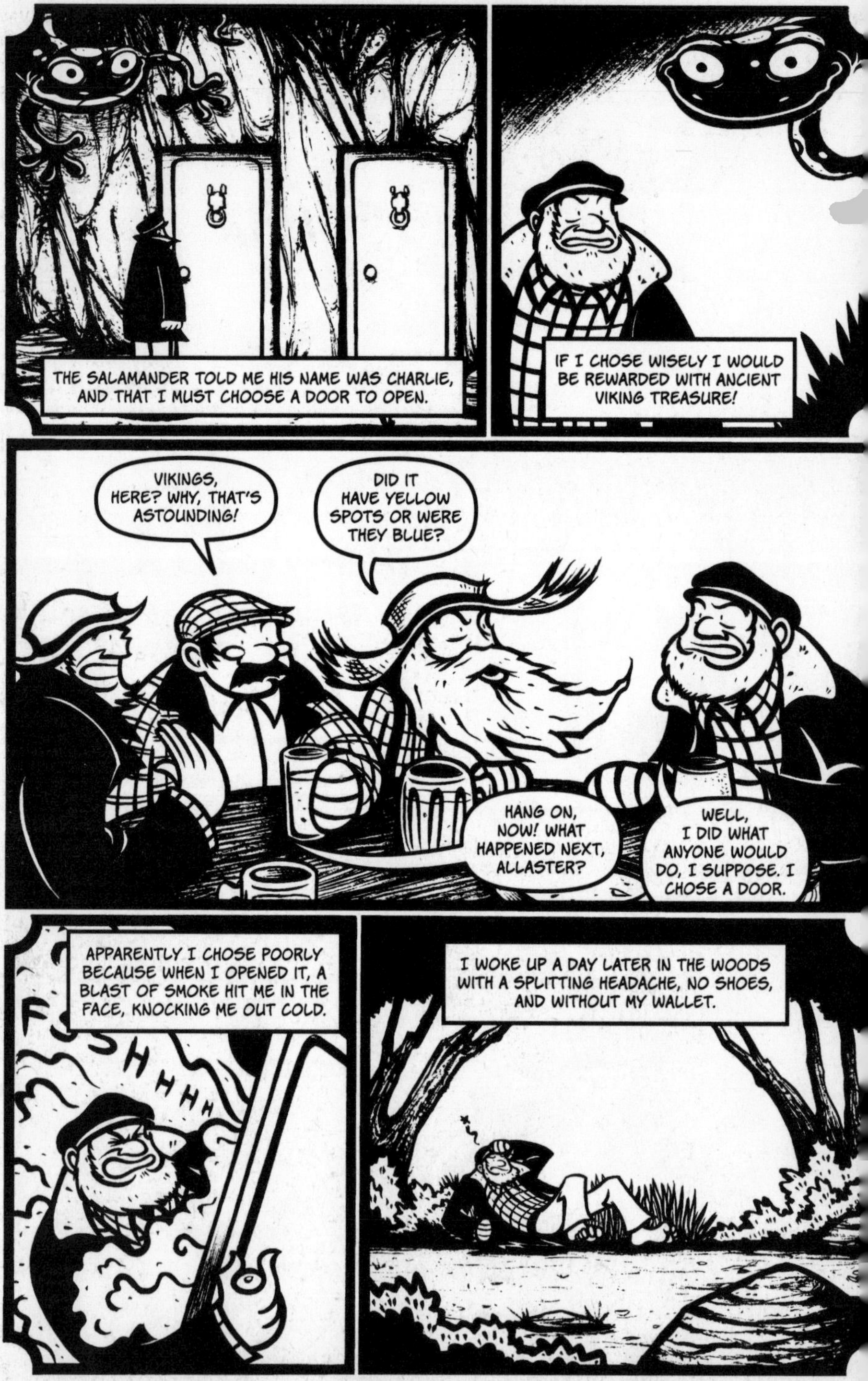
THE SALAMANDER TOLD ME HIS NAME WAS CHARLIE, AND THAT I MUST CHOOSE A DOOR TO OPEN.
IF I CHOSE WISELY I WOULD BE REWARDED WITH ANCIENT VIKING TREASURE!
VIKINGS, HERE? WHY, THAT'S ASTOUNDING!
DID IT HAVE YELLOW SPOTS OR WERE THEY BLUE?
HANG ON, NOW! WHAT HAPPENED NEXT, ALLASTER?
WELL, I DID WHAT ANYONE WOULD DO, I SUPPOSE. I CHOSE A DOOR.
APPARENTLY I CHOSE POORLY BECAUSE WHEN I OPENED IT, A BLAST OF SMOKE HIT ME IN THE FACE, KNOCKING ME OUT COLD.
FSSHHHHH
I WOKE UP A DAY LATER IN THE WOODS WITH A SPLITTING HEADACHE, NO SHOES, AND WITHOUT MY WALLET.

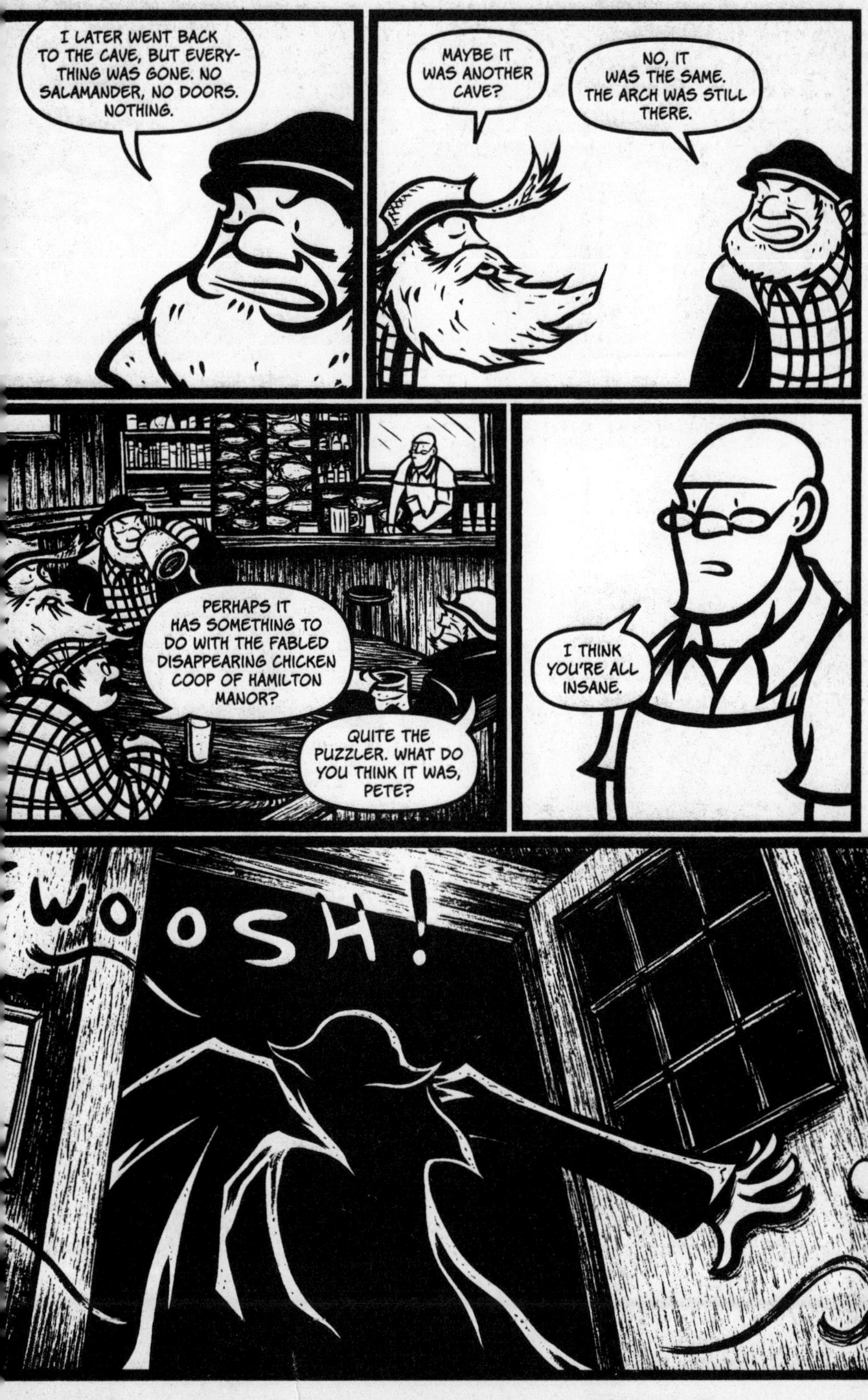
I LATER WENT BACK TO THE CAVE, BUT EVERY-THING WAS GONE. NO SALAMANDER, NO DOORS. NOTHING.
MAYBE IT WAS ANOTHER CAVE?
NO, IT WAS THE SAME. THE ARCH WAS STILL THERE.
PERHAPS IT HAS SOMETHING TO DO WITH THE FABLED DISAPPEARING CHICKEN COOP OF HAMILTON MANOR?
QUITE THE PUZZLER. WHAT DO YOU THINK IT WAS, PETE?
I THINK YOU'RE ALL INSANE.
WOOSH!

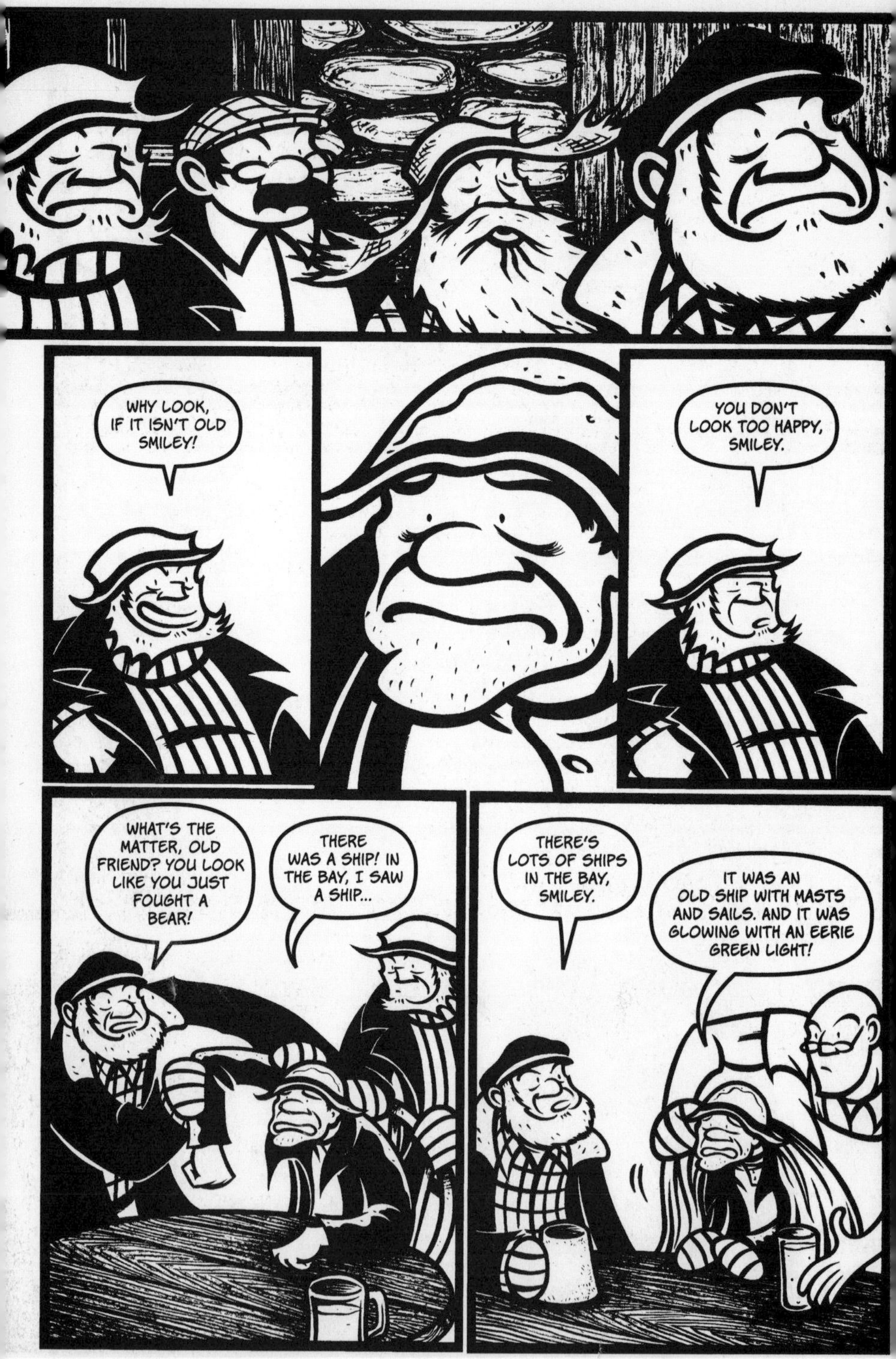
WHY LOOK, IF IT ISN'T OLD SMILEY!
YOU DON'T LOOK TOO HAPPY, SMILEY.
WHAT'S THE MATTER, OLD FRIEND? YOU LOOK LIKE YOU JUST FOUGHT A BEAR!
THERE WAS A SHIP! IN THE BAY, I SAW A SHIP...
THERE'S LOTS OF SHIPS IN THE BAY, SMILEY.
IT WAS AN OLD SHIP WITH MASTS AND SAILS. AND IT WAS GLOWING WITH AN EERIE GREEN LIGHT!

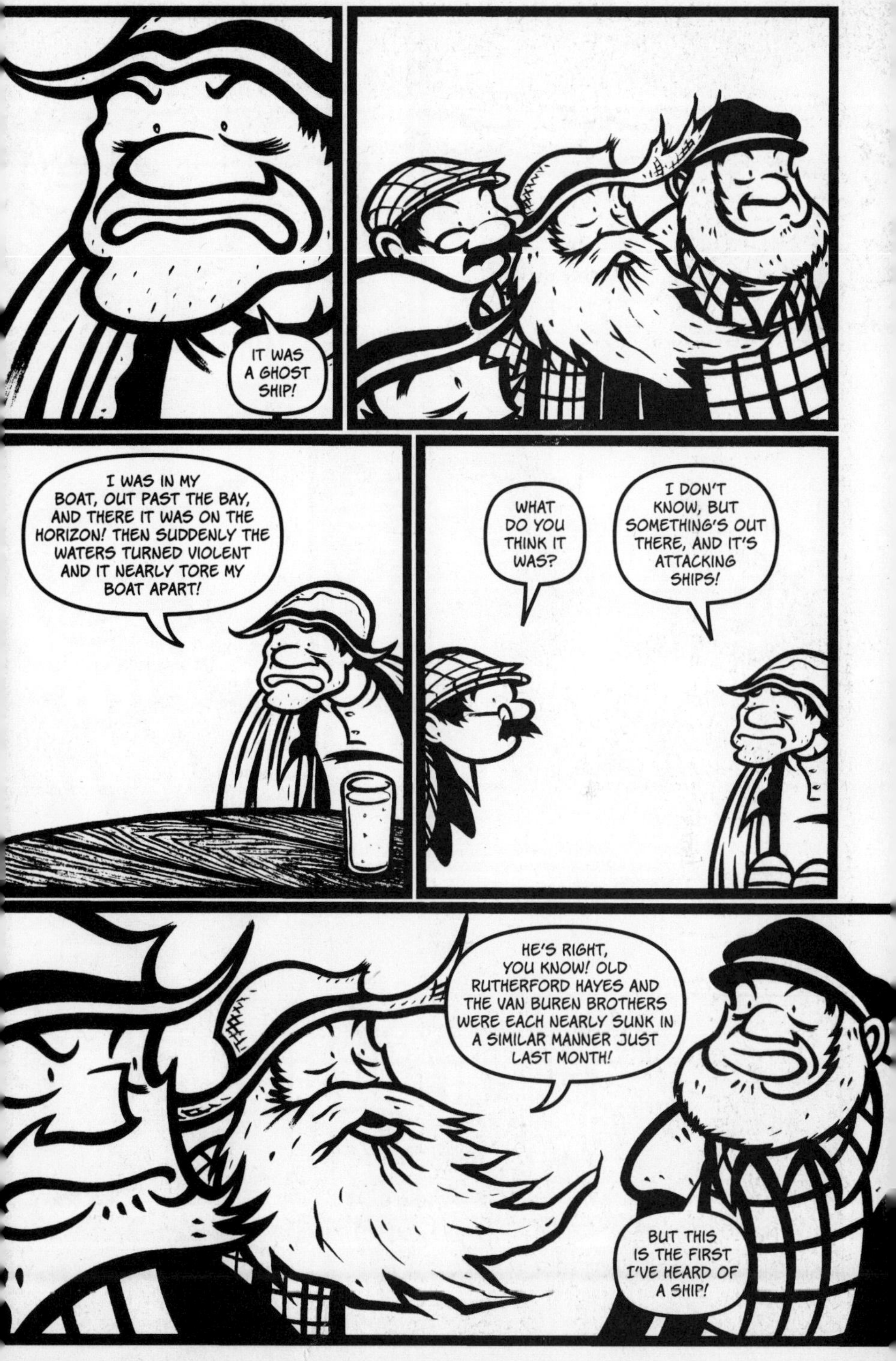
IT WAS A GHOST SHIP!
I WAS IN MY BOAT, OUT PAST THE BAY, AND THERE IT WAS ON THE HORIZON! THEN SUDDENLY THE WATERS TURNED VIOLENT AND IT NEARLY TORE MY BOAT APART!
WHAT DO YOU THINK IT WAS?
I DON'T KNOW, BUT SOMETHING'S OUT THERE, AND IT'S ATTACKING SHIPS!
HE'S RIGHT, YOU KNOW! OLD RUTHERFORD HAYES AND THE VAN BUREN BROTHERS WERE EACH NEARLY SUNK IN A SIMILAR MANNER JUST LAST MONTH!
BUT THIS IS THE FIRST I'VE HEARD OF A SHIP!

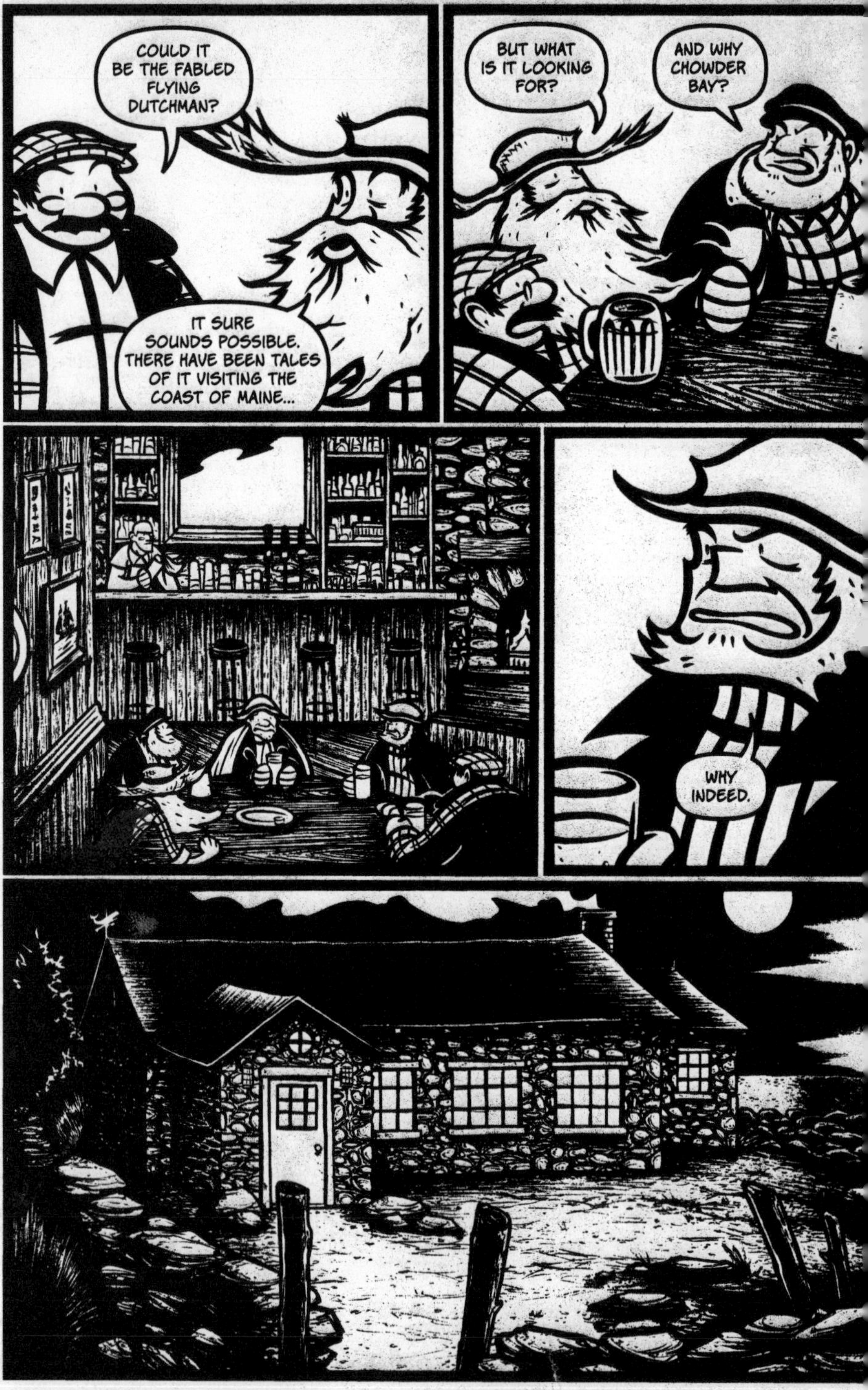
COULD IT BE THE FABLED FLYING DUTCHMAN?
IT SURE SOUNDS POSSIBLE. THERE HAVE BEEN TALES OF IT VISITING THE COAST OF MAINE...
BUT WHAT IS IT LOOKING FOR?
AND WHY CHOWDER BAY?
WHY INDEED.

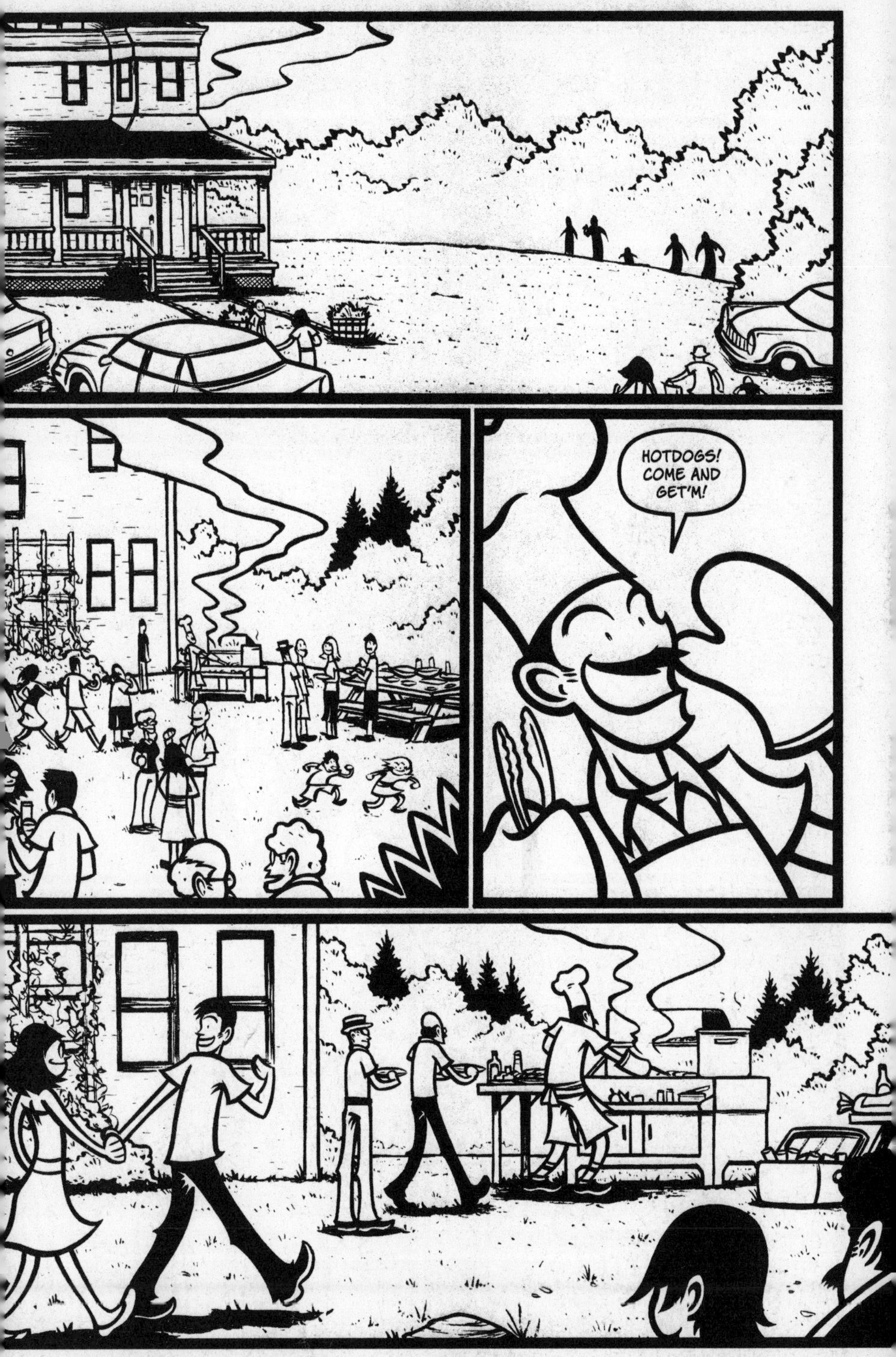
HOTDOGS! COME AND GET'M!

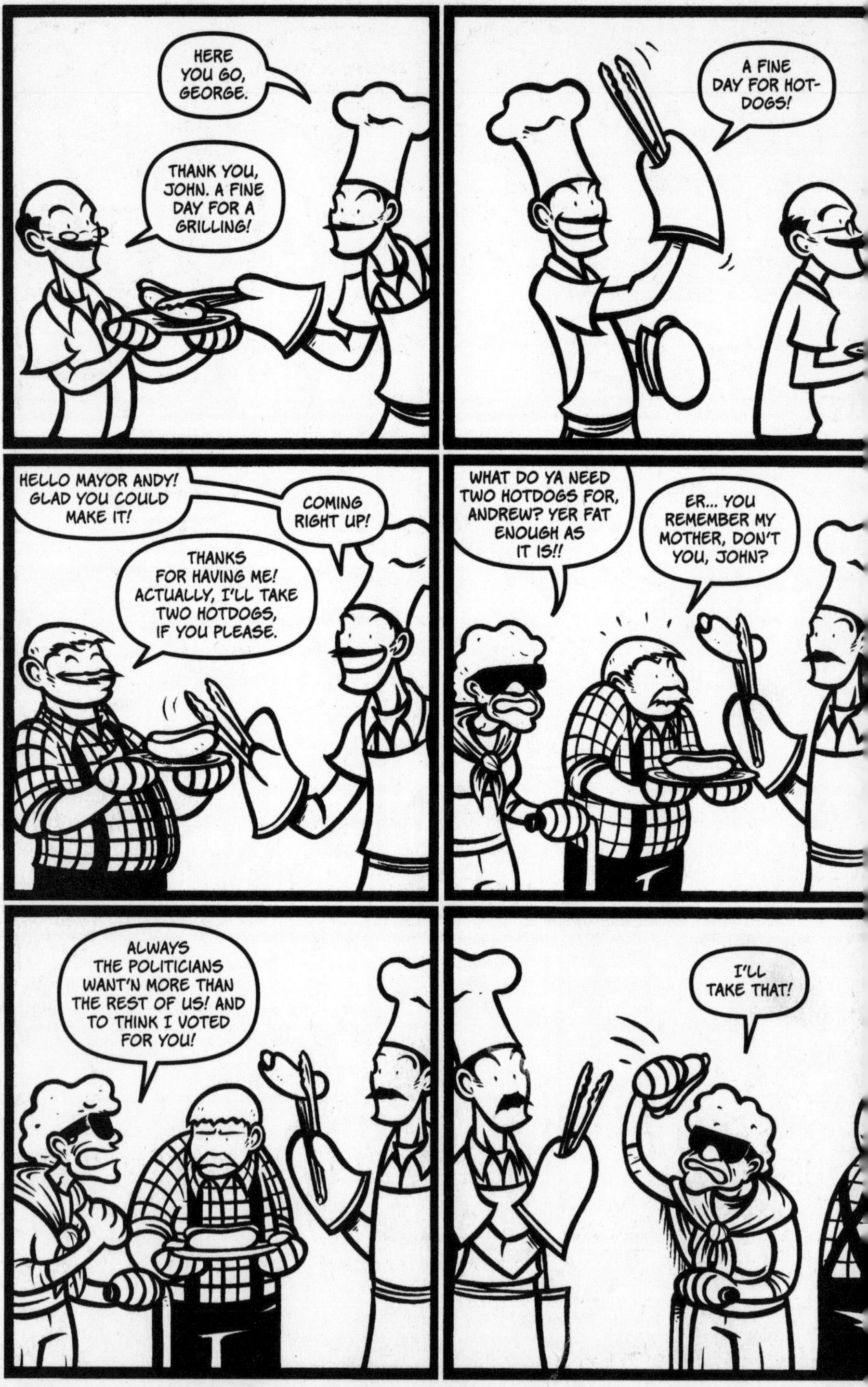
HERE YOU GO, GEORGE.
THANK YOU, JOHN. A FINE DAY FOR A GRILLING!
A FINE DAY FOR HOT-DOGS!
HELLO MAYOR ANDY! GLAD YOU COULD MAKE IT!
THANKS FOR HAVING ME! ACTUALLY, I'LL TAKE TWO HOTDOGS, IF YOU PLEASE.
COMING RIGHT UP!
WHAT DO YA NEED TWO HOTDOGS FOR, ANDREW? YER FAT ENOUGH AS IT IS!!
ER... YOU REMEMBER MY MOTHER, DON'T YOU, JOHN?
ALWAYS THE POLITICIANS WANT'N MORE THAN THE REST OF US! AND TO THINK I VOTED FOR YOU!
I'LL TAKE THAT!

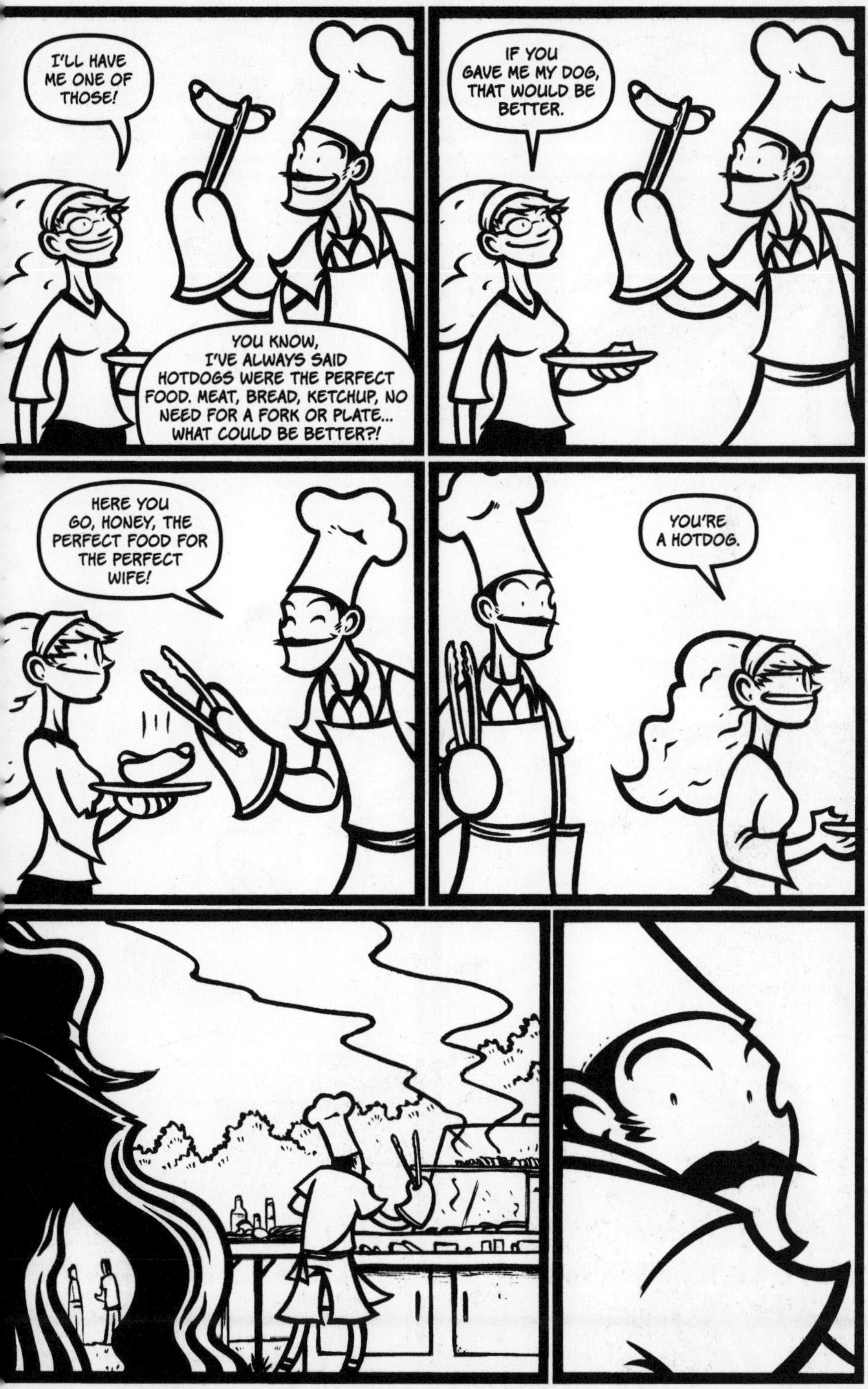
I'LL HAVE ME ONE OF THOSE!
YOU KNOW, I'VE ALWAYS SAID HOTDOGS WERE THE PERFECT FOOD. MEAT, BREAD, KETCHUP, NO NEED FOR A FORK OR PLATE... WHAT COULD BE BETTER?!
IF YOU GAVE ME MY DOG, THAT WOULD BE BETTER.
HERE YOU GO, HONEY, THE PERFECT FOOD FOR THE PERFECT WIFE!
YOU'RE A HOTDOG.

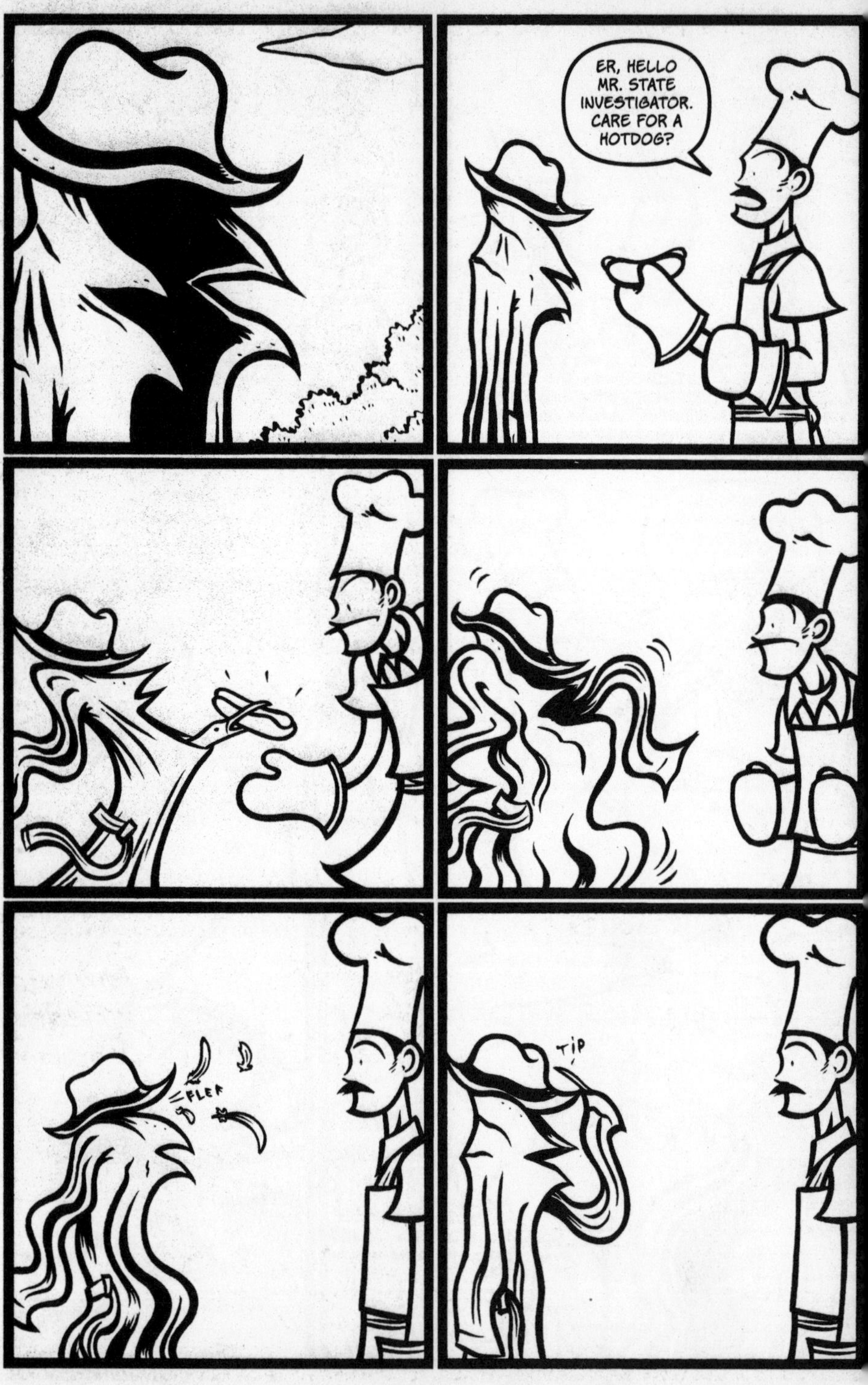
ER, HELLO MR. STATE INVESTIGATOR. CARE FOR A HOTDOG?
FLEF
TIP

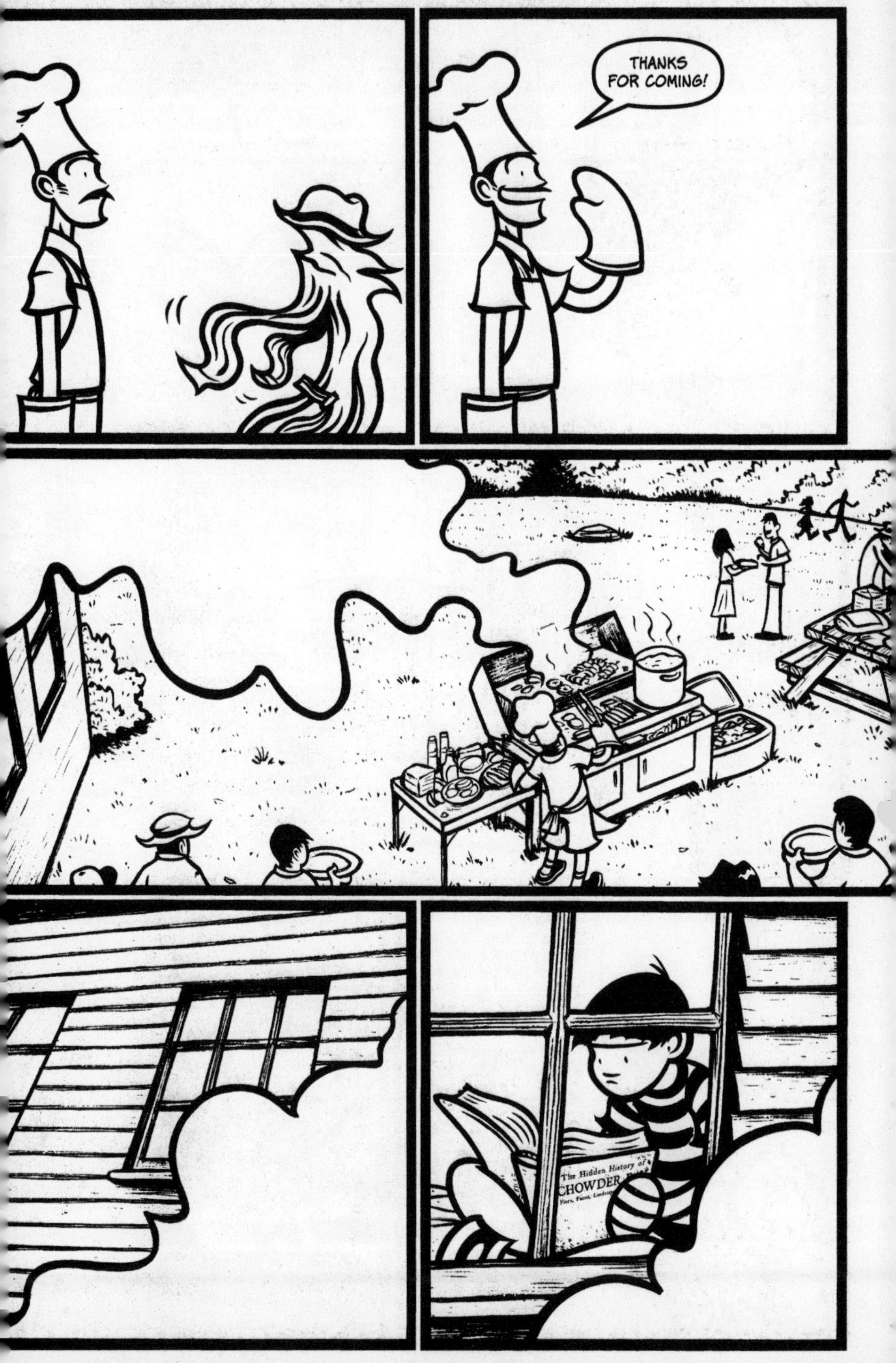
THANKS FOR COMING!
The Hidden History of
CHOWDER
Flora, Fauna,

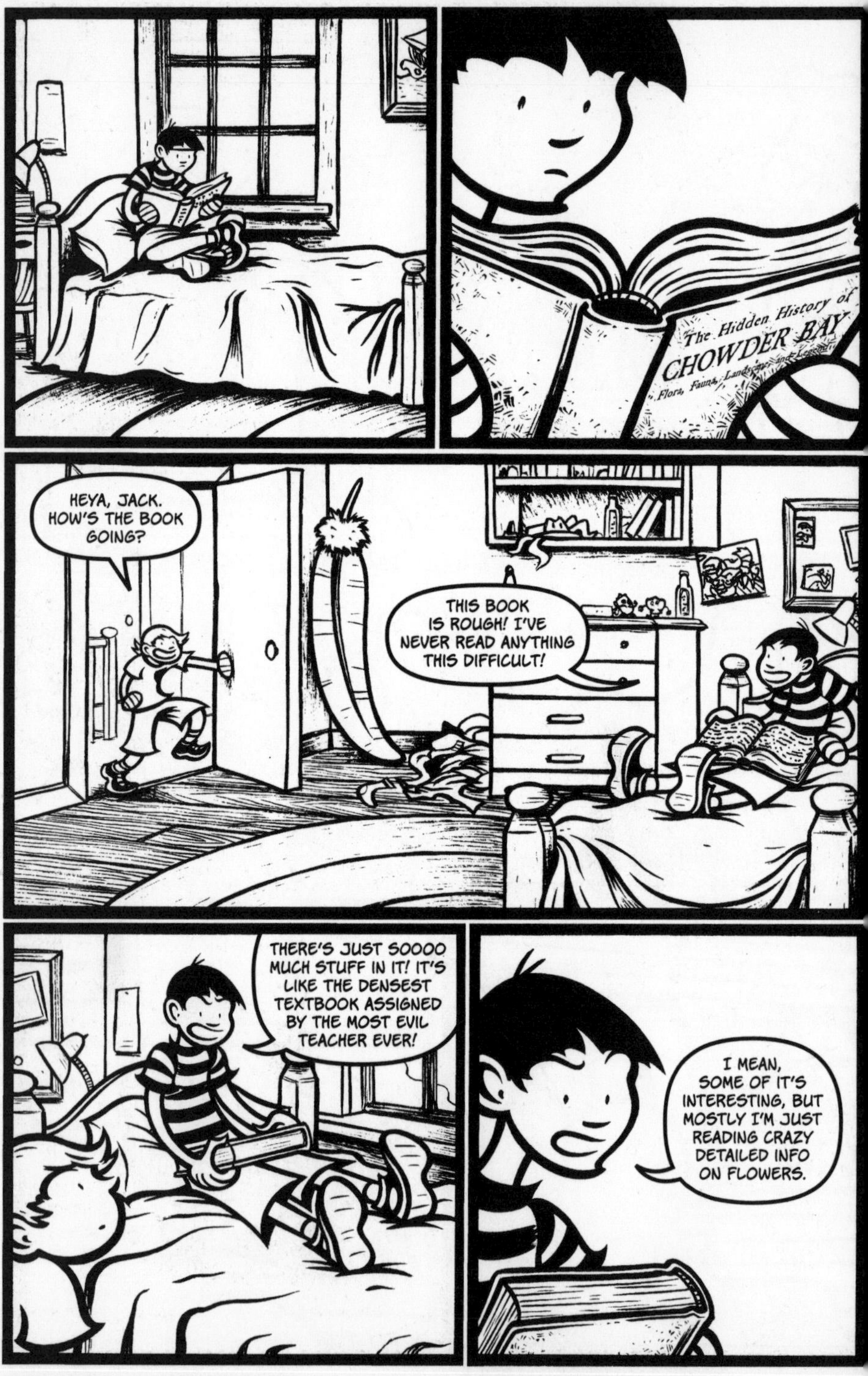
The Hidden History of
CHOWDER BAY
Flora, Fauna, Landscape and Legends
HEYA, JACK. HOW'S THE BOOK GOING?
THIS BOOK IS ROUGH! I'VE NEVER READ ANYTHING THIS DIFFICULT!
THERE'S JUST SOOOO MUCH STUFF IN IT! IT'S LIKE THE DENSEST TEXTBOOK ASSIGNED BY THE MOST EVIL TEACHER EVER!
I MEAN, SOME OF IT'S INTERESTING, BUT MOSTLY I'M JUST READING CRAZY DETAILED INFO ON FLOWERS.

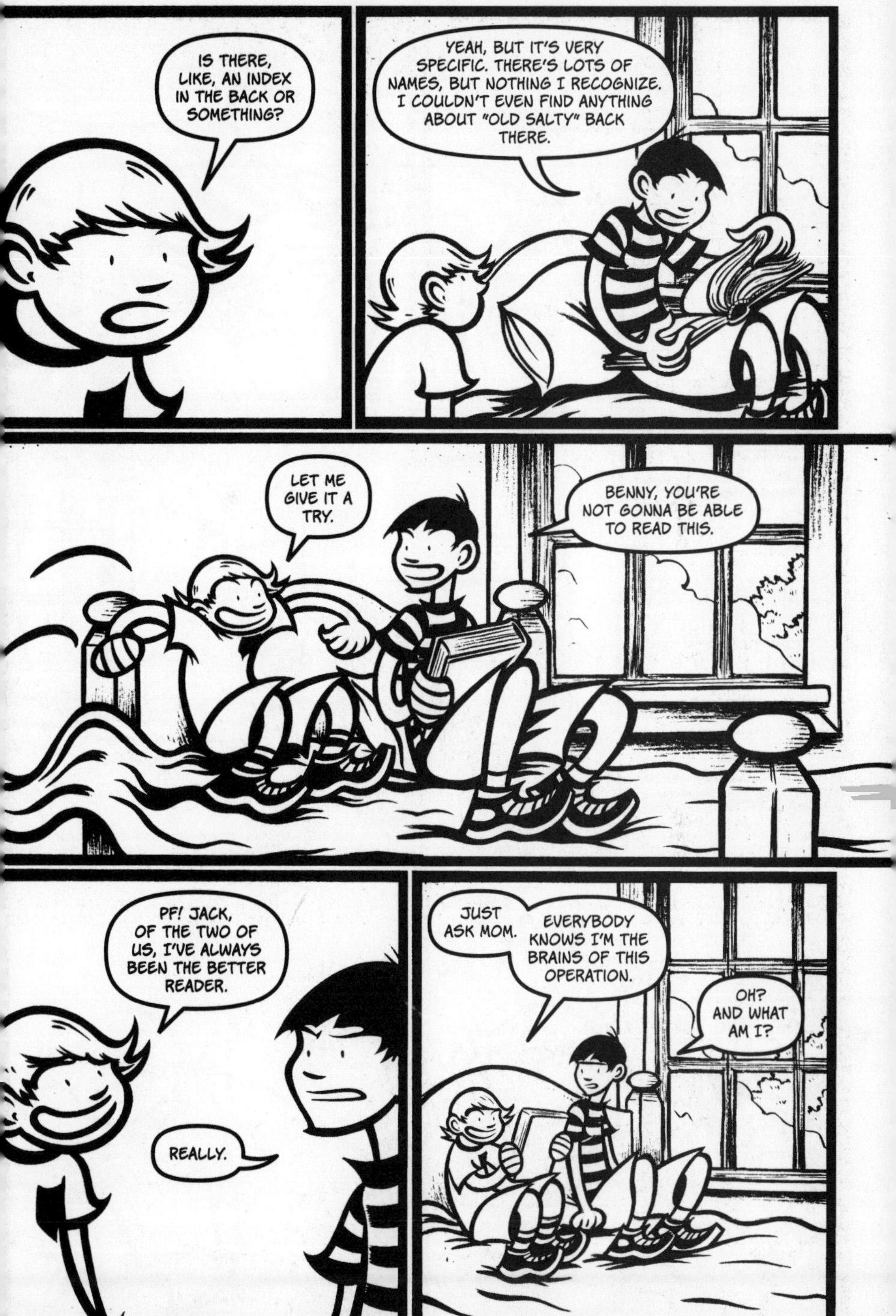
IS THERE, LIKE, AN INDEX IN THE BACK OR SOMETHING?
YEAH, BUT IT'S VERY SPECIFIC. THERE'S LOTS OF NAMES, BUT NOTHING I RECOGNIZE. I COULDN'T EVEN FIND ANYTHING ABOUT "OLD SALTY" BACK THERE.
LET ME GIVE IT A TRY.
BENNY, YOU'RE NOT GONNA BE ABLE TO READ THIS.
PF! JACK, OF THE TWO OF US, I'VE ALWAYS BEEN THE BETTER READER.
REALLY.
JUST ASK MOM.
EVERYBODY KNOWS I'M THE BRAINS OF THIS OPERATION.
OH? AND WHAT AM I?

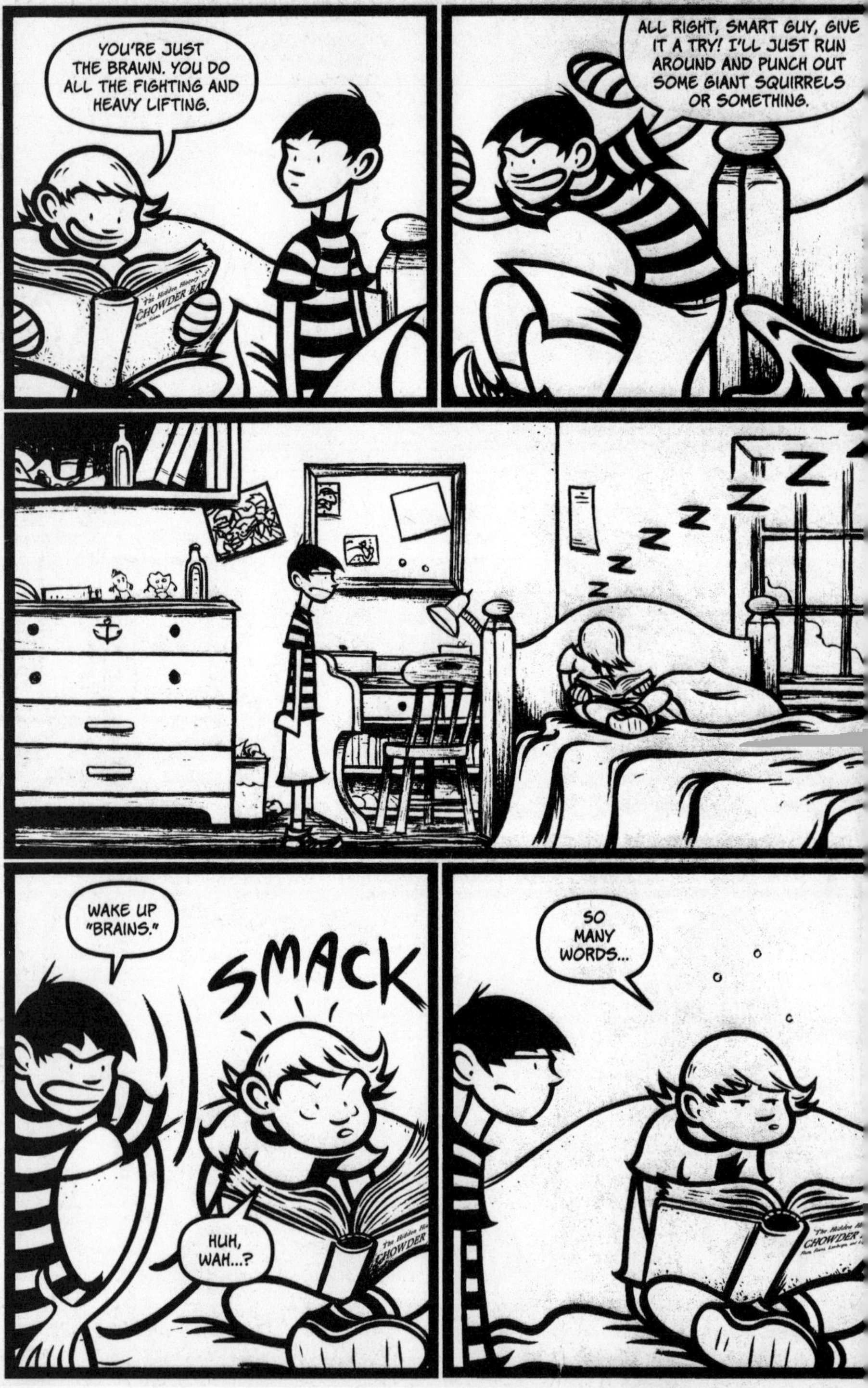
YOU'RE JUST THE BRAWN. YOU DO ALL THE FIGHTING AND HEAVY LIFTING.
The Hidden History of CHOWDER BAY
ALL RIGHT, SMART GUY, GIVE IT A TRY! I'LL JUST RUN AROUND AND PUNCH OUT SOME GIANT SQUIRRELS OR SOMETHING.
Z Z Z Z Z Z Z Z
WAKE UP "BRAINS."
SMACK
HUH, WAH...?
SO MANY WORDS...

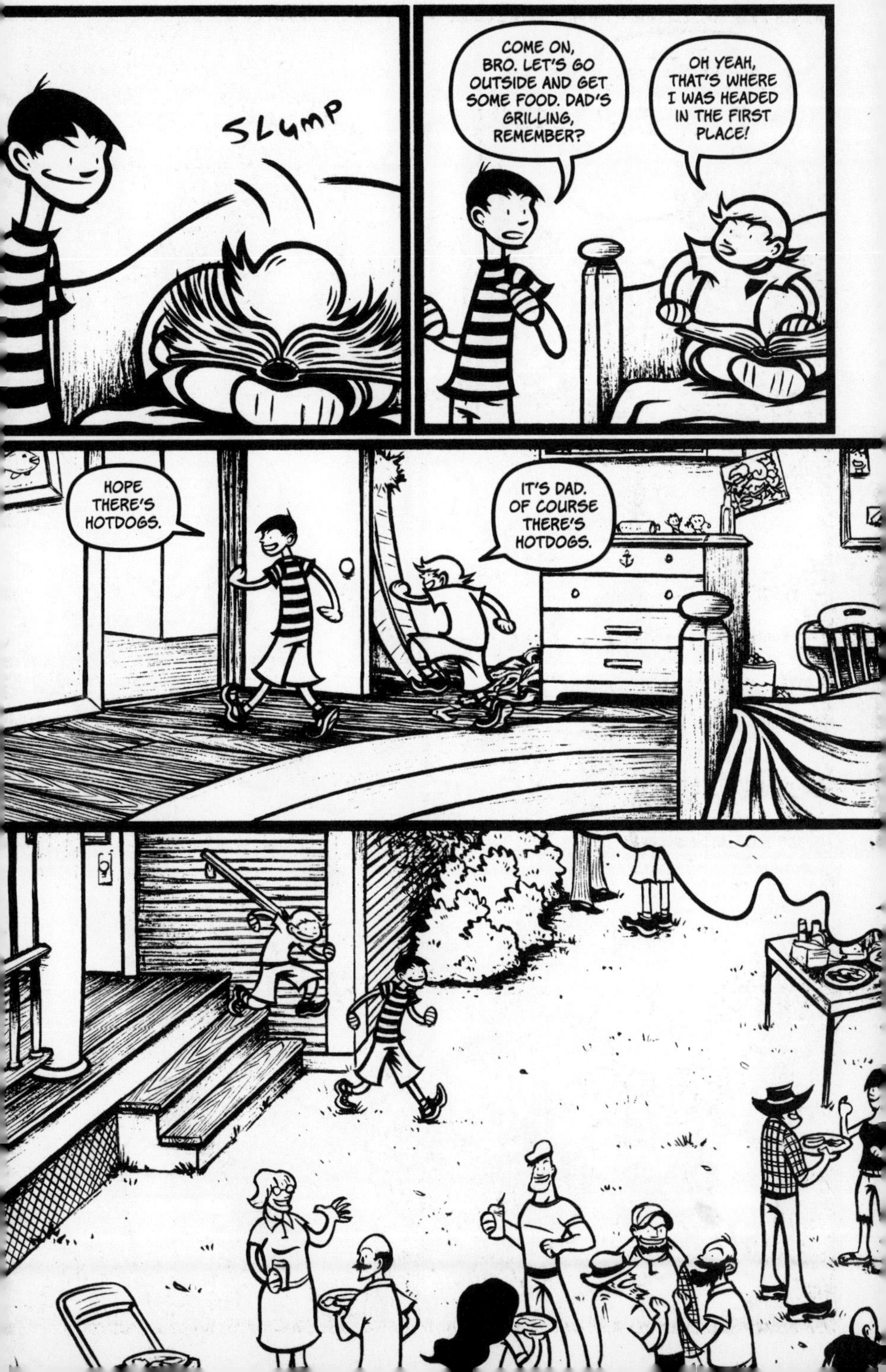
SLUMP
COME ON, BRO. LET'S GO OUTSIDE AND GET SOME FOOD. DAD'S GRILLING, REMEMBER?
OH YEAH, THAT'S WHERE I WAS HEADED IN THE FIRST PLACE!
HOPE THERE'S HOTDOGS.
IT'S DAD. OF COURSE THERE'S HOTDOGS.

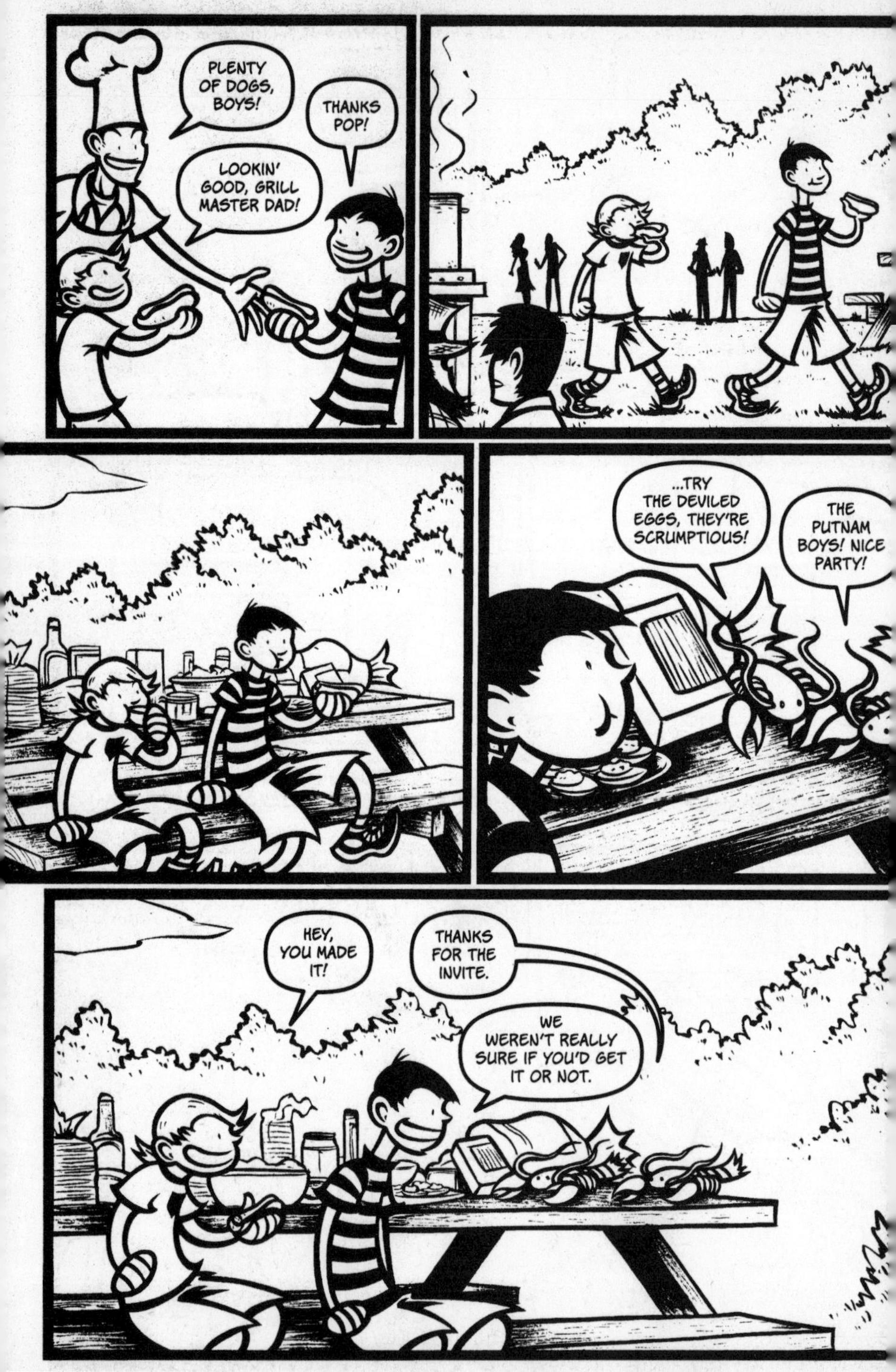
PLENTY OF DOGS, BOYS!
THANKS POP!
LOOKIN' GOOD, GRILL MASTER DAD!
...TRY THE DEVILED EGGS, THEY'RE SCRUMPTIOUS!
THE PUTNAM BOYS! NICE PARTY!
HEY, YOU MADE IT!
THANKS FOR THE INVITE.
WE WEREN'T REALLY SURE IF YOU'D GET IT OR NOT.

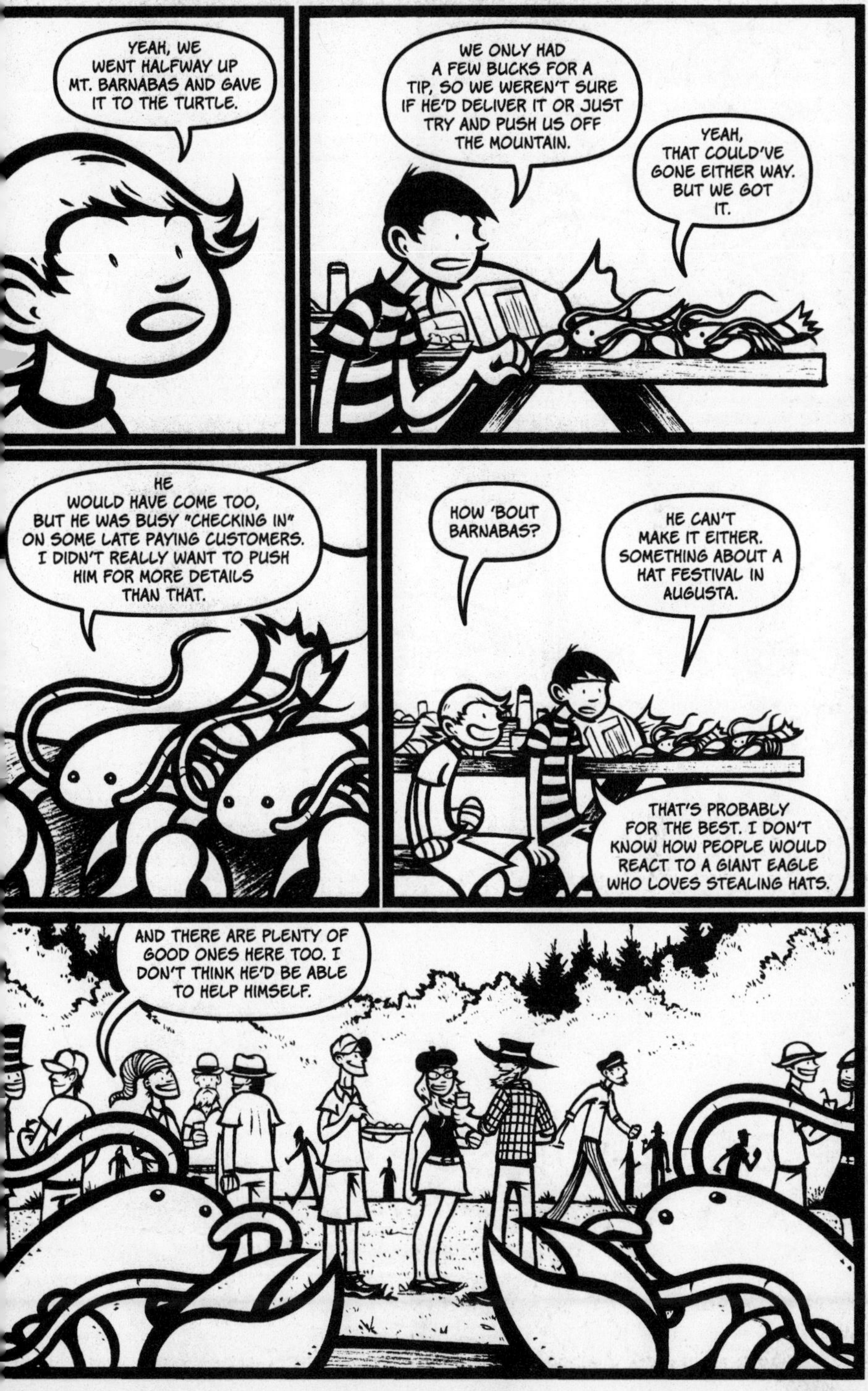
YEAH, WE WENT HALFWAY UP MT. BARNABAS AND GAVE IT TO THE TURTLE.
WE ONLY HAD A FEW BUCKS FOR A TIP, SO WE WEREN'T SURE IF HE'D DELIVER IT OR JUST TRY AND PUSH US OFF THE MOUNTAIN.
YEAH, THAT COULD'VE GONE EITHER WAY. BUT WE GOT IT.
HE WOULD HAVE COME TOO, BUT HE WAS BUSY "CHECKING IN" ON SOME LATE PAYING CUSTOMERS. I DIDN'T REALLY WANT TO PUSH HIM FOR MORE DETAILS THAN THAT.
HOW 'BOUT BARNABAS?
HE CAN'T MAKE IT EITHER. SOMETHING ABOUT A HAT FESTIVAL IN AUGUSTA.
THAT'S PROBABLY FOR THE BEST. I DON'T KNOW HOW PEOPLE WOULD REACT TO A GIANT EAGLE WHO LOVES STEALING HATS.
AND THERE ARE PLENTY OF GOOD ONES HERE TOO. I DON'T THINK HE'D BE ABLE TO HELP HIMSELF.

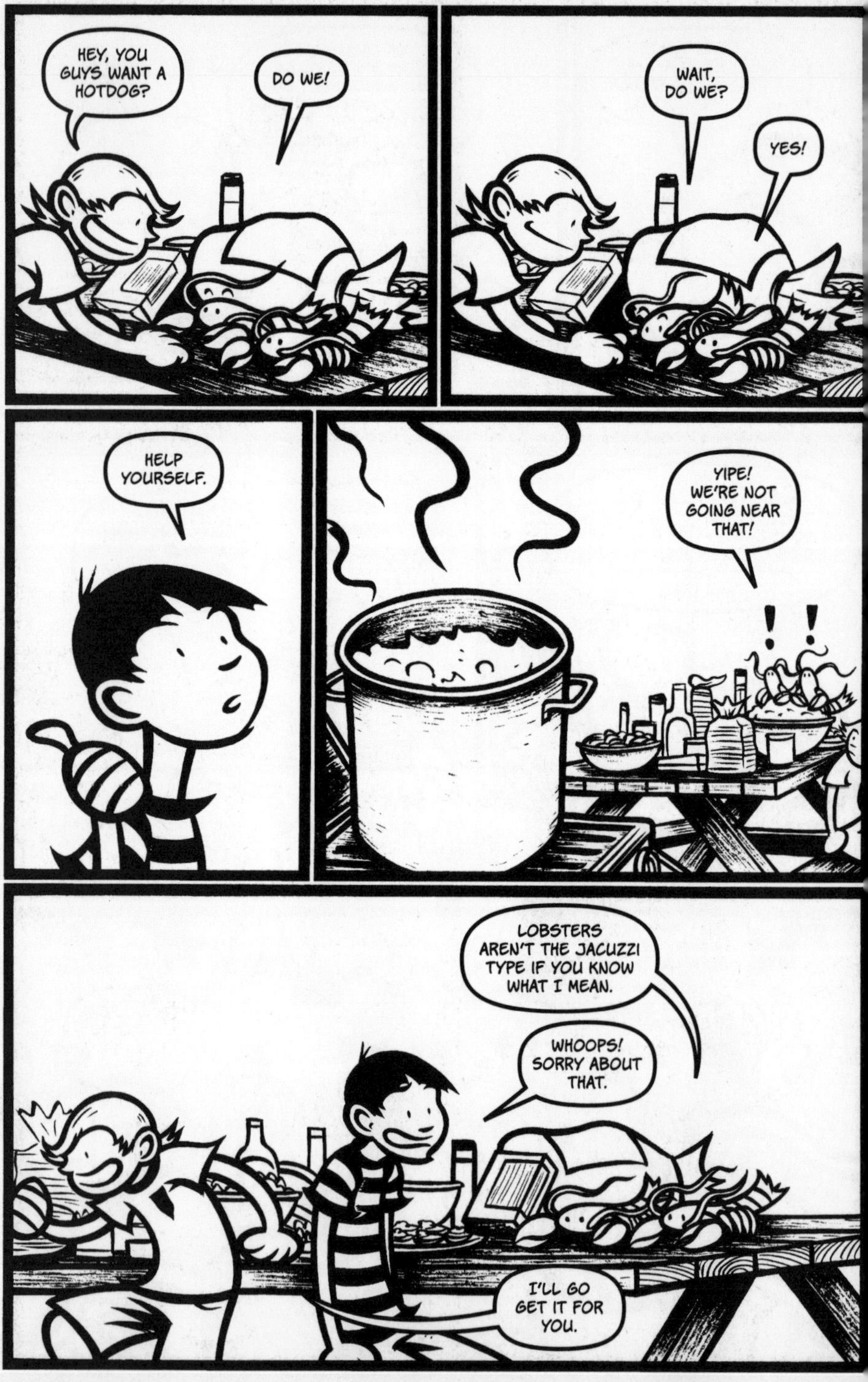
HEY, YOU GUYS WANT A HOTDOG?
DO WE!
WAIT, DO WE?
YES!
HELP YOURSELF.
YIPE! WE'RE NOT GOING NEAR THAT!
! !
LOBSTERS AREN'T THE JACUZZI TYPE IF YOU KNOW WHAT I MEAN.
WHOOPS! SORRY ABOUT THAT.
I'LL GO GET IT FOR YOU.

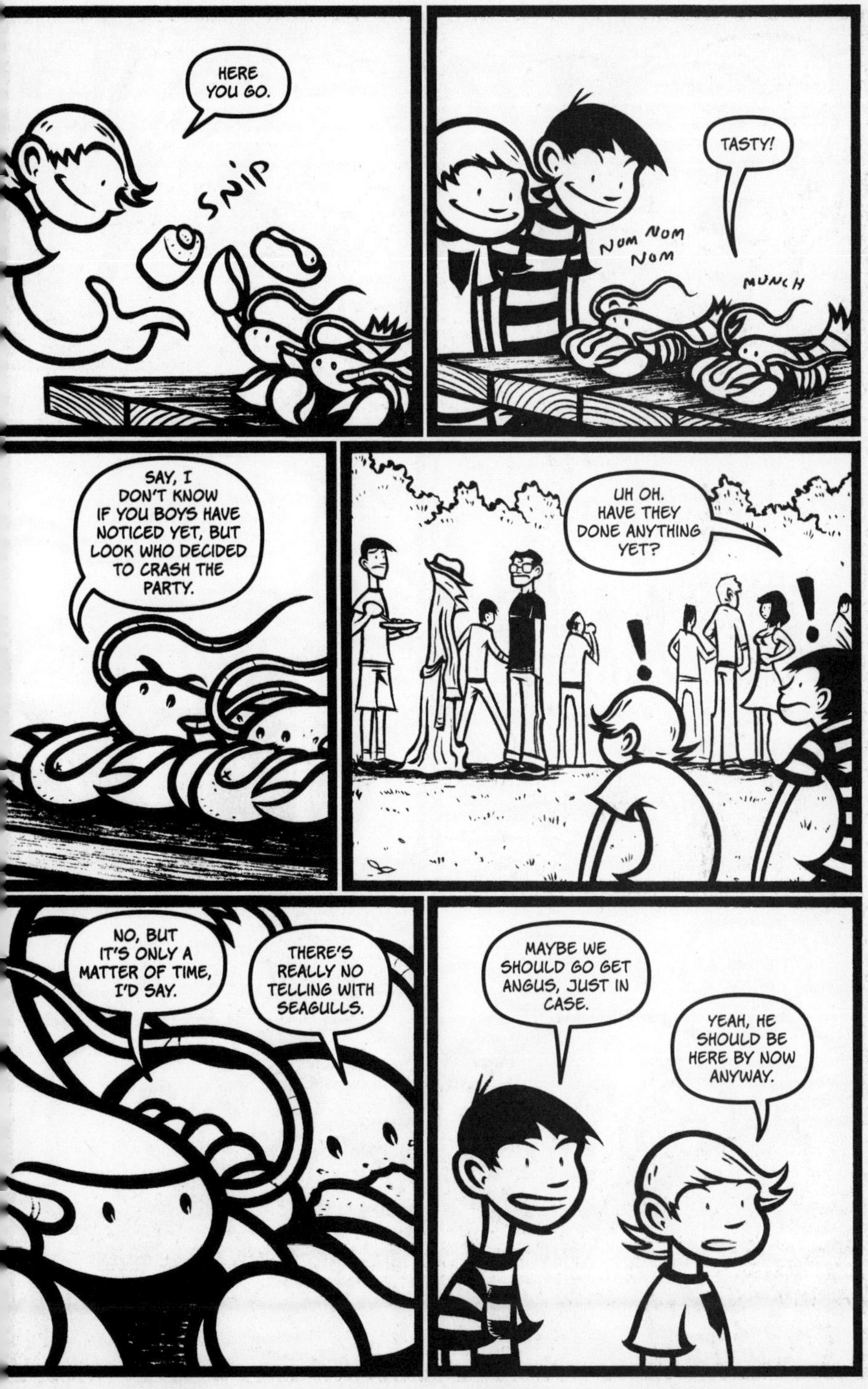
HERE YOU GO.
SNIP
NOM NOM NOM
TASTY!
MUNCH
SAY, I DON'T KNOW IF YOU BOYS HAVE NOTICED YET, BUT LOOK WHO DECIDED TO CRASH THE PARTY.
UH OH. HAVE THEY DONE ANYTHING YET?
!
!
NO, BUT IT'S ONLY A MATTER OF TIME, I'D SAY.
THERE'S REALLY NO TELLING WITH SEAGULLS.
MAYBE WE SHOULD GO GET ANGUS, JUST IN CASE.
YEAH, HE SHOULD BE HERE BY NOW ANYWAY.

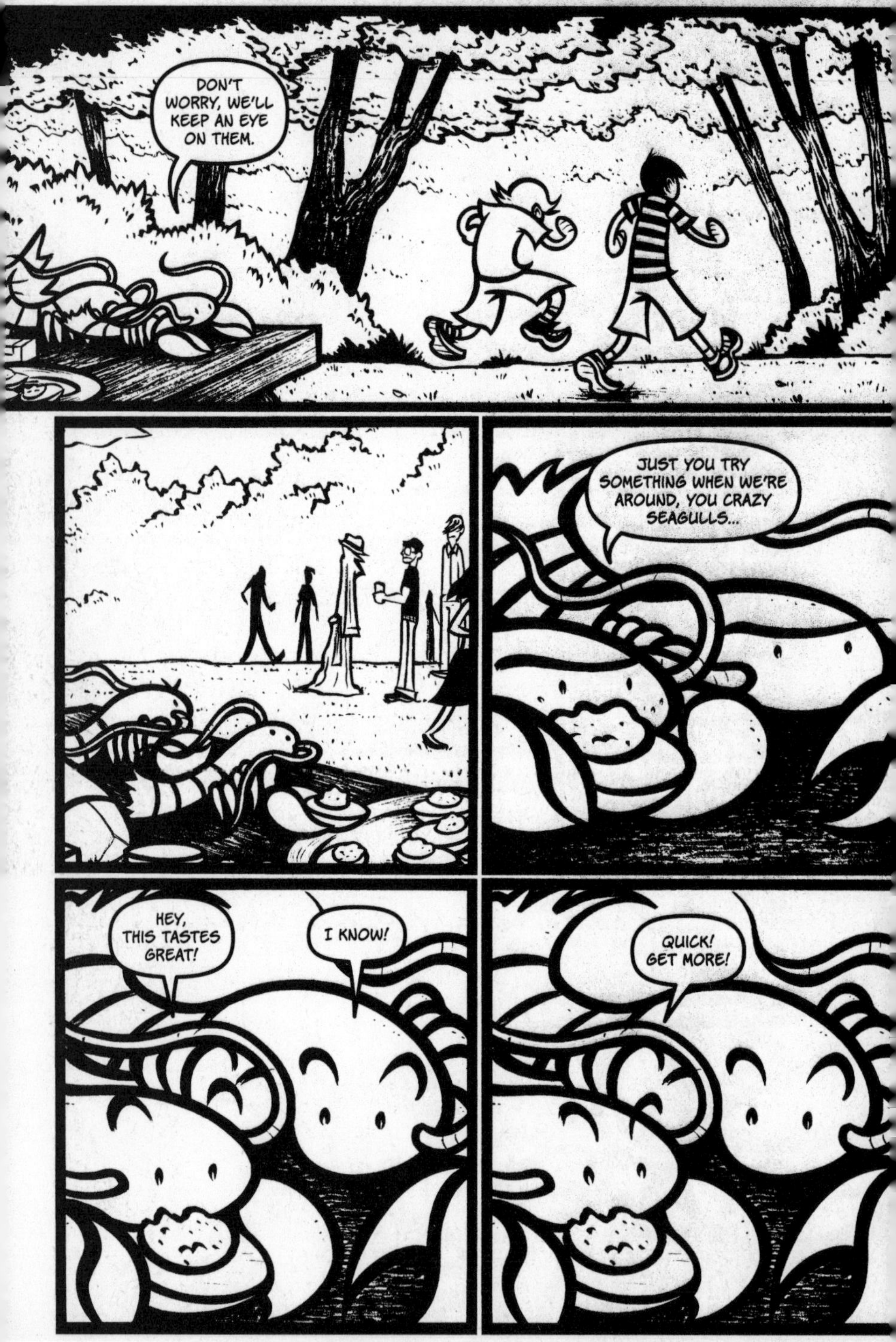
DON'T WORRY, WE'LL KEEP AN EYE ON THEM.
JUST YOU TRY SOMETHING WHEN WE'RE AROUND, YOU CRAZY SEAGULLS...
HEY, THIS TASTES GREAT!
I KNOW!
QUICK! GET MORE!

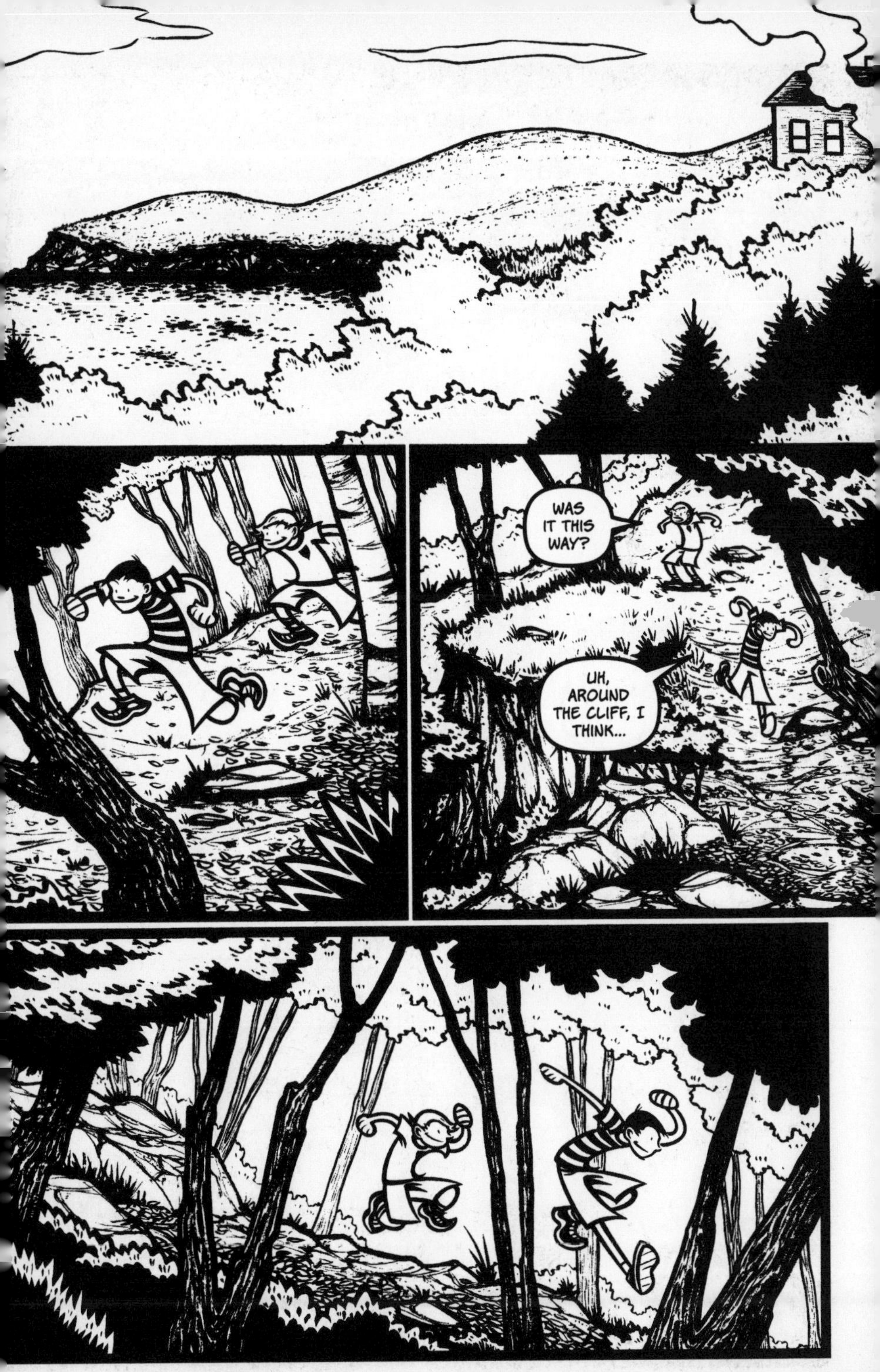
WAS IT THIS WAY?
UH, AROUND THE CLIFF, I THINK...

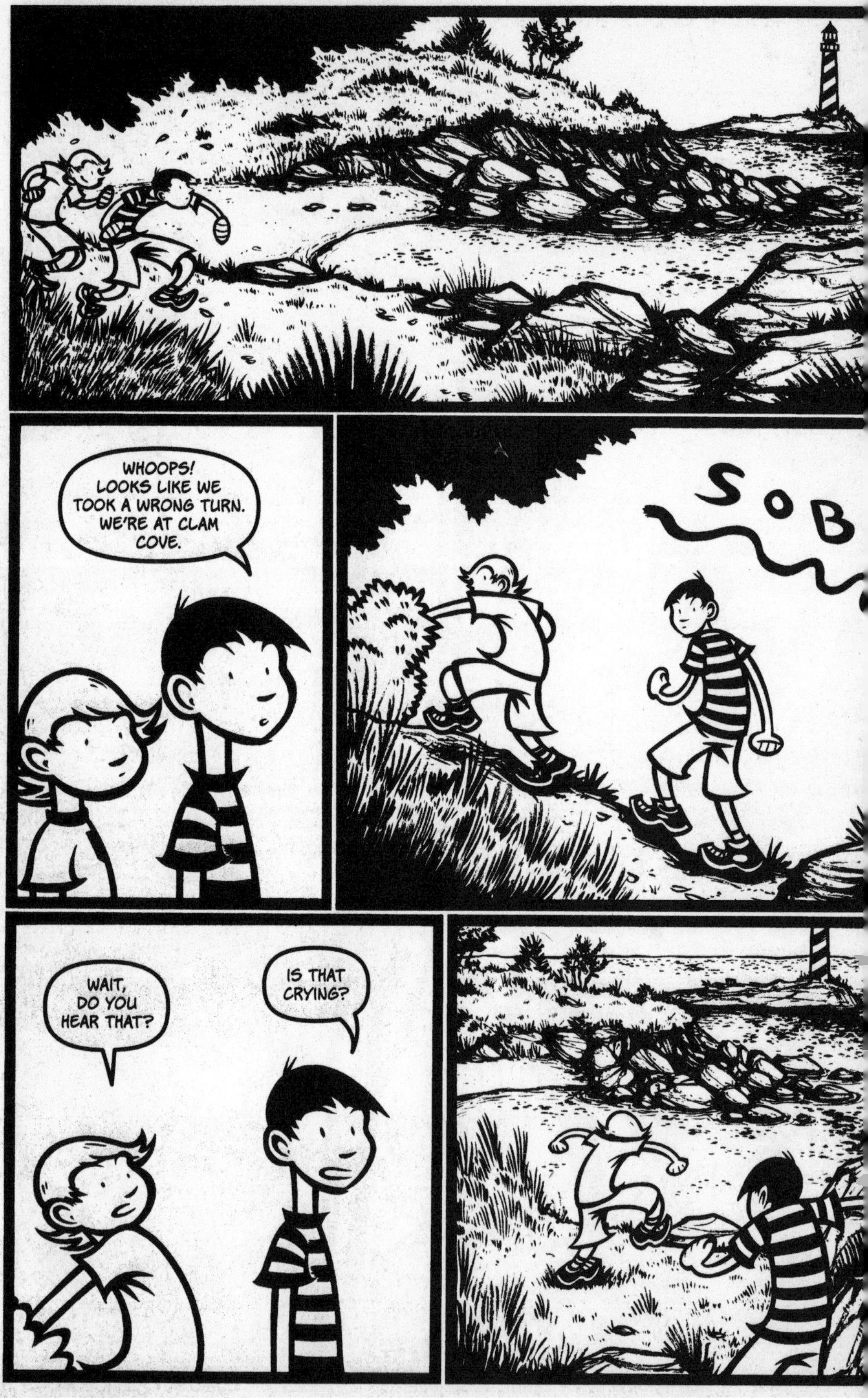
WHOOPS! LOOKS LIKE WE TOOK A WRONG TURN. WE'RE AT CLAM COVE.
SOB
WAIT, DO YOU HEAR THAT?
IS THAT CRYING?

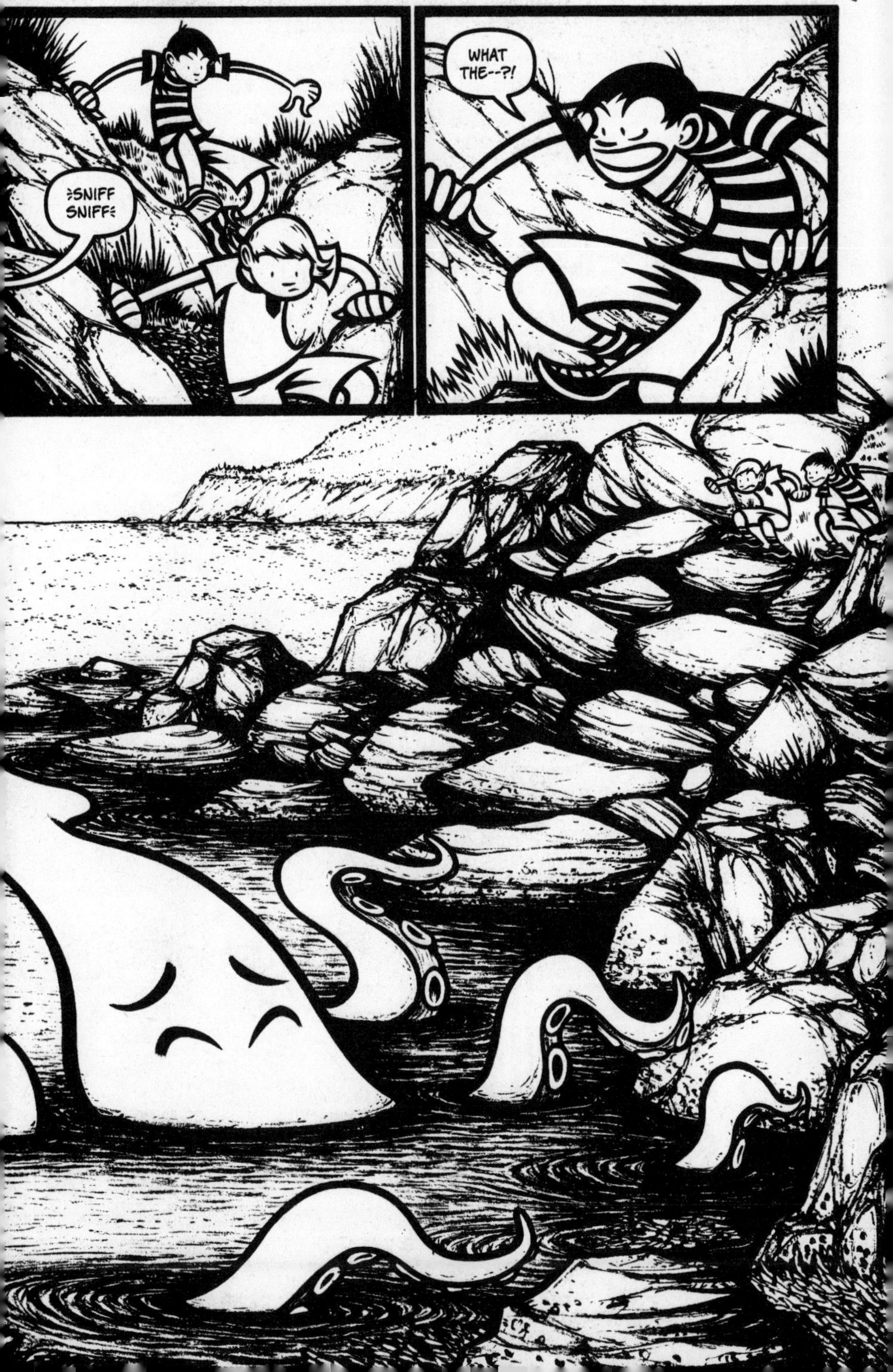
SNIFF SNIFF
WHAT THE--?!

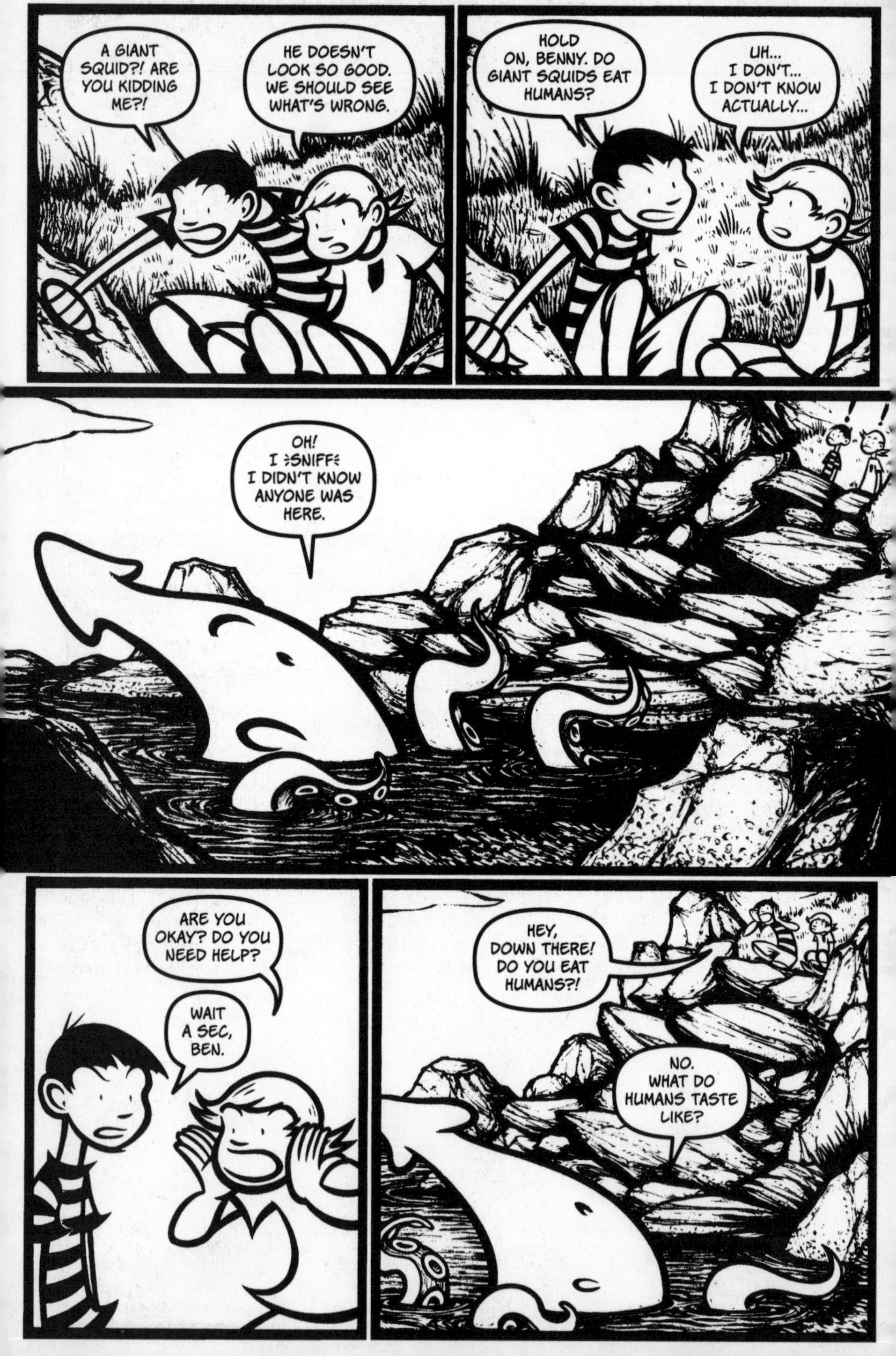
A GIANT SQUID?! ARE YOU KIDDING ME?!
HE DOESN'T LOOK SO GOOD. WE SHOULD SEE WHAT'S WRONG.
HOLD ON, BENNY. DO GIANT SQUIDS EAT HUMANS?
UH... I DON'T... I DON'T KNOW ACTUALLY...
!
!
OH! I ≷SNIFF≶ I DIDN'T KNOW ANYONE WAS HERE.
ARE YOU OKAY? DO YOU NEED HELP?
WAIT A SEC, BEN.
HEY, DOWN THERE! DO YOU EAT HUMANS?!
NO. WHAT DO HUMANS TASTE LIKE?

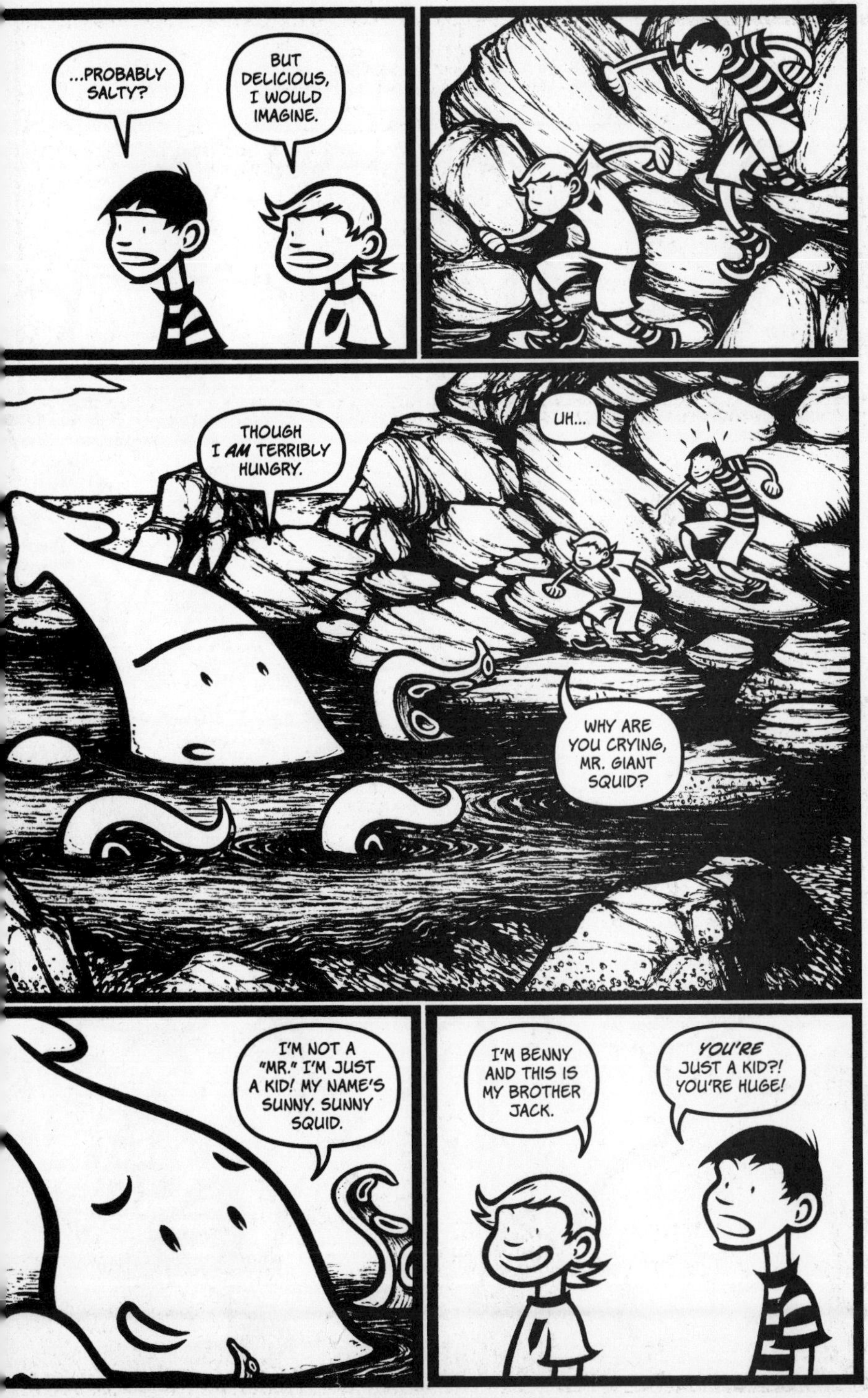
...PROBABLY SALTY?
BUT DELICIOUS, I WOULD IMAGINE.
THOUGH I *AM* TERRIBLY HUNGRY.
UH...
WHY ARE YOU CRYING, MR. GIANT SQUID?
I'M NOT A "MR." I'M JUST A KID! MY NAME'S SUNNY. SUNNY SQUID.
I'M BENNY AND THIS IS MY BROTHER JACK.
YOU'RE JUST A KID?! YOU'RE HUGE!

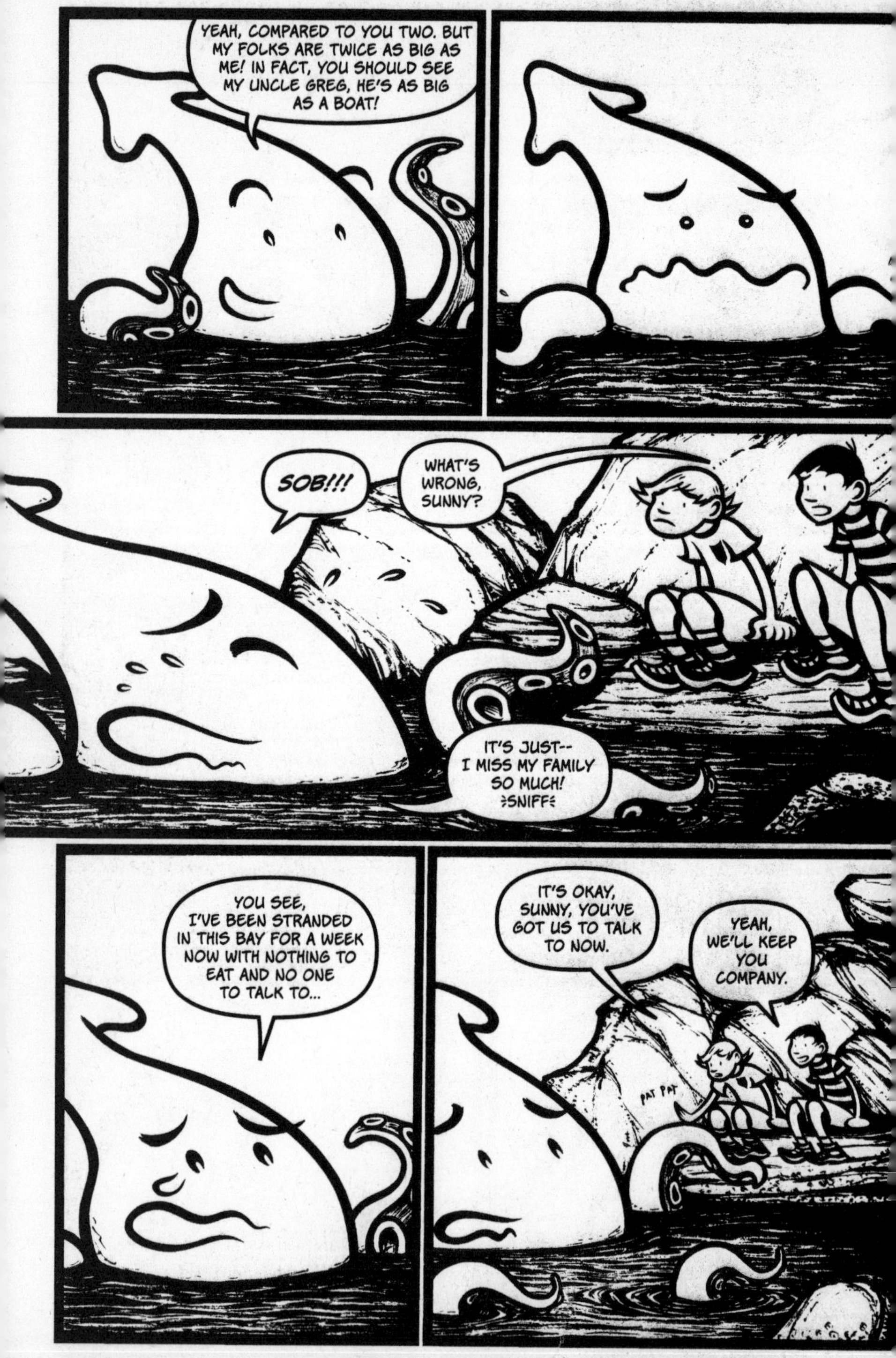
YEAH, COMPARED TO YOU TWO. BUT MY FOLKS ARE TWICE AS BIG AS ME! IN FACT, YOU SHOULD SEE MY UNCLE GREG, HE'S AS BIG AS A BOAT!
SOB!!!
WHAT'S WRONG, SUNNY?
IT'S JUST-- I MISS MY FAMILY SO MUCH! SNIFF
YOU SEE, I'VE BEEN STRANDED IN THIS BAY FOR A WEEK NOW WITH NOTHING TO EAT AND NO ONE TO TALK TO...
IT'S OKAY, SUNNY, YOU'VE GOT US TO TALK TO NOW.
YEAH, WE'LL KEEP YOU COMPANY.
PAT PAT

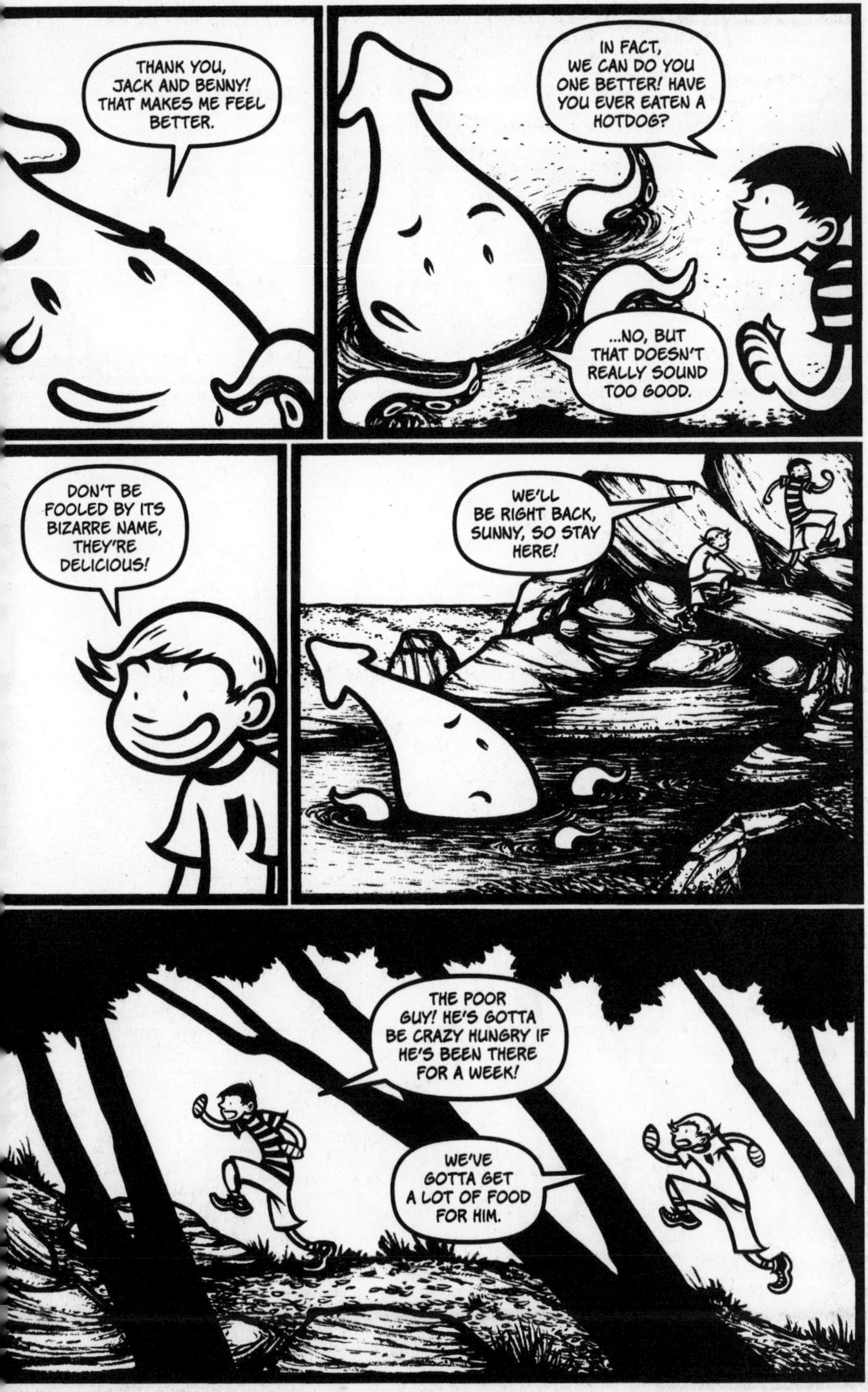
THANK YOU, JACK AND BENNY! THAT MAKES ME FEEL BETTER.
IN FACT, WE CAN DO YOU ONE BETTER! HAVE YOU EVER EATEN A HOTDOG?
...NO, BUT THAT DOESN'T REALLY SOUND TOO GOOD.
DON'T BE FOOLED BY ITS BIZARRE NAME, THEY'RE DELICIOUS!
WE'LL BE RIGHT BACK, SUNNY, SO STAY HERE!
THE POOR GUY! HE'S GOTTA BE CRAZY HUNGRY IF HE'S BEEN THERE FOR A WEEK!
WE'VE GOTTA GET A LOT OF FOOD FOR HIM.

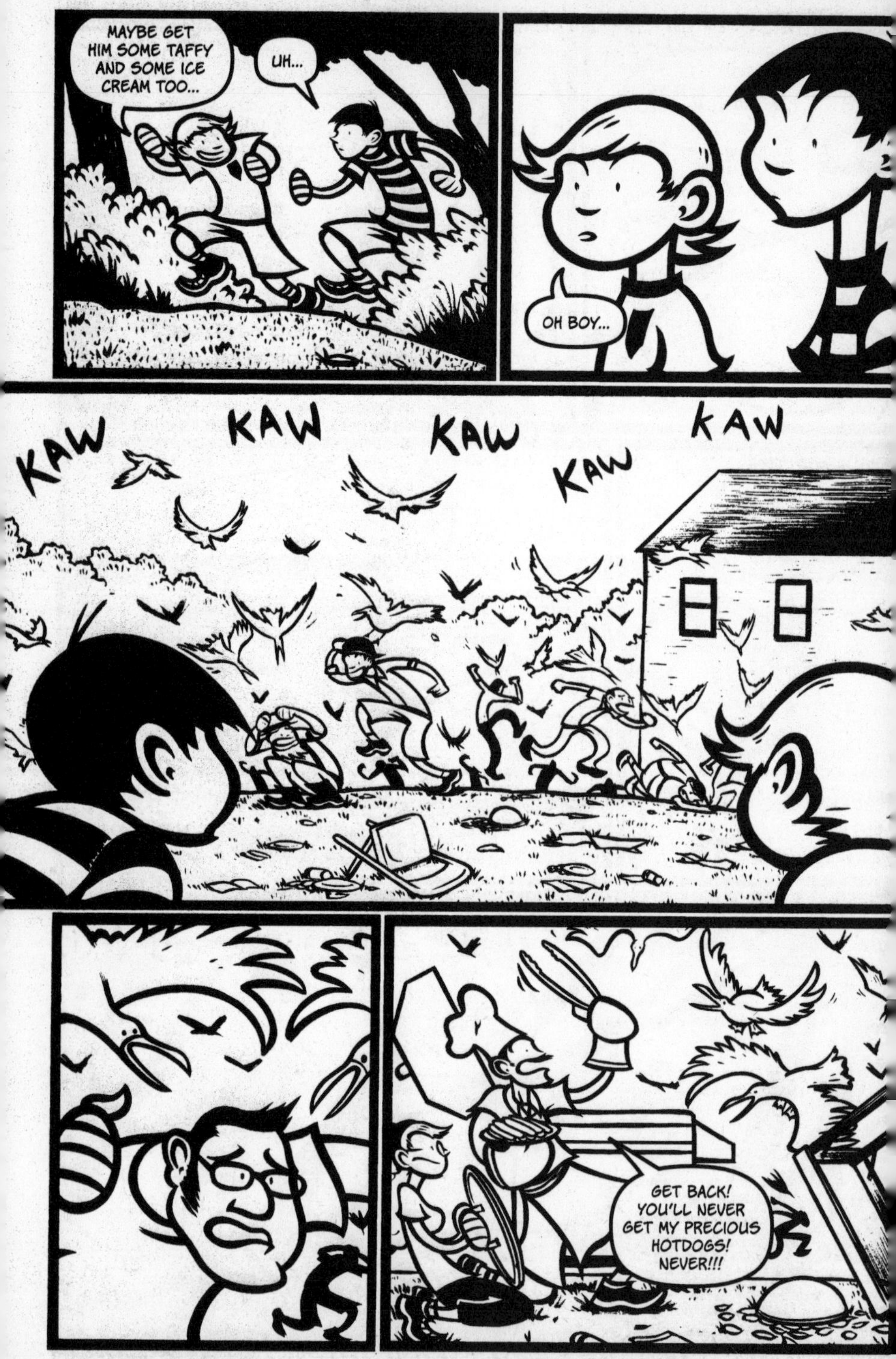
MAYBE GET HIM SOME TAFFY AND SOME ICE CREAM TOO...
UH...
OH BOY...
KAW
KAW
KAW
KAW
KAW
GET BACK! YOU'LL NEVER GET MY PRECIOUS HOTDOGS! NEVER!!!

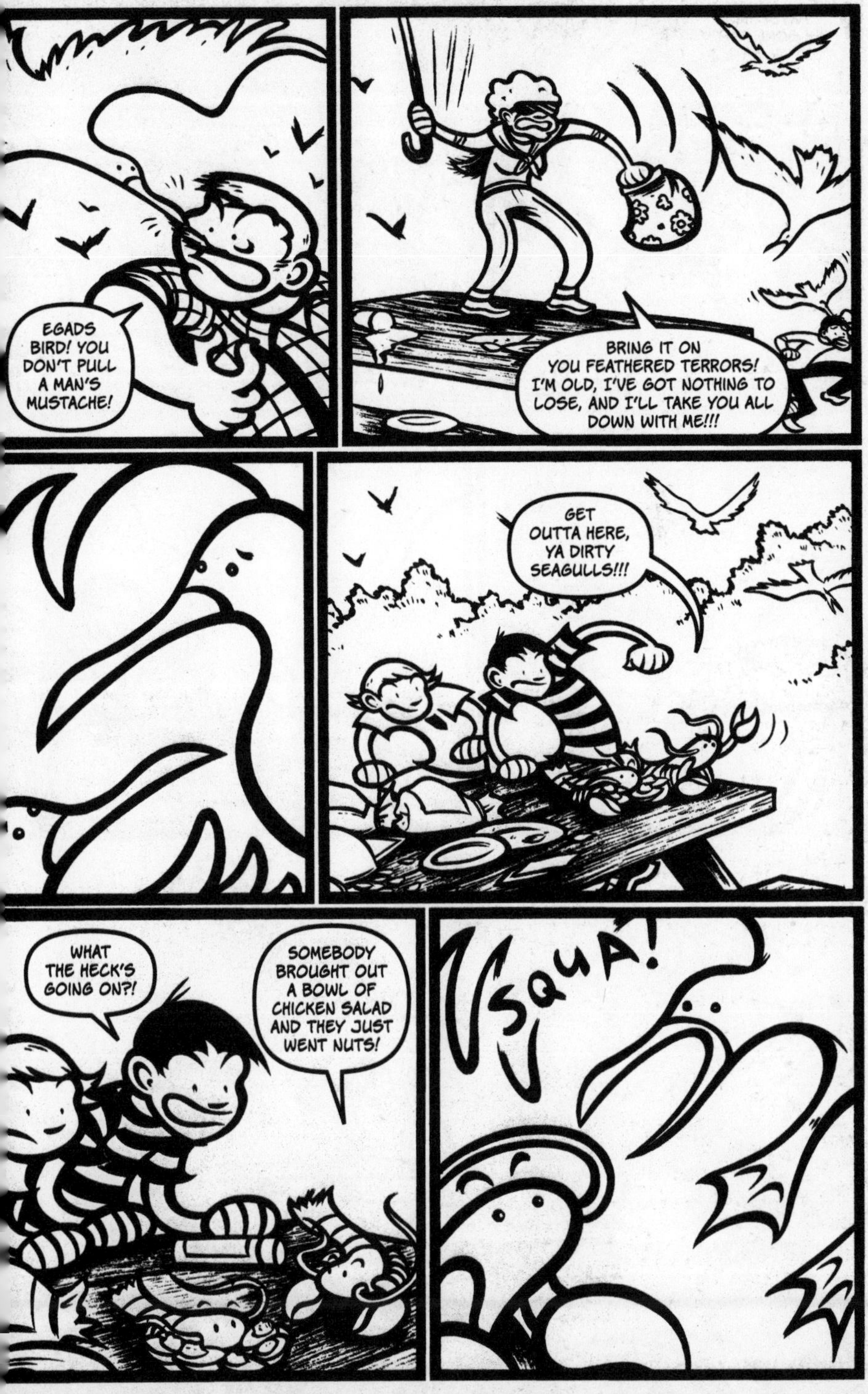
EGADS BIRD! YOU DON'T PULL A MAN'S MUSTACHE!
BRING IT ON YOU FEATHERED TERRORS! I'M OLD, I'VE GOT NOTHING TO LOSE, AND I'LL TAKE YOU ALL DOWN WITH ME!!!
GET OUTTA HERE, YA DIRTY SEAGULLS!!!
WHAT THE HECK'S GOING ON?!
SOMEBODY BROUGHT OUT A BOWL OF CHICKEN SALAD AND THEY JUST WENT NUTS!
SQUA!

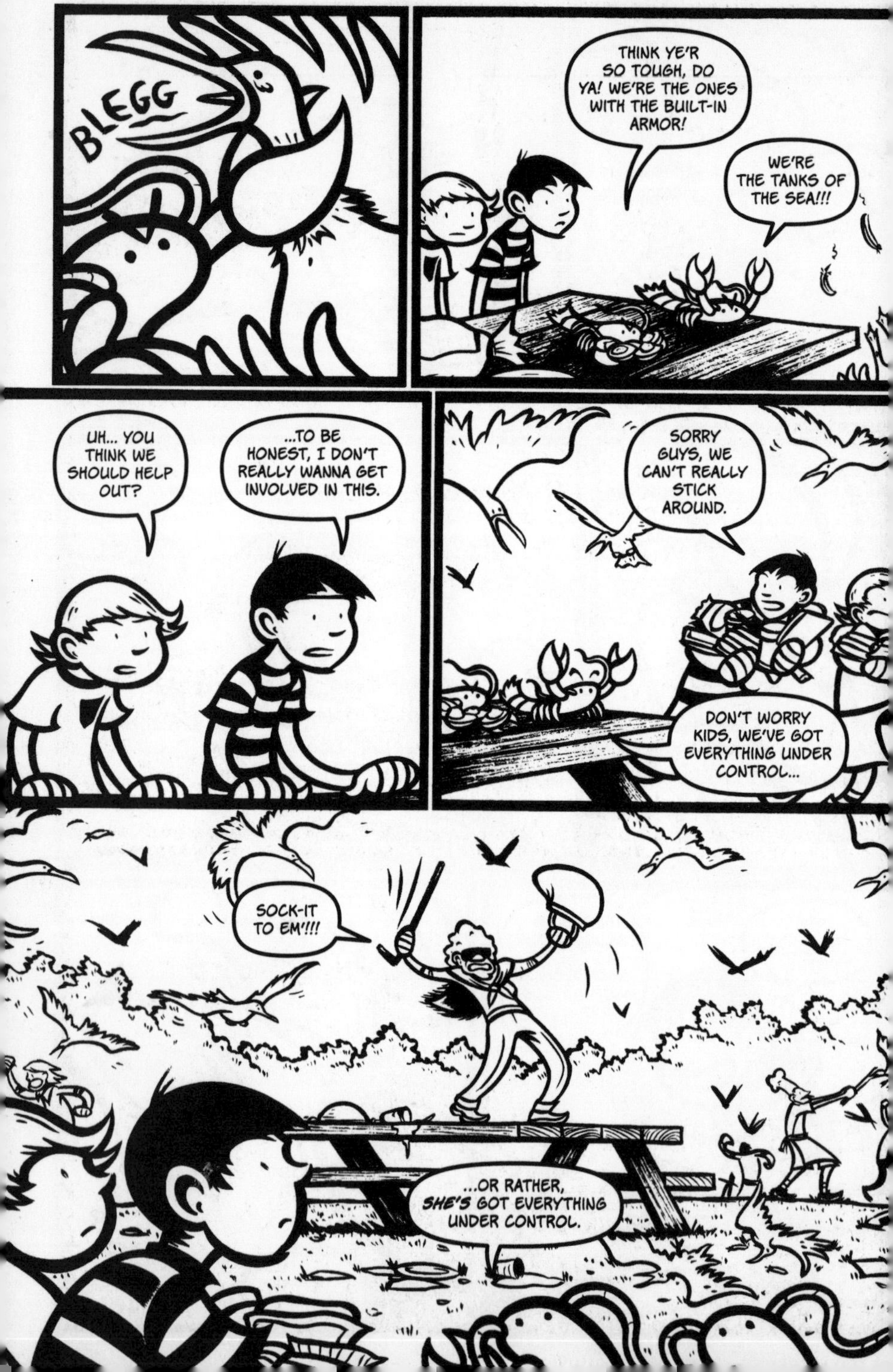
BLEGG
THINK YE'R SO TOUGH, DO YA! WE'RE THE ONES WITH THE BUILT-IN ARMOR!
WE'RE THE TANKS OF THE SEA!!!
UH... YOU THINK WE SHOULD HELP OUT?
...TO BE HONEST, I DON'T REALLY WANNA GET INVOLVED IN THIS.
SORRY GUYS, WE CAN'T REALLY STICK AROUND.
DON'T WORRY KIDS, WE'VE GOT EVERYTHING UNDER CONTROL...
SOCK-IT TO EM'!!!
...OR RATHER, *SHE'S* GOT EVERYTHING UNDER CONTROL.

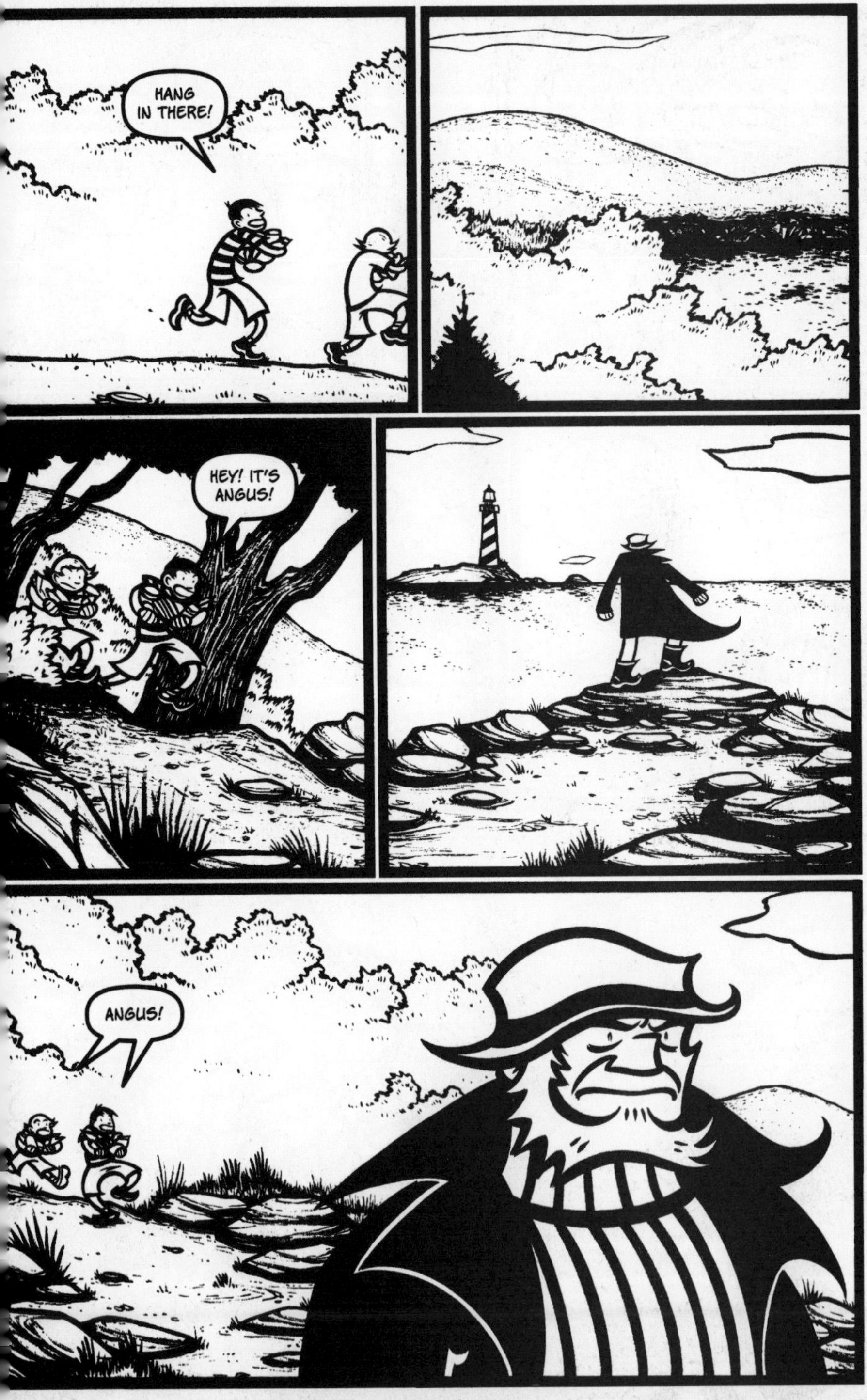
HANG IN THERE!
HEY! IT'S ANGUS!
ANGUS!

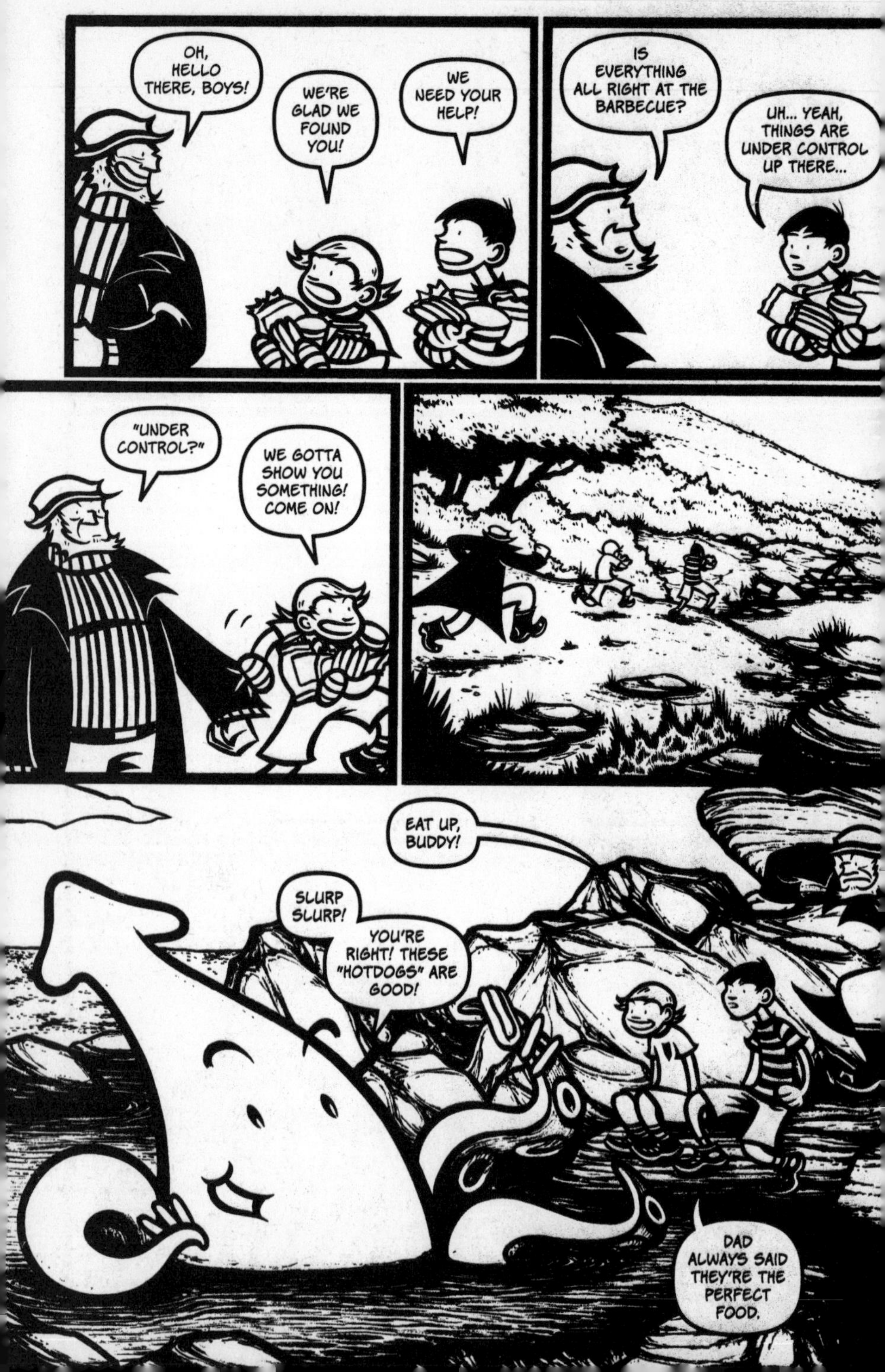
OH, HELLO THERE, BOYS!
WE'RE GLAD WE FOUND YOU!
WE NEED YOUR HELP!
IS EVERYTHING ALL RIGHT AT THE BARBECUE?
UH... YEAH, THINGS ARE UNDER CONTROL UP THERE...
"UNDER CONTROL?"
WE GOTTA SHOW YOU SOMETHING! COME ON!
EAT UP, BUDDY!
SLURP SLURP!
YOU'RE RIGHT! THESE "HOTDOGS" ARE GOOD!
DAD ALWAYS SAID THEY'RE THE PERFECT FOOD.

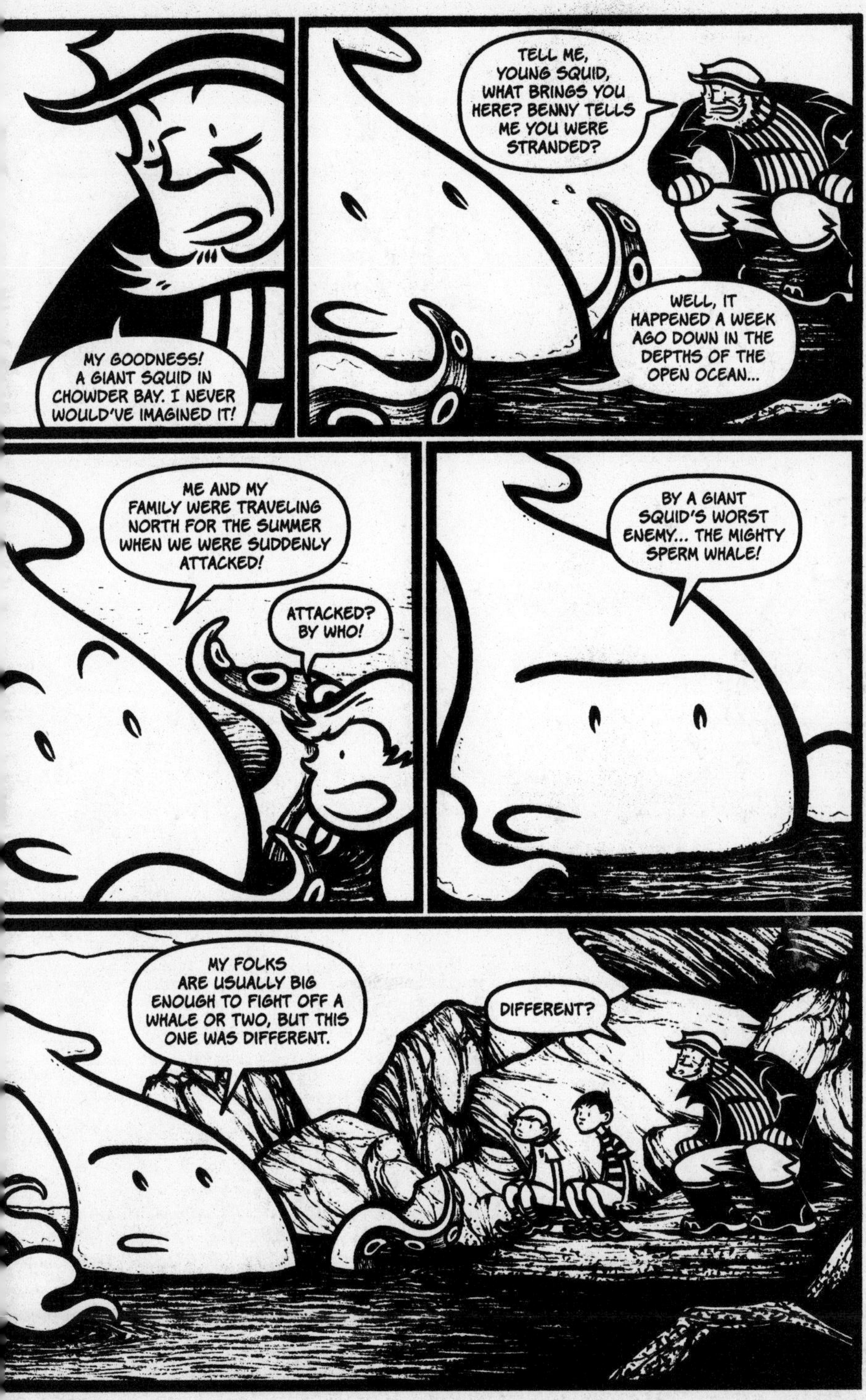
MY GOODNESS! A GIANT SQUID IN CHOWDER BAY. I NEVER WOULD'VE IMAGINED IT!
TELL ME, YOUNG SQUID, WHAT BRINGS YOU HERE? BENNY TELLS ME YOU WERE STRANDED?
WELL, IT HAPPENED A WEEK AGO DOWN IN THE DEPTHS OF THE OPEN OCEAN...
ME AND MY FAMILY WERE TRAVELING NORTH FOR THE SUMMER WHEN WE WERE SUDDENLY ATTACKED!
ATTACKED? BY WHO!
BY A GIANT SQUID'S WORST ENEMY... THE MIGHTY SPERM WHALE!
MY FOLKS ARE USUALLY BIG ENOUGH TO FIGHT OFF A WHALE OR TWO, BUT THIS ONE WAS DIFFERENT.
DIFFERENT?

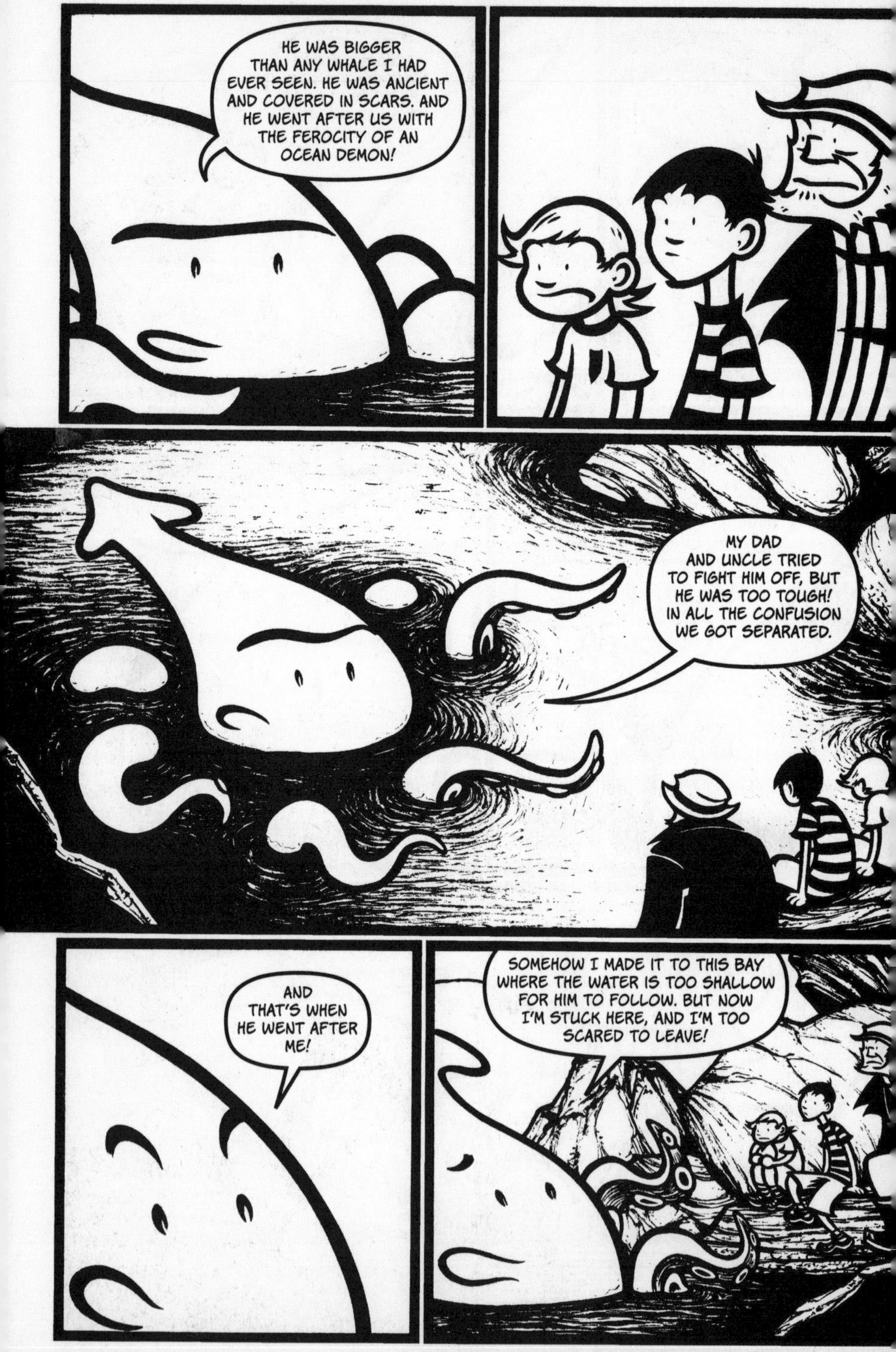
HE WAS BIGGER THAN ANY WHALE I HAD EVER SEEN. HE WAS ANCIENT AND COVERED IN SCARS. AND HE WENT AFTER US WITH THE FEROCITY OF AN OCEAN DEMON!
MY DAD AND UNCLE TRIED TO FIGHT HIM OFF, BUT HE WAS TOO TOUGH! IN ALL THE CONFUSION WE GOT SEPARATED.
AND THAT'S WHEN HE WENT AFTER ME!
SOMEHOW I MADE IT TO THIS BAY WHERE THE WATER IS TOO SHALLOW FOR HIM TO FOLLOW. BUT NOW I'M STUCK HERE, AND I'M TOO SCARED TO LEAVE!

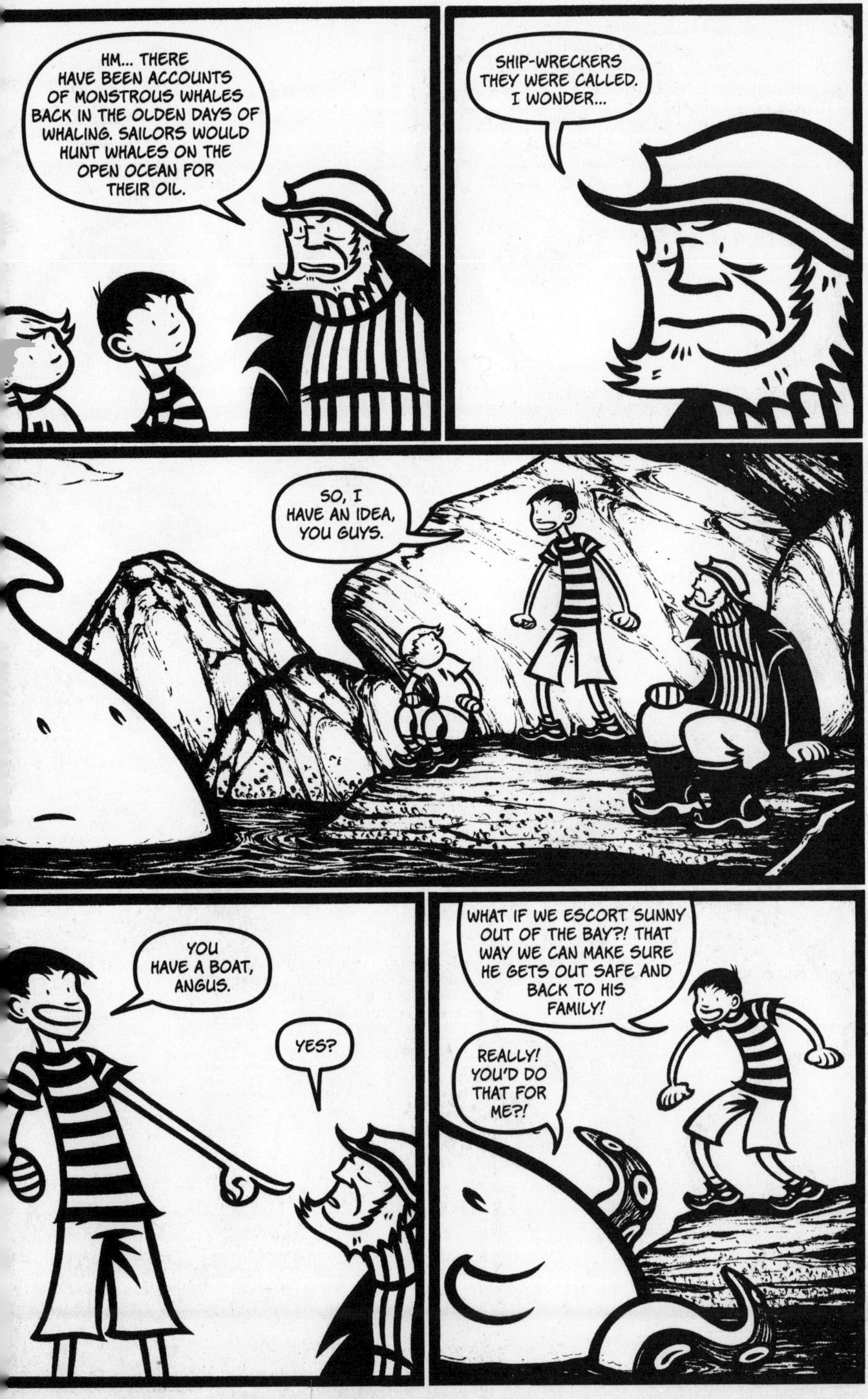
HM... THERE HAVE BEEN ACCOUNTS OF MONSTROUS WHALES BACK IN THE OLDEN DAYS OF WHALING. SAILORS WOULD HUNT WHALES ON THE OPEN OCEAN FOR THEIR OIL.
SHIP-WRECKERS THEY WERE CALLED. I WONDER...
SO, I HAVE AN IDEA, YOU GUYS.
YOU HAVE A BOAT, ANGUS.
YES?
WHAT IF WE ESCORT SUNNY OUT OF THE BAY?! THAT WAY WE CAN MAKE SURE HE GETS OUT SAFE AND BACK TO HIS FAMILY!
REALLY! YOU'D DO THAT FOR ME?!

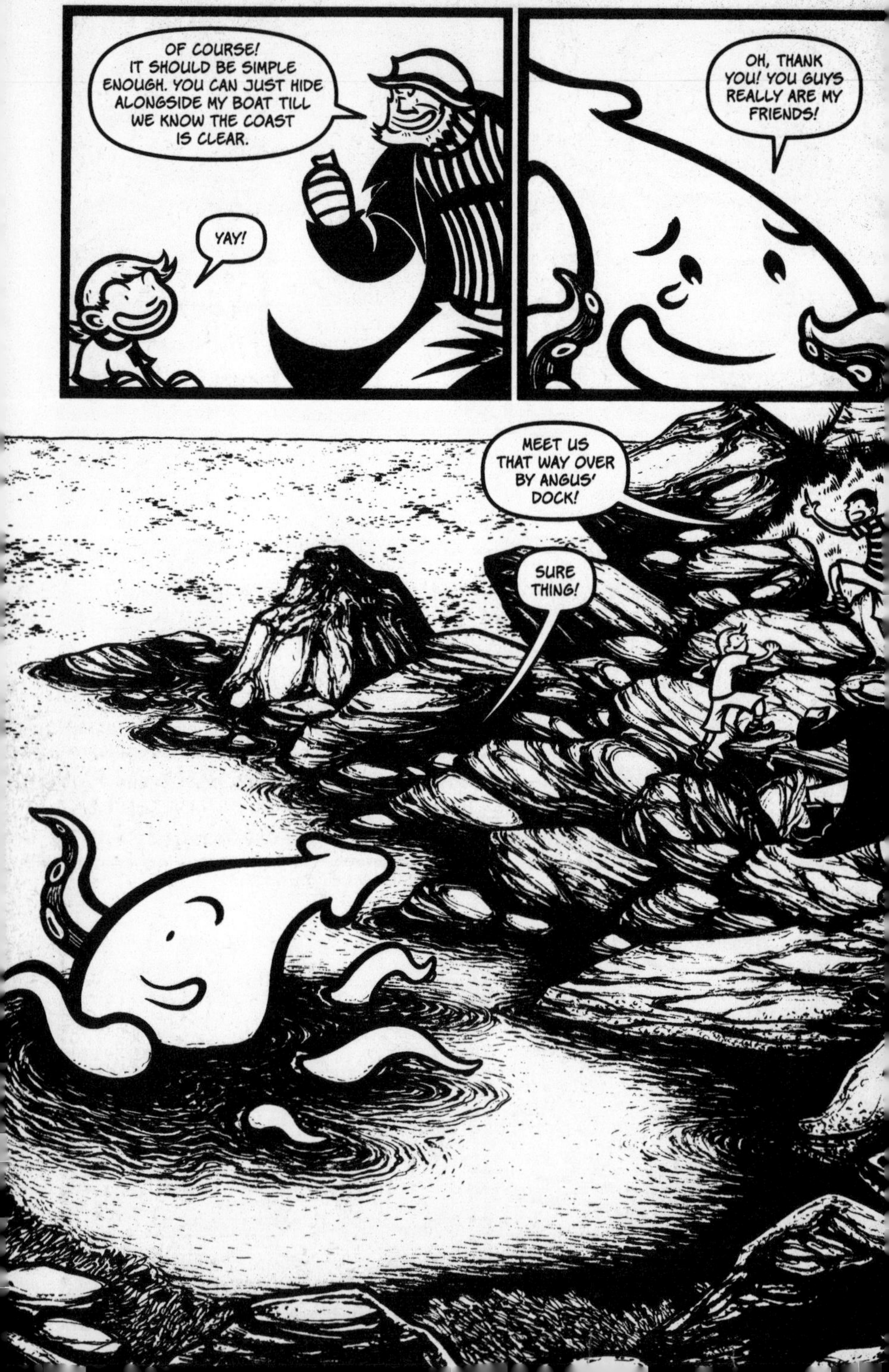
OF COURSE! IT SHOULD BE SIMPLE ENOUGH. YOU CAN JUST HIDE ALONGSIDE MY BOAT TILL WE KNOW THE COAST IS CLEAR.
YAY!
OH, THANK YOU! YOU GUYS REALLY ARE MY FRIENDS!
MEET US THAT WAY OVER BY ANGUS' DOCK!
SURE THING!

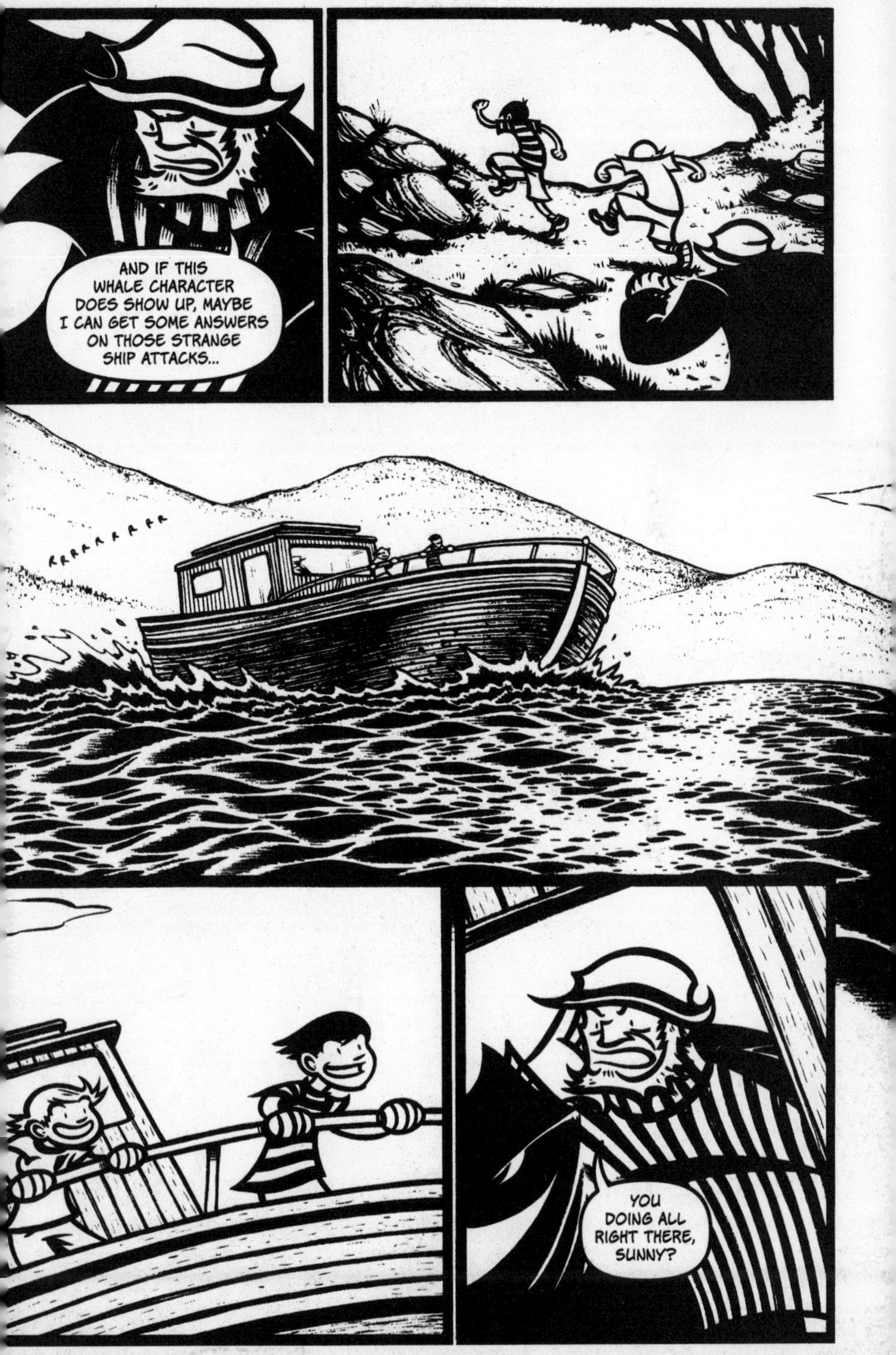
AND IF THIS WHALE CHARACTER DOES SHOW UP, MAYBE I CAN GET SOME ANSWERS ON THOSE STRANGE SHIP ATTACKS...
RRRRRRRRRR
YOU DOING ALL RIGHT THERE, SUNNY?

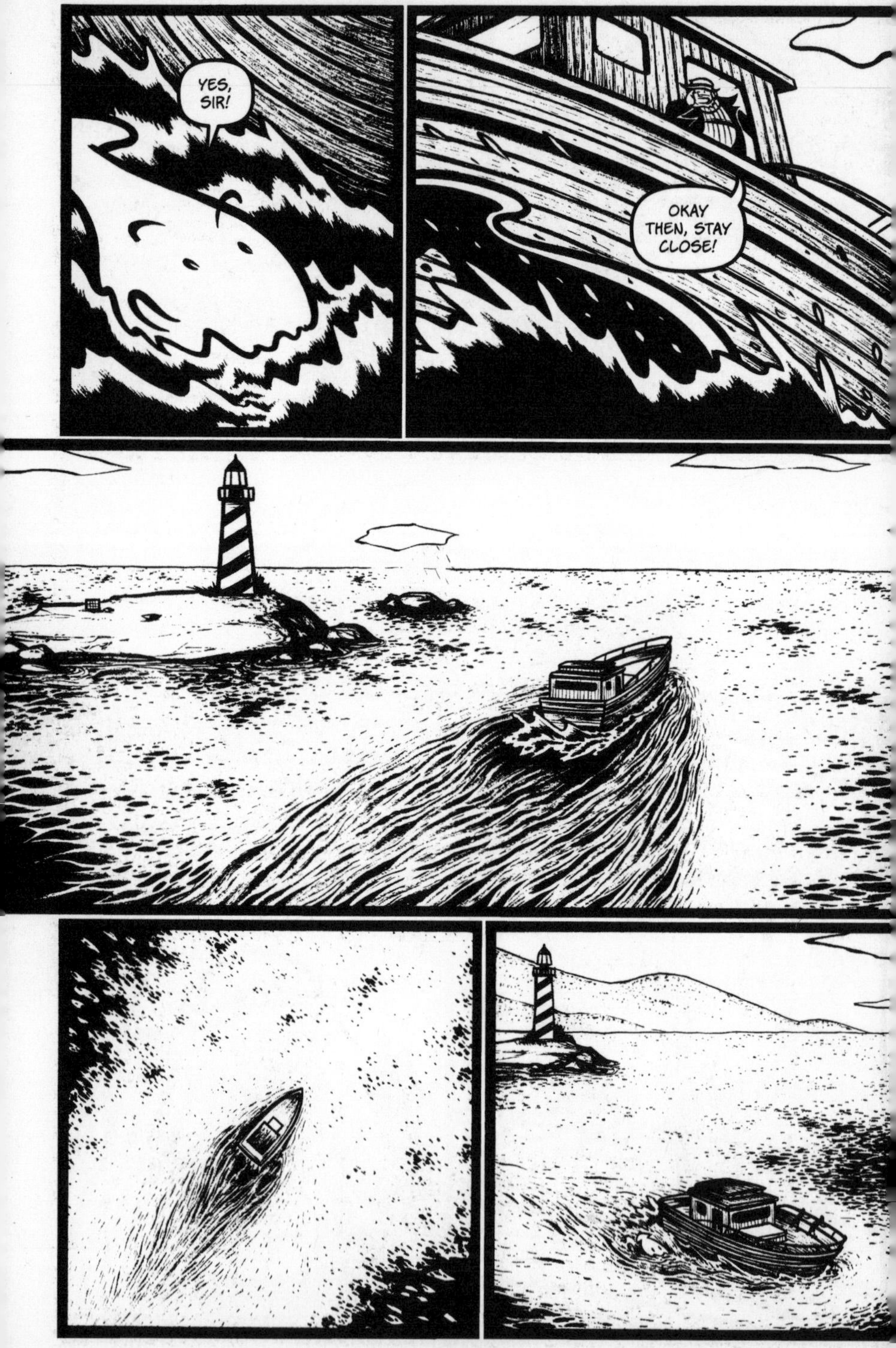
YES, SIR!
OKAY THEN, STAY CLOSE!

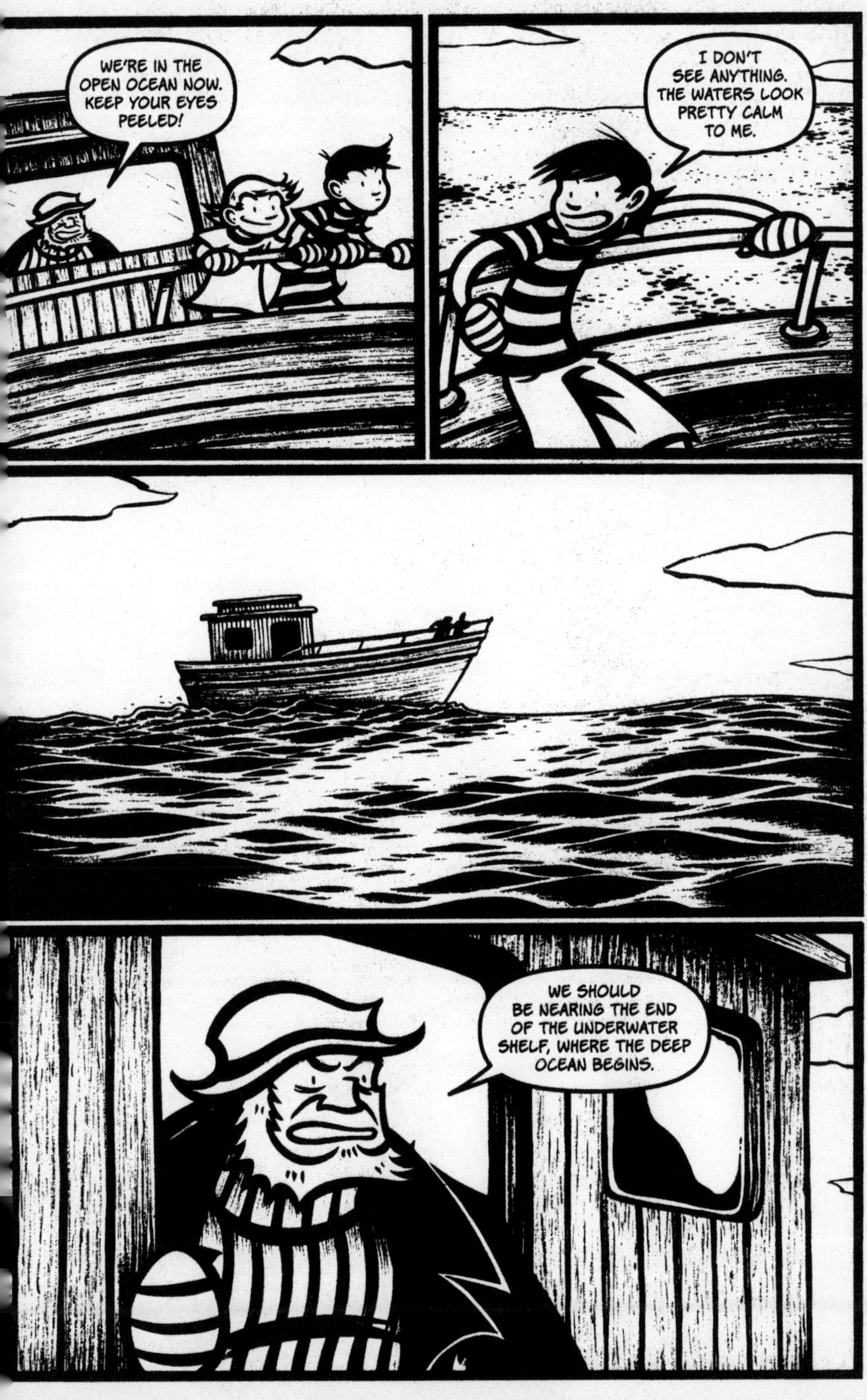
WE'RE IN THE OPEN OCEAN NOW. KEEP YOUR EYES PEELED!
I DON'T SEE ANYTHING. THE WATERS LOOK PRETTY CALM TO ME.
WE SHOULD BE NEARING THE END OF THE UNDERWATER SHELF, WHERE THE DEEP OCEAN BEGINS.

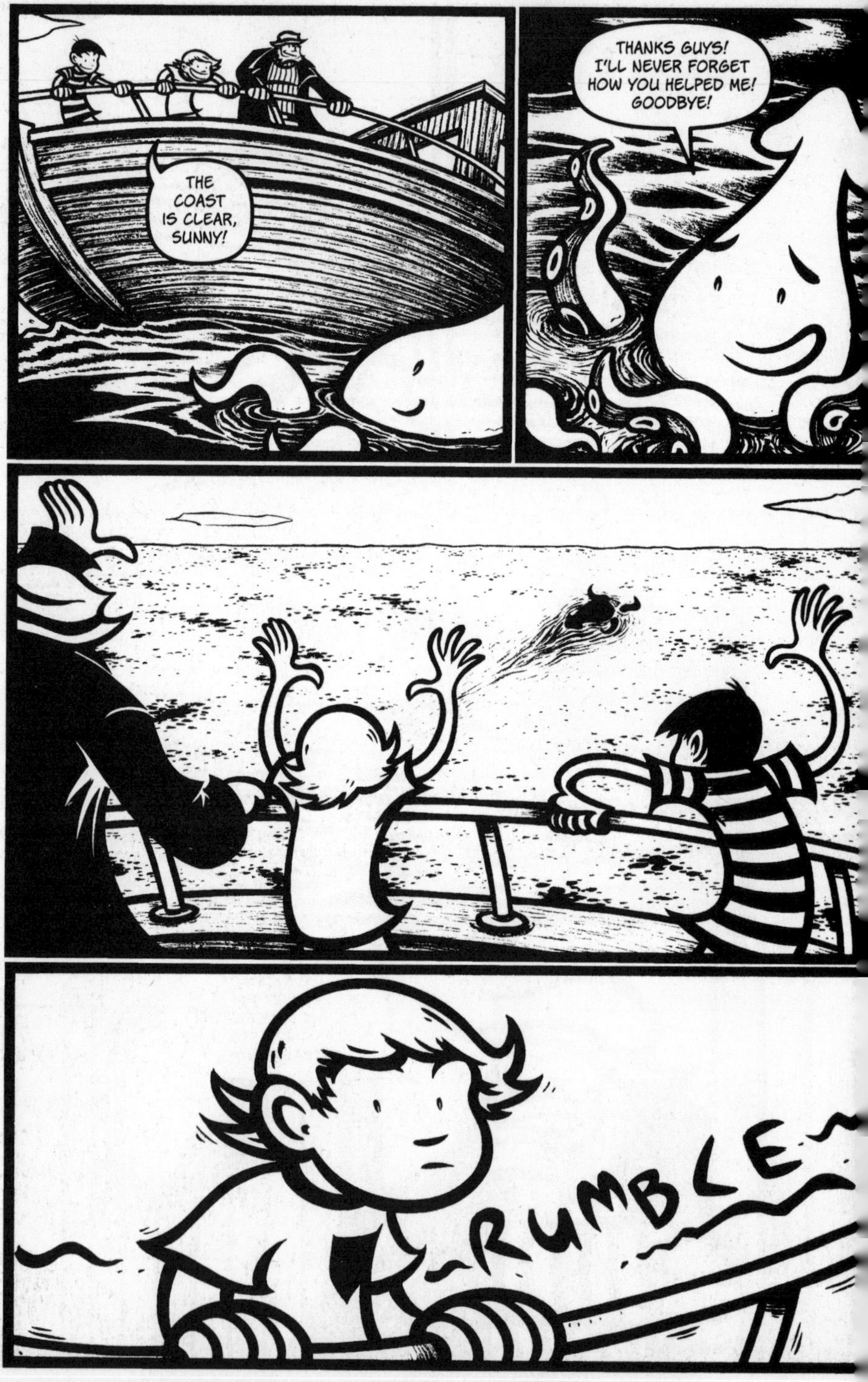
THE COAST IS CLEAR, SUNNY!
THANKS GUYS! I'LL NEVER FORGET HOW YOU HELPED ME! GOODBYE!
~RUMBLE~

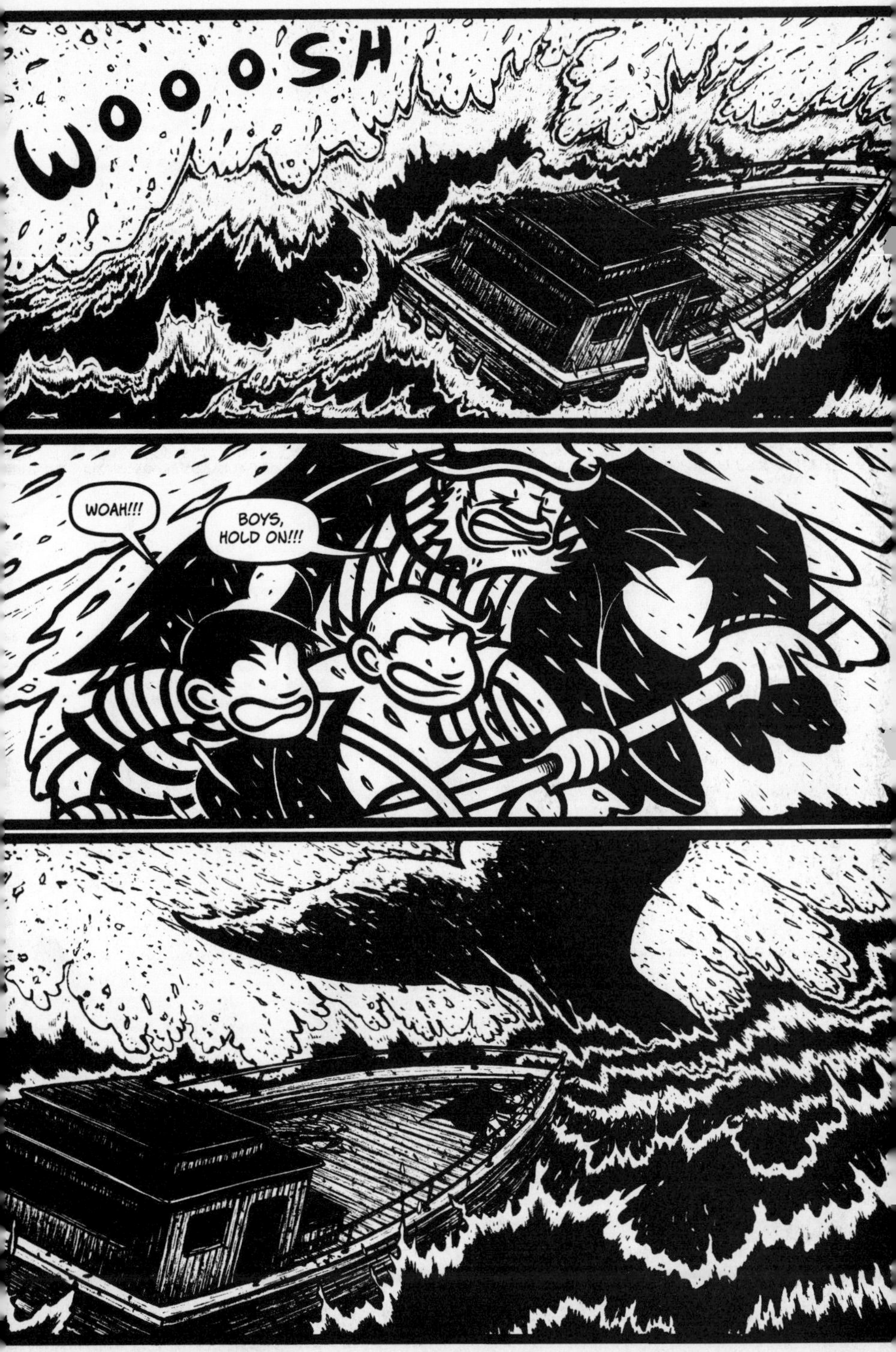
WOOOSH
WOAH!!!
BOYS, HOLD ON!!!

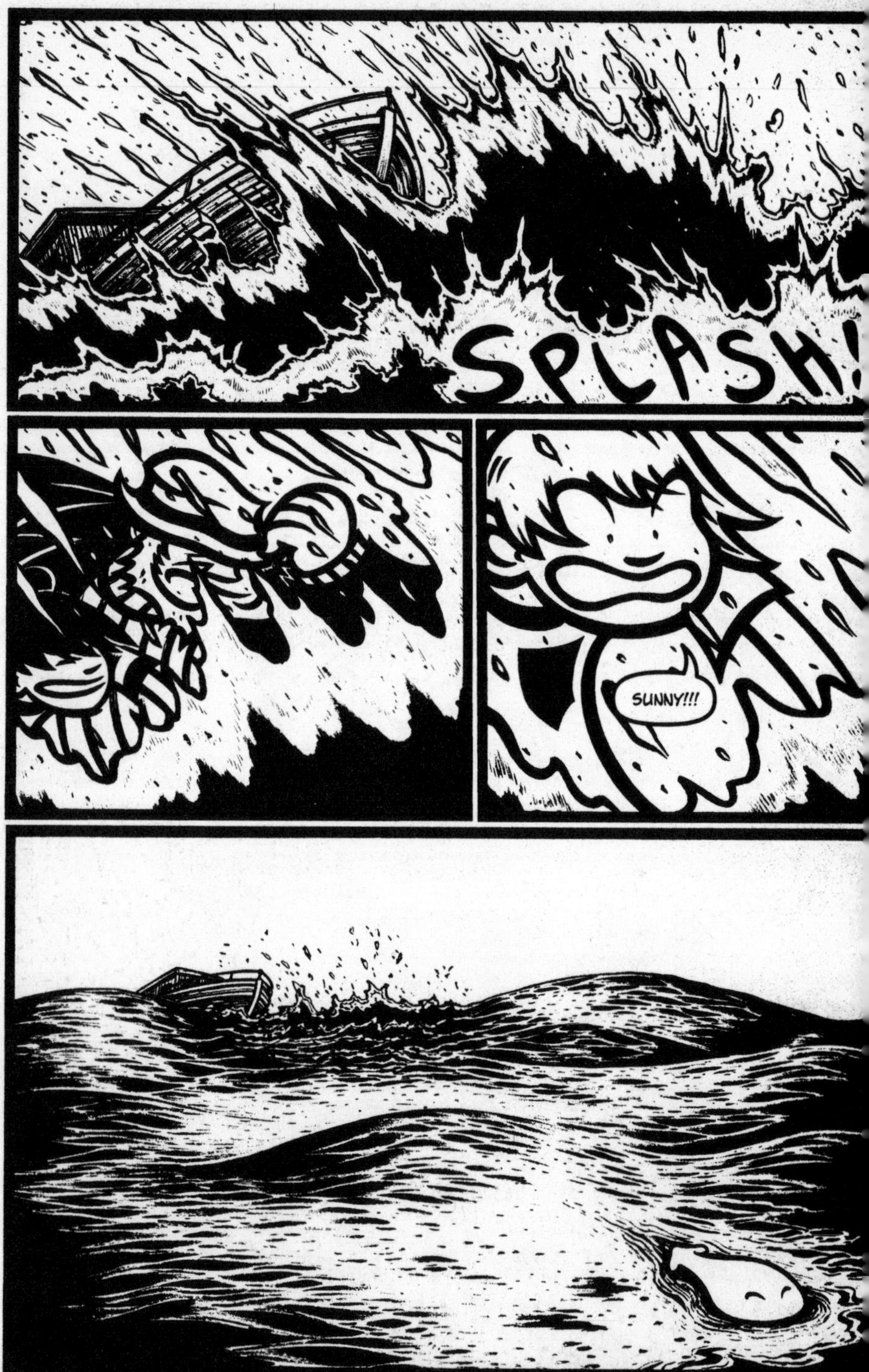
SPLASH!
SUNNY!!!

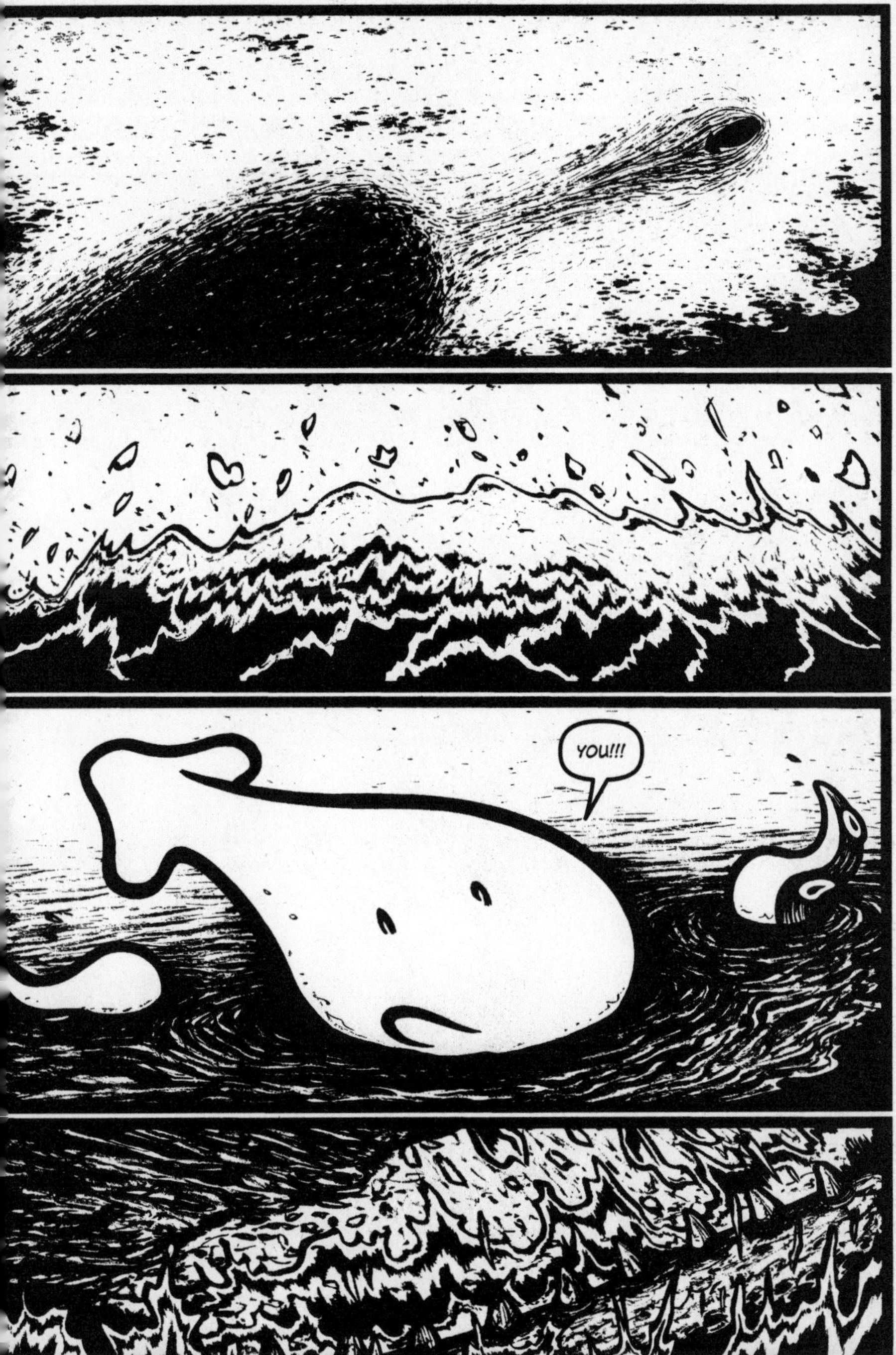
YOU!!!

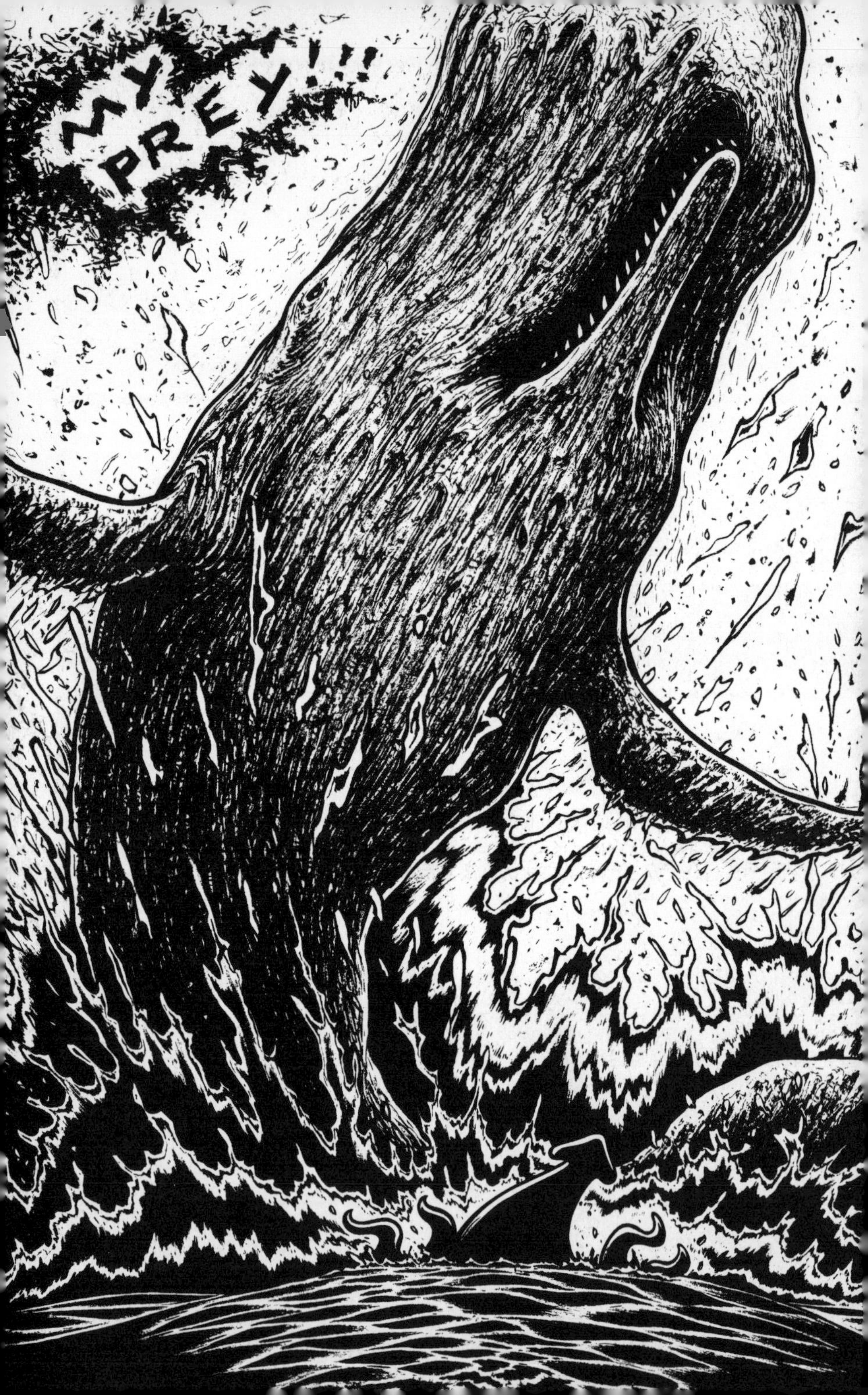
MY PREY!!!

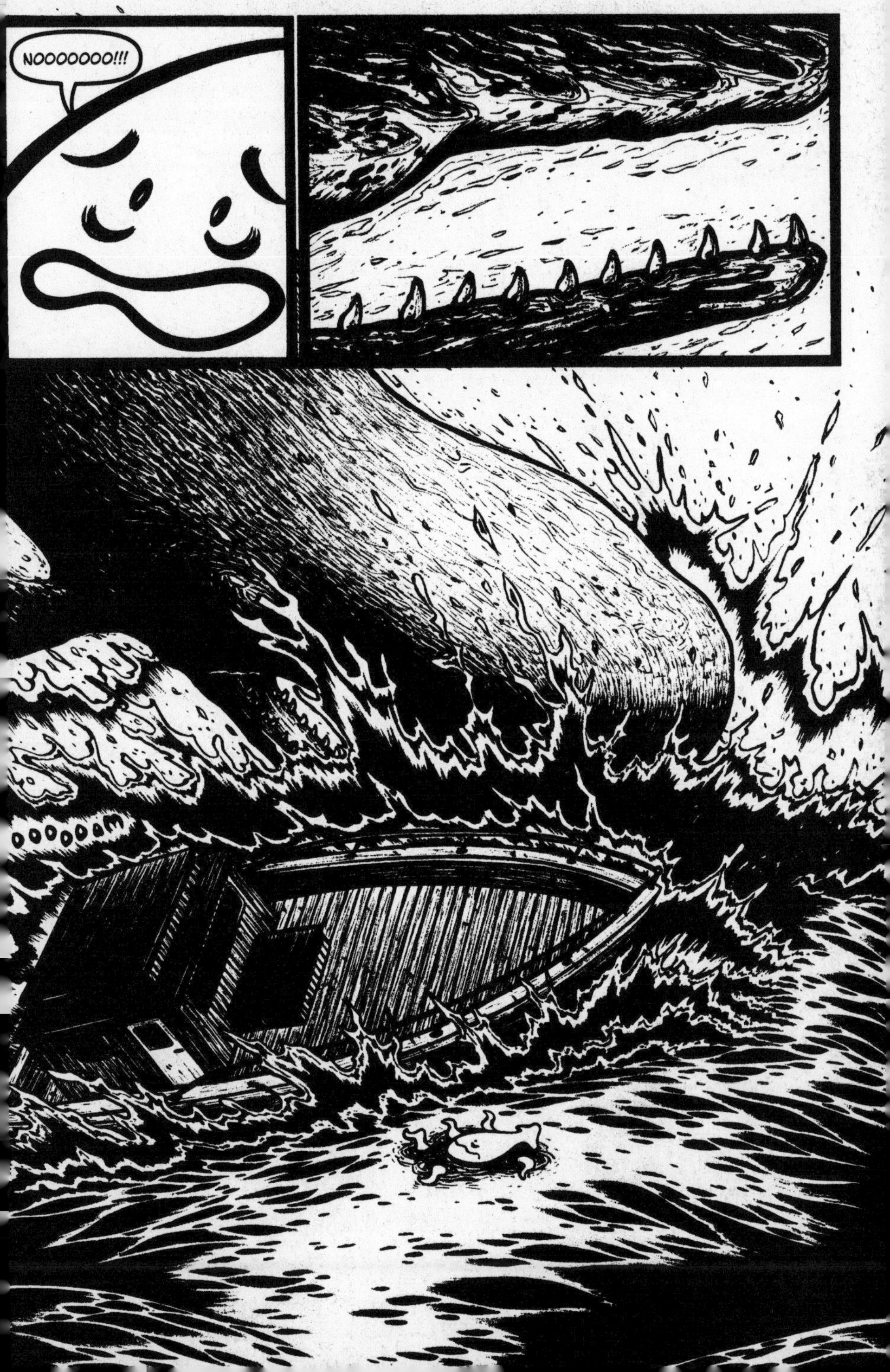
NOOOOOOO!!!
OOOOOOOM

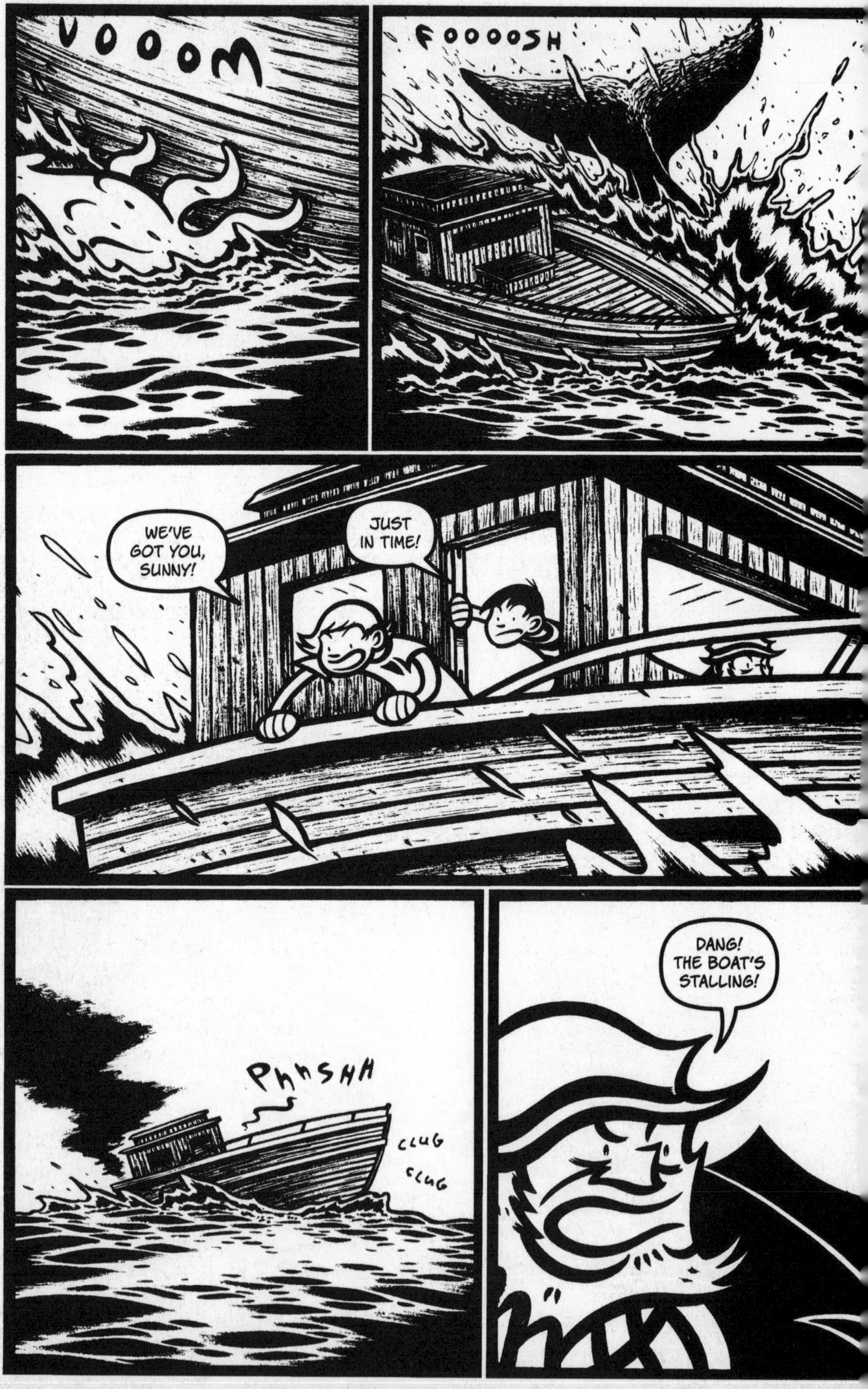
VOOOM
FOOOOSH
WE'VE GOT YOU, SUNNY!
JUST IN TIME!
PHHSHH
CLUG
CLUG
DANG! THE BOAT'S STALLING!

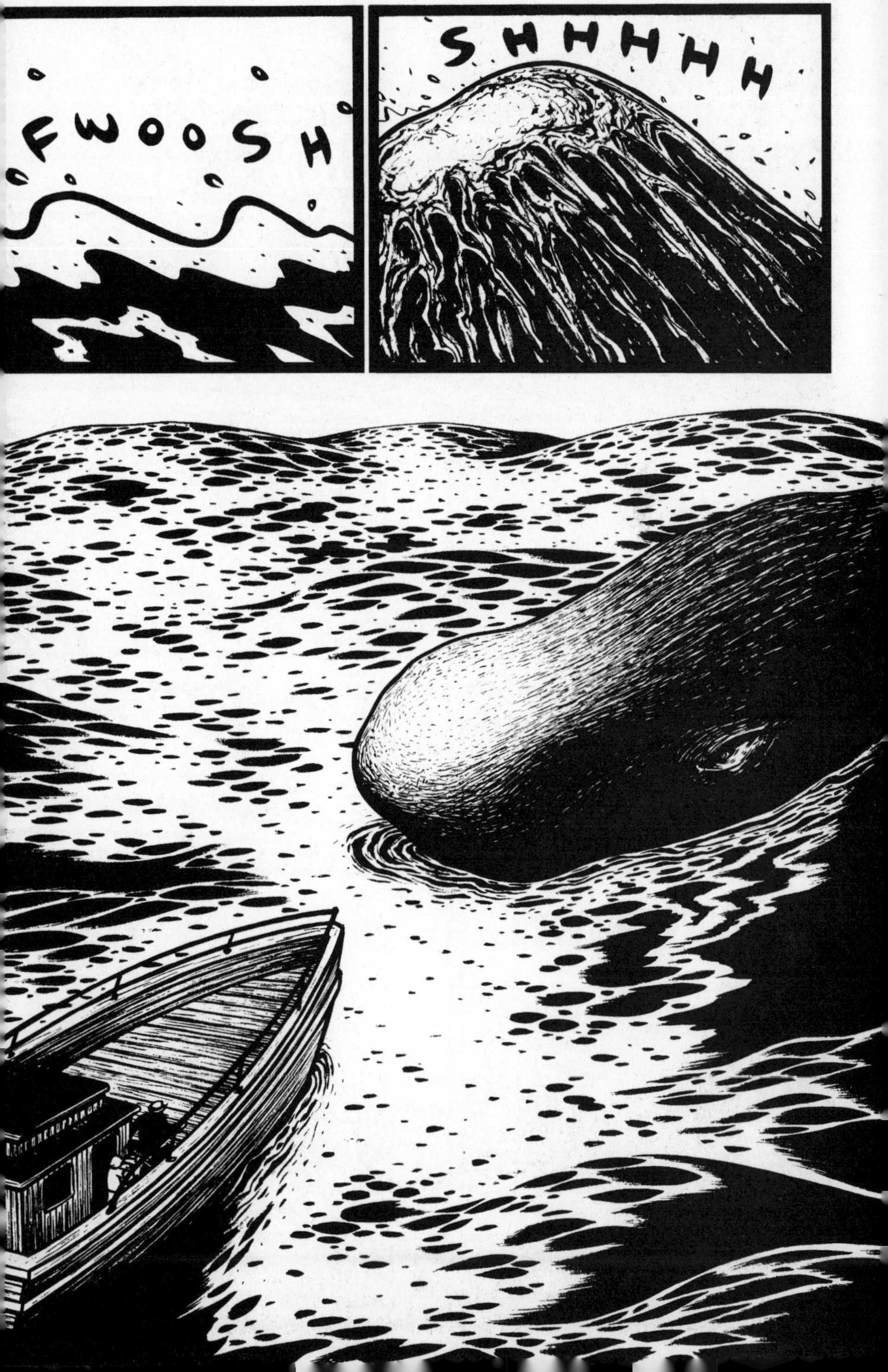
FWOOSH
SHHHHH

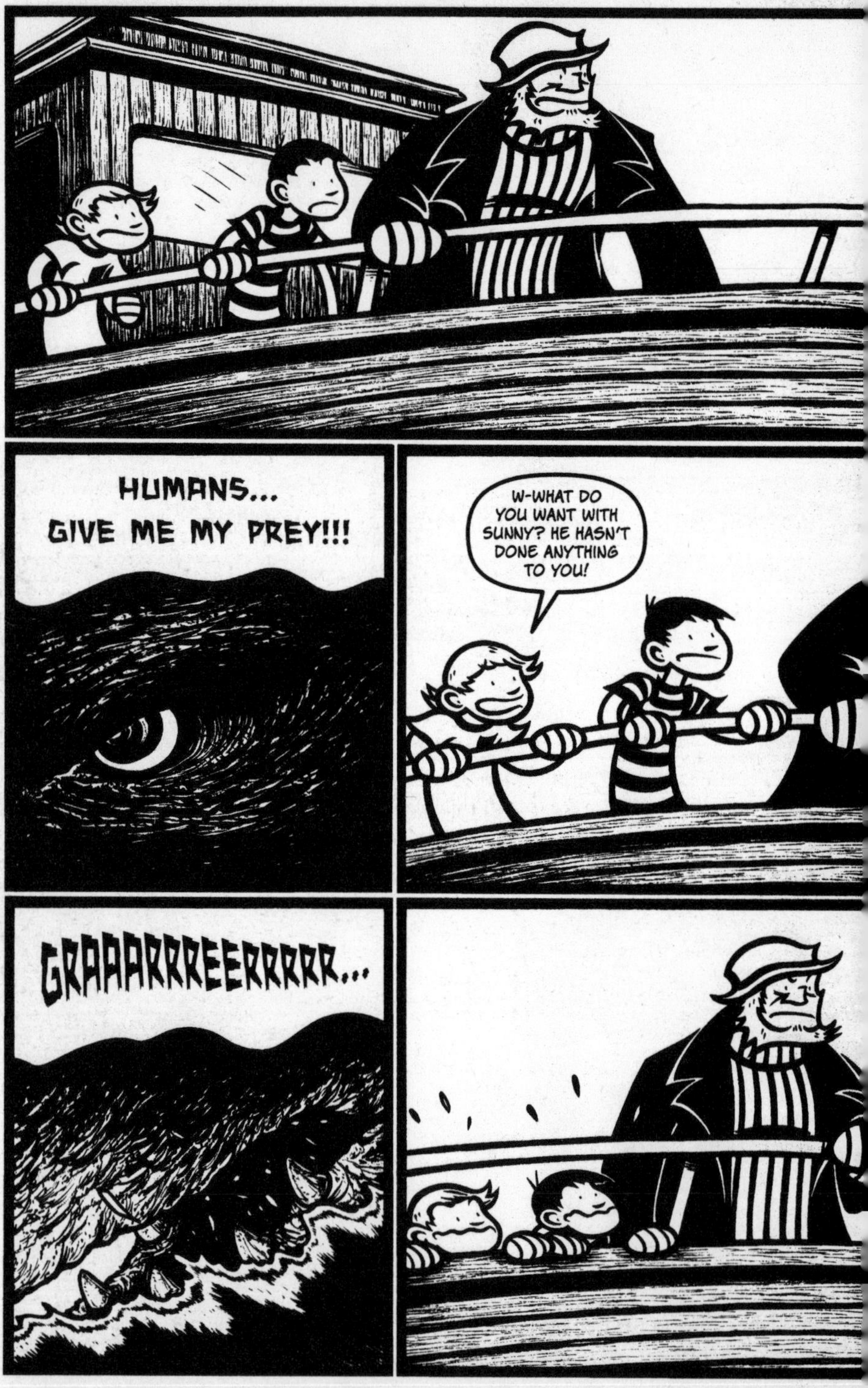
HUMANS... GIVE ME MY PREY!!!
W-WHAT DO YOU WANT WITH SUNNY? HE HASN'T DONE ANYTHING TO YOU!
GRAAARRREERRRR...

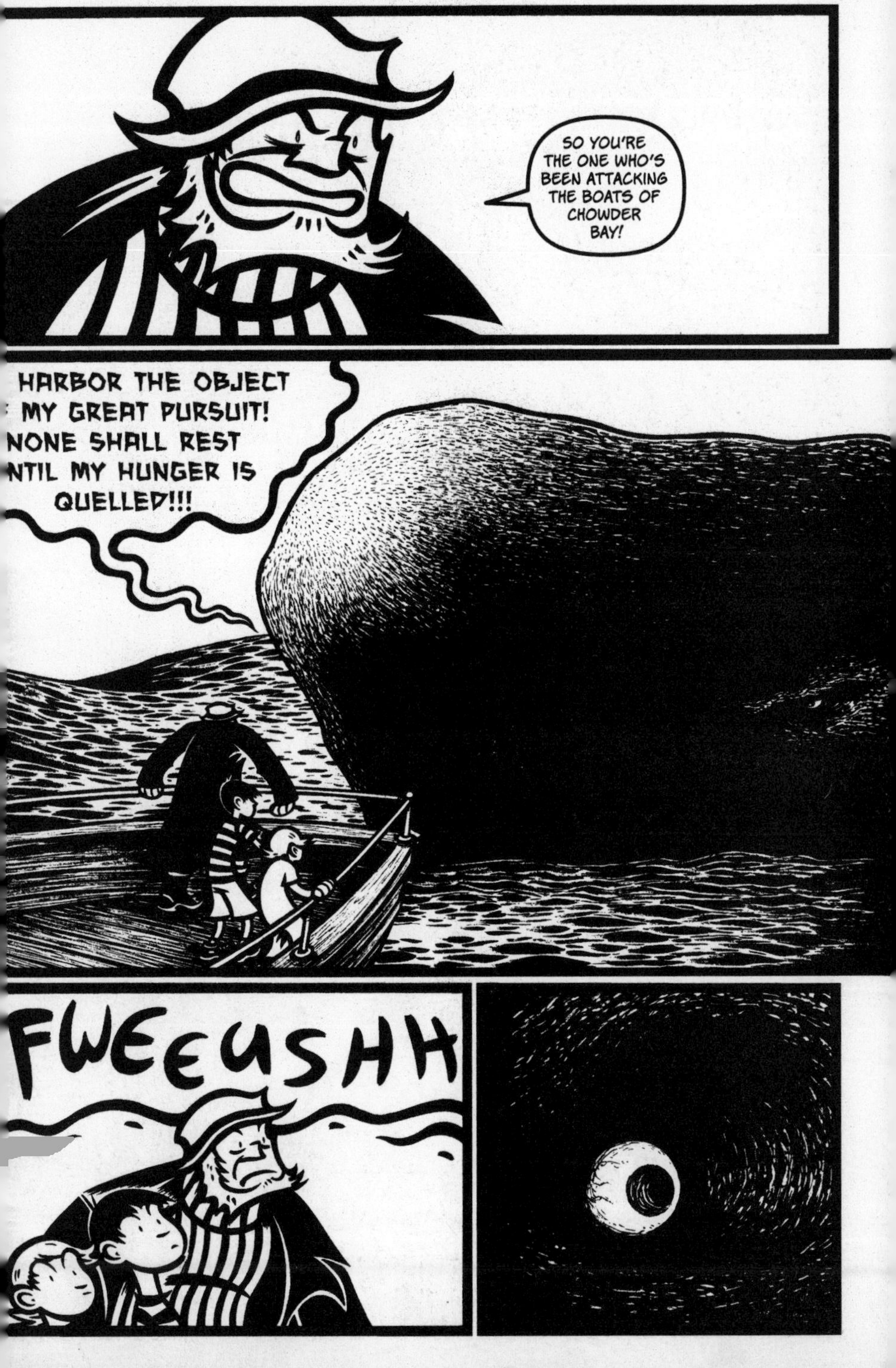
SO YOU'RE THE ONE WHO'S BEEN ATTACKING THE BOATS OF CHOWDER BAY!
HARBOR THE OBJECT MY GREAT PURSUIT! NONE SHALL REST NTIL MY HUNGER IS QUELLED!!!
FWEEUSHH

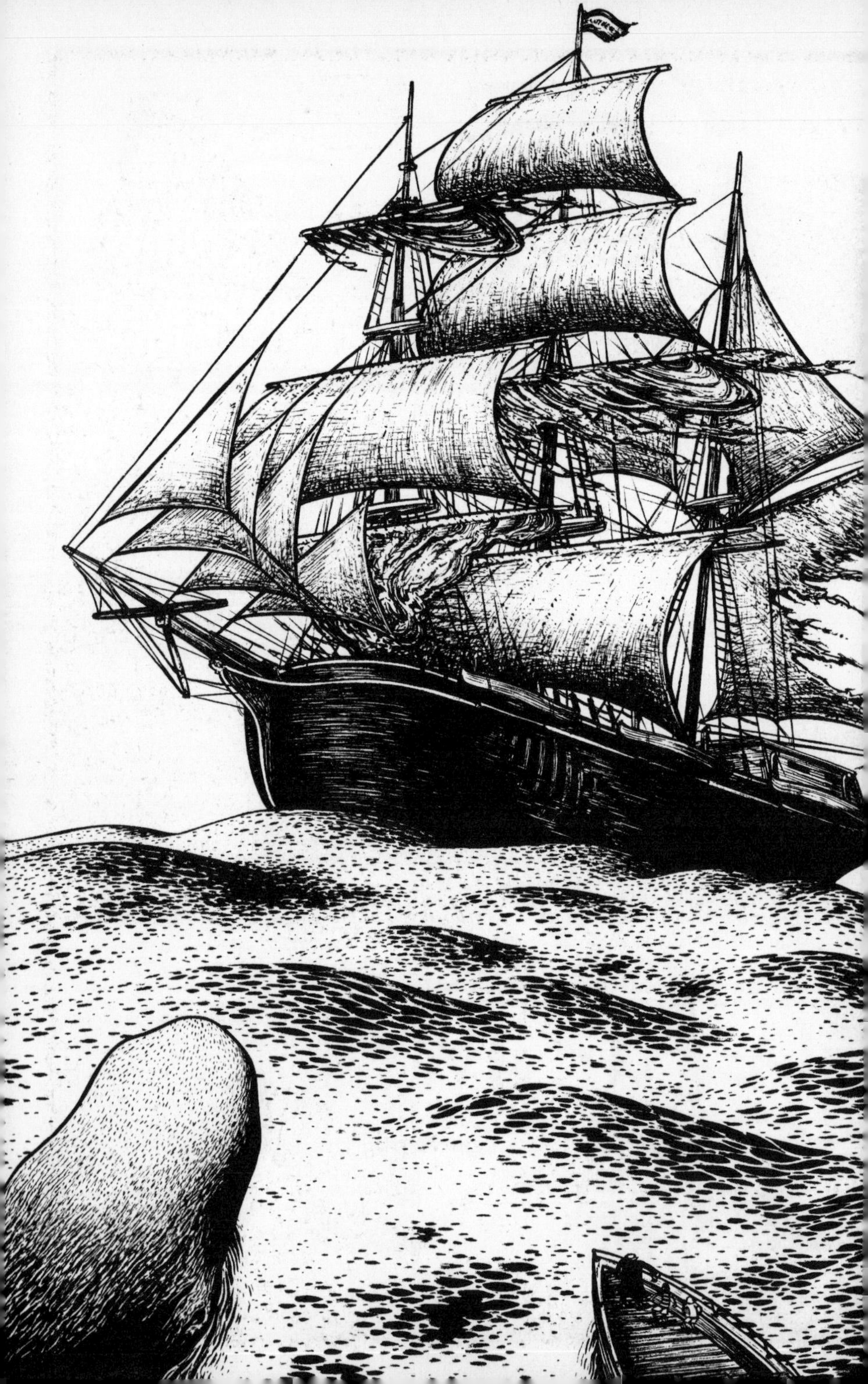

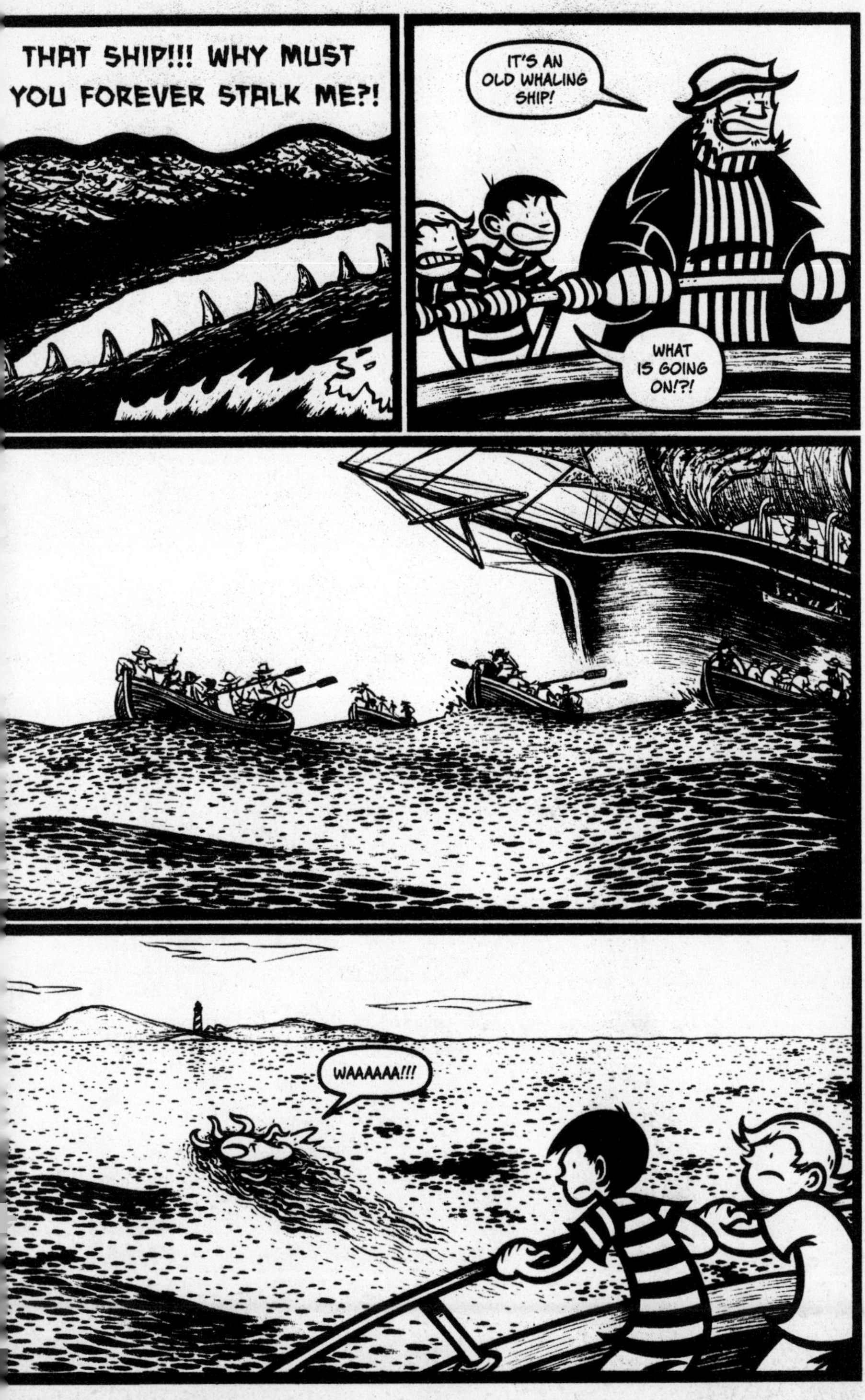
THAT SHIP!!! WHY MUST YOU FOREVER STALK ME?!
IT'S AN OLD WHALING SHIP!
WHAT IS GOING ON!?!
WAAAAAA!!!

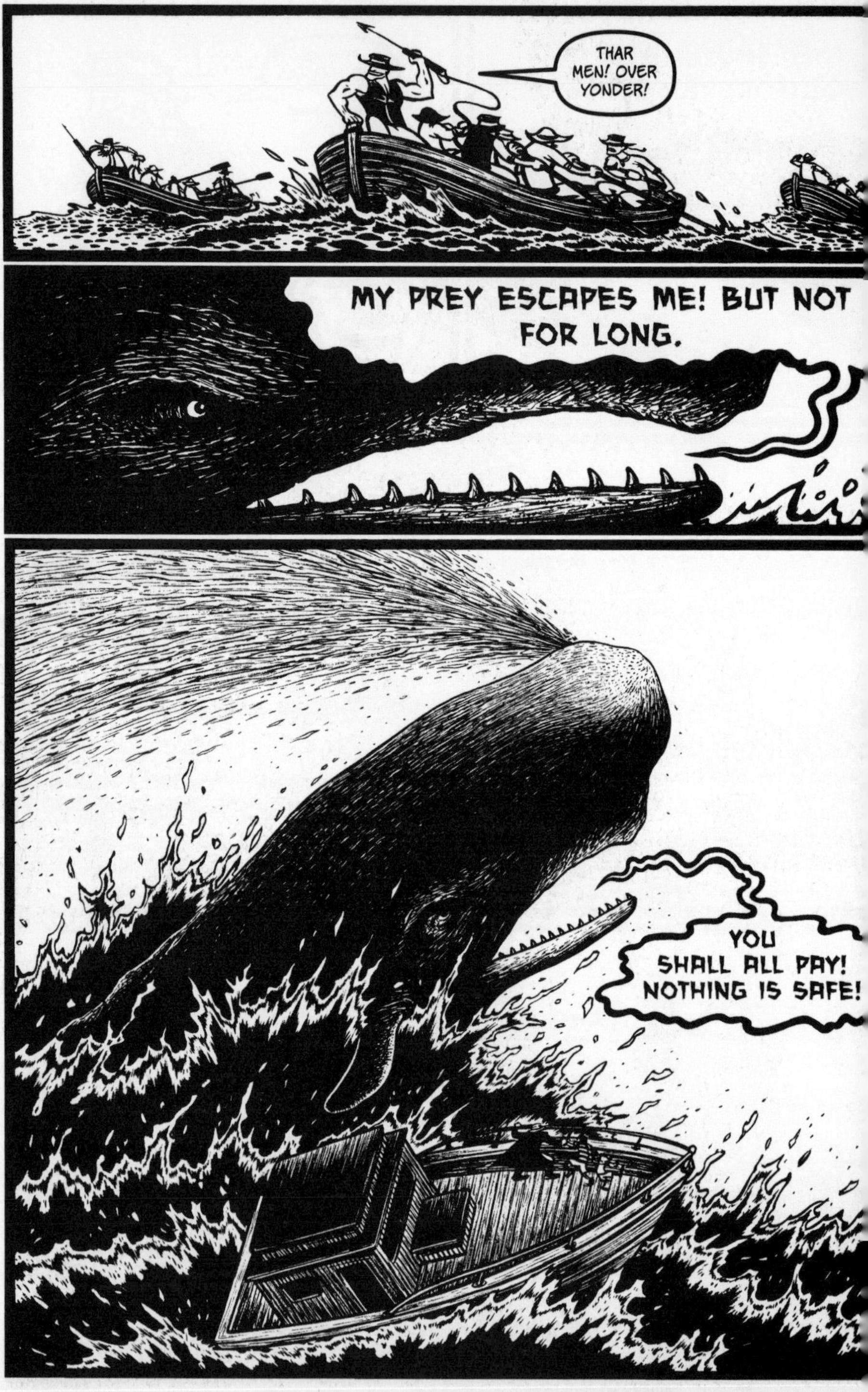
THAR MEN! OVER YONDER!
MY PREY ESCAPES ME! BUT NOT FOR LONG.
YOU SHALL ALL PAY! NOTHING IS SAFE!

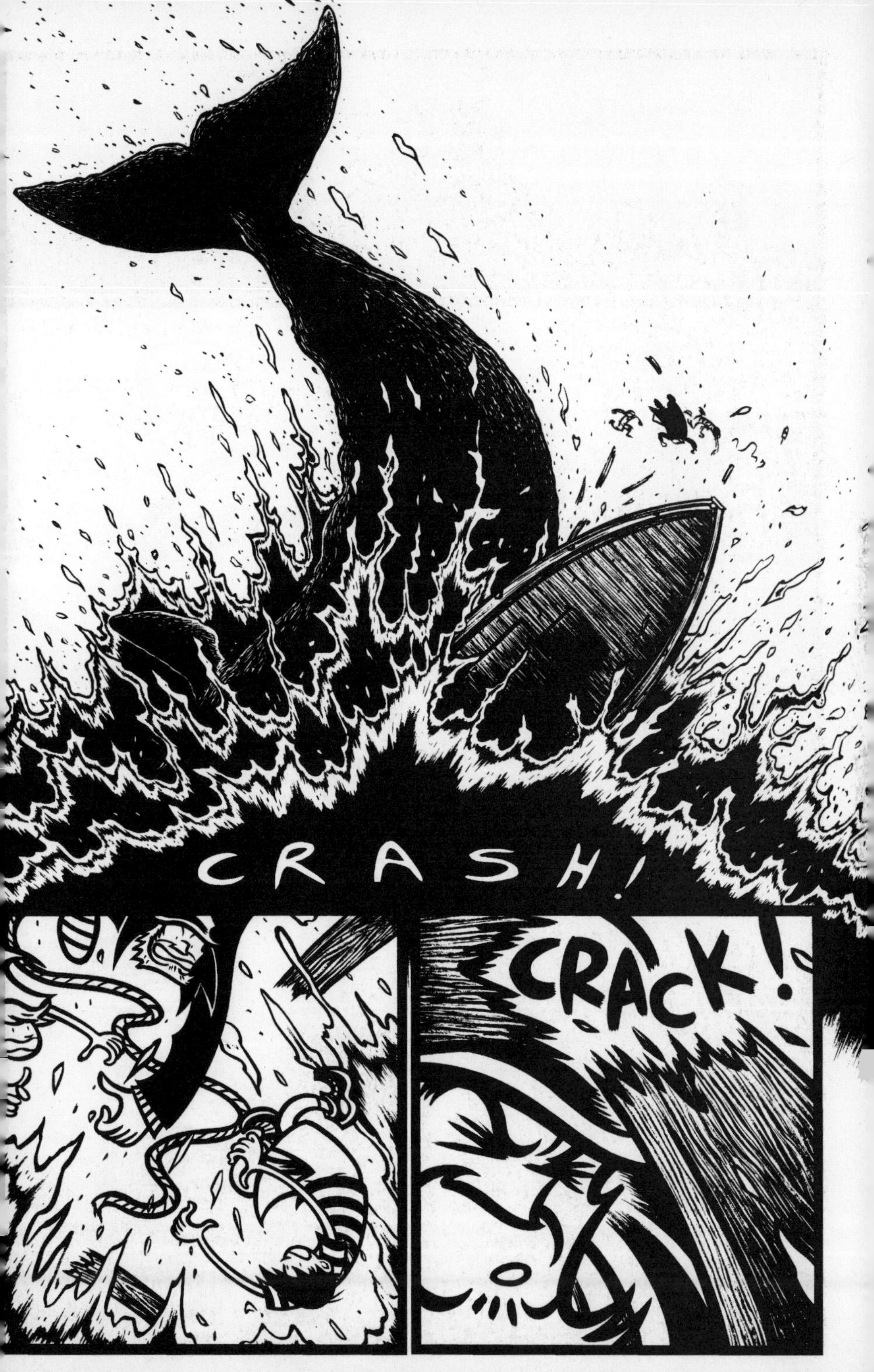
CRASH!
CRACK!

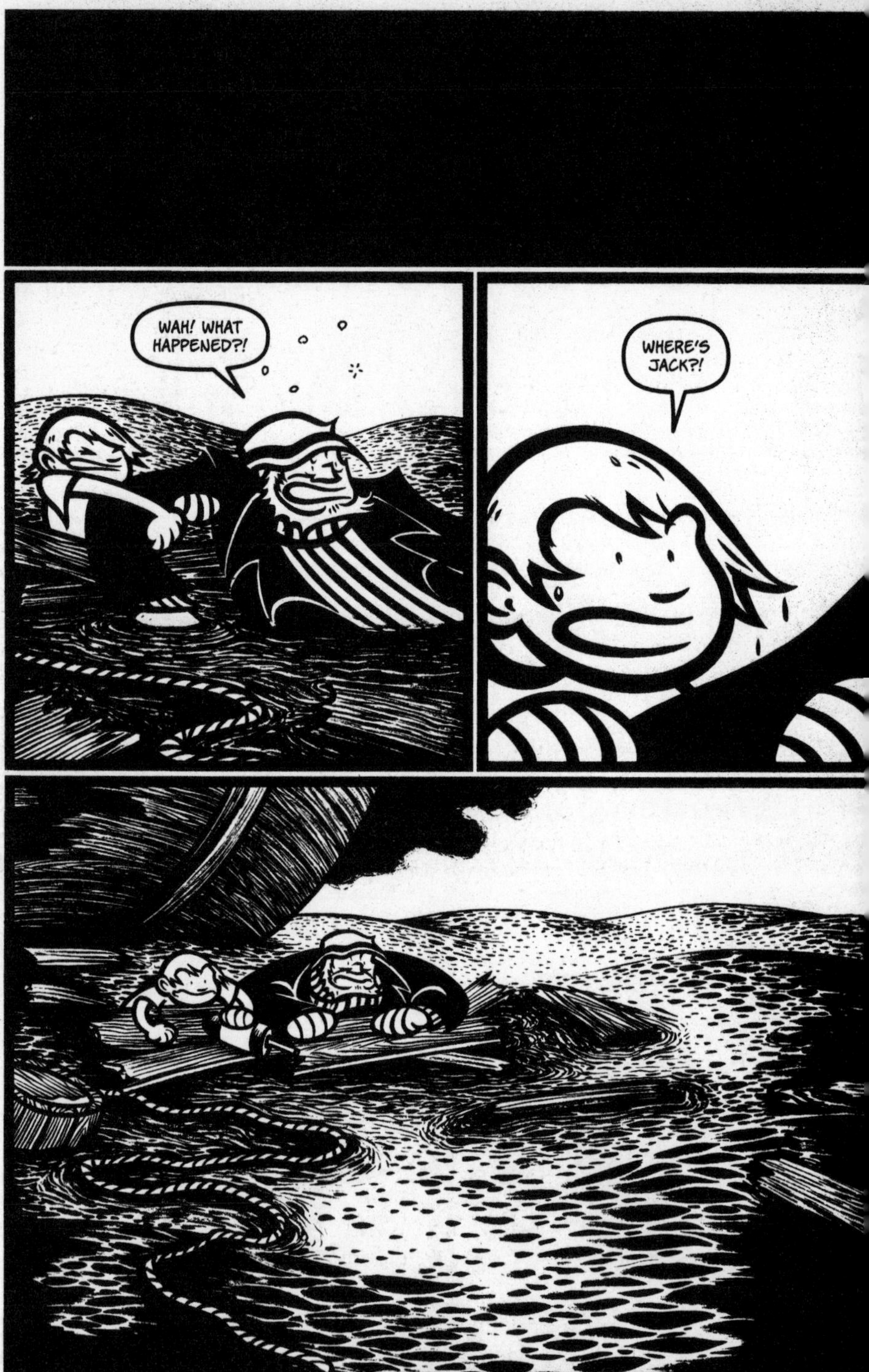
WAH! WHAT HAPPENED?!
WHERE'S JACK?!

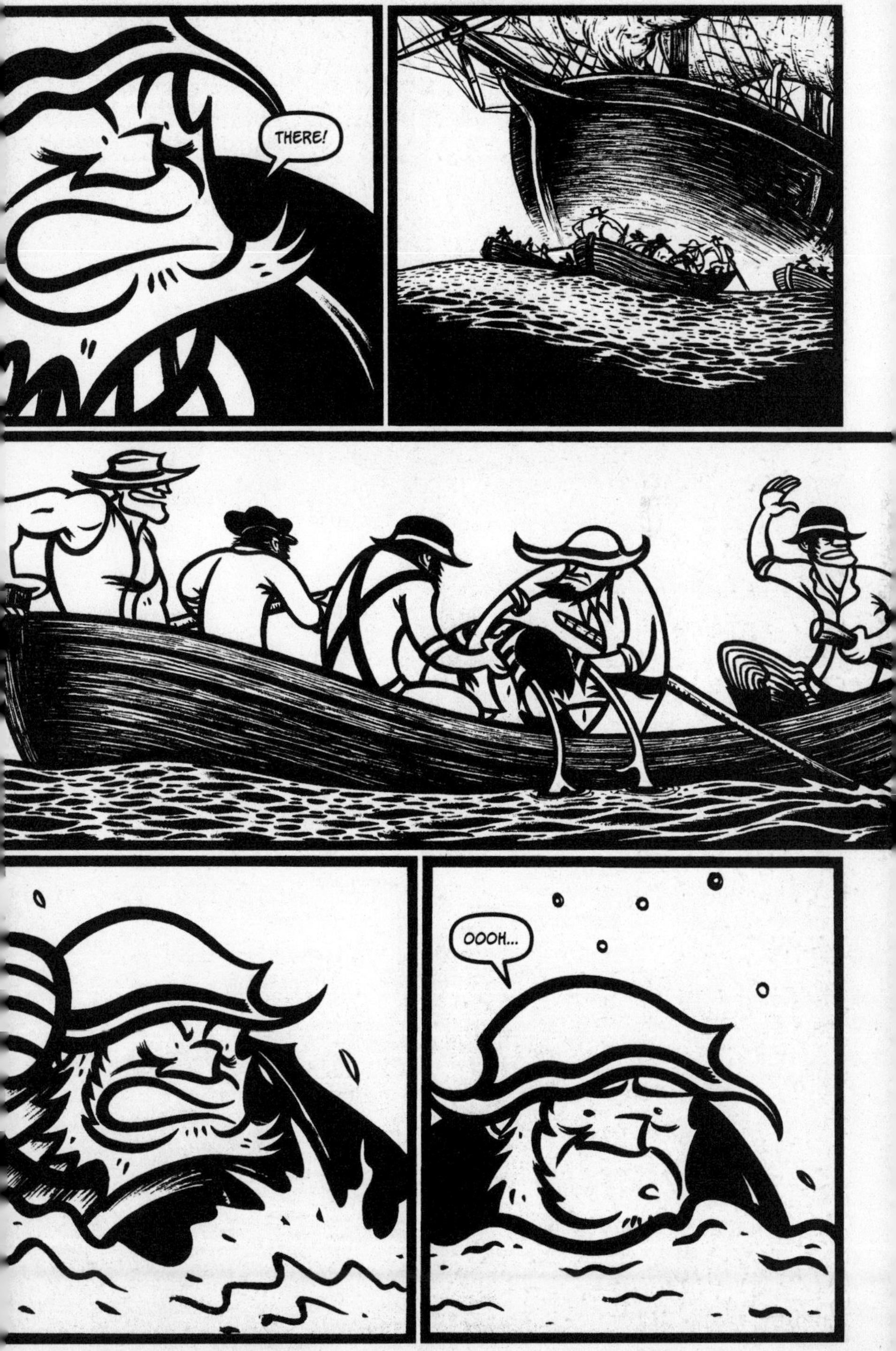
THERE!
OOOH...

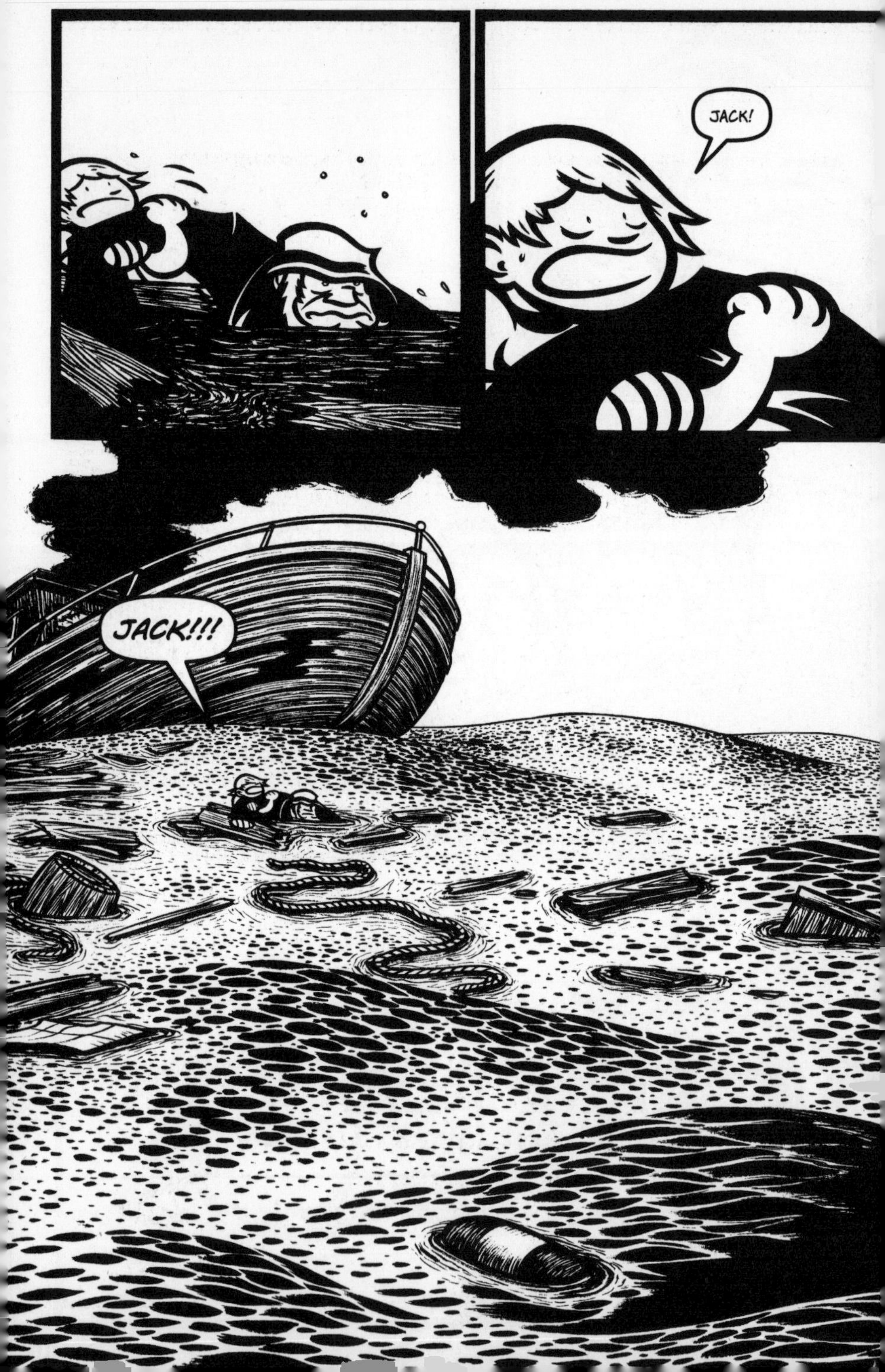
JACK!
JACK!!!

Next time. . .

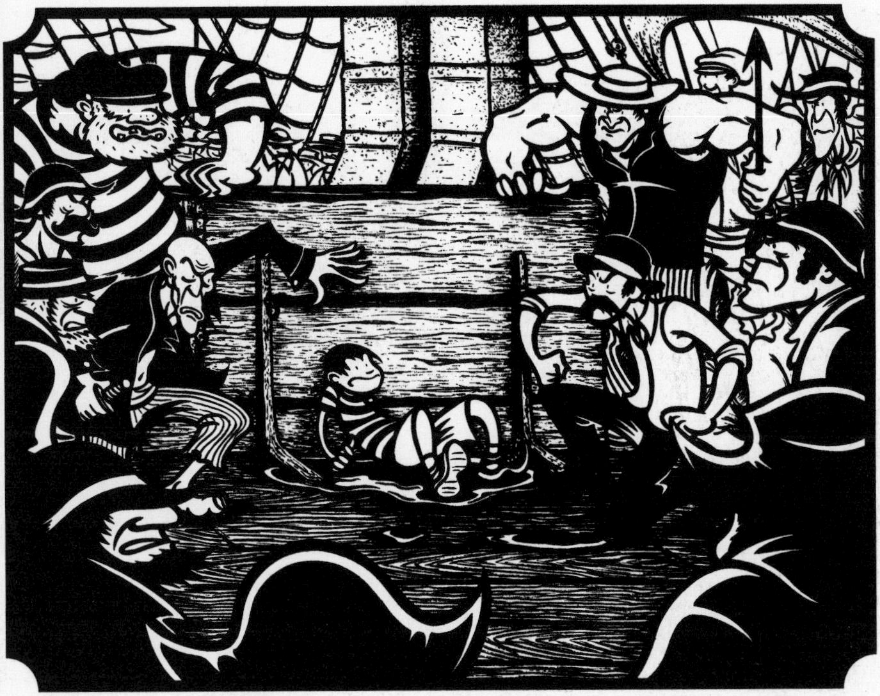

Jack has been abducted by 19th century whalers while Benny and Angus are left stranded on the high seas! Can Jack handle life aboard a ghost ship and will they solve the mystery of this mighty whale before it attacks them again?

FIND OUT IN VOLUME FIVE OF

SALT WATER TAFFY

THE SEASIDE ADVENTURES OF

JACK AND BENNY

CALDERA'S REVENGE PART 2

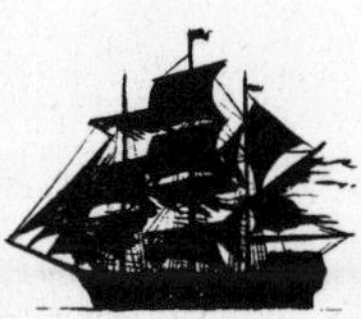

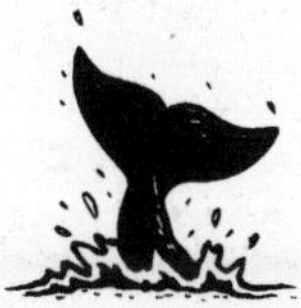

And now...

AN

EXCITING ADVENTURE

WITH

DAN the WOLF

Written by

MATTHEW LOUX

Illustrated by

BRIAN STONE

Lettered by

DOUGLAS E. SHERWOOD

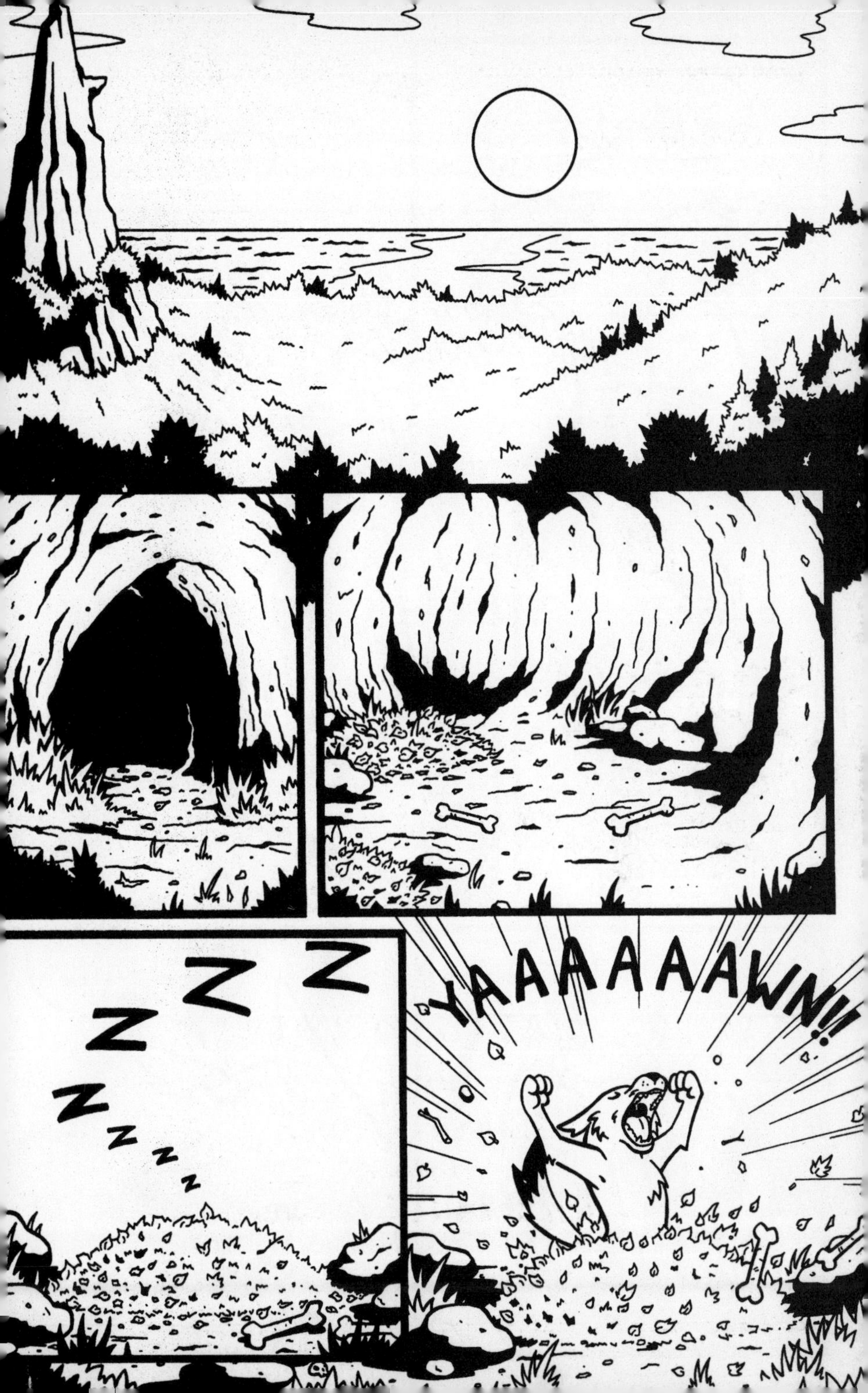
Z Z Z Z z z z
YAAAAAAAWN!!

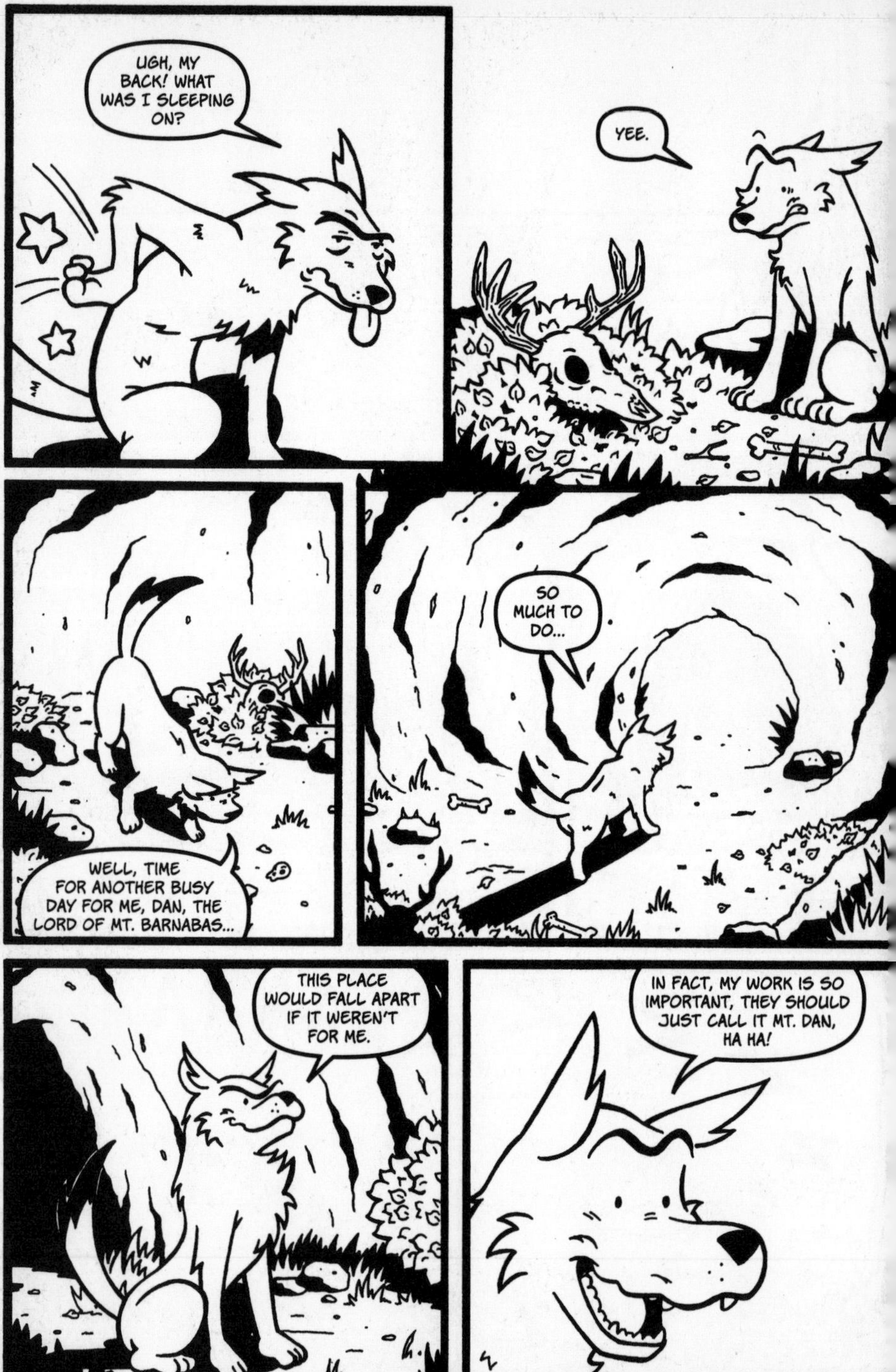
UGH, MY BACK! WHAT WAS I SLEEPING ON?
YEE.
WELL, TIME FOR ANOTHER BUSY DAY FOR ME, DAN, THE LORD OF MT. BARNABAS...
SO MUCH TO DO...
THIS PLACE WOULD FALL APART IF IT WEREN'T FOR ME.
IN FACT, MY WORK IS SO IMPORTANT, THEY SHOULD JUST CALL IT MT. DAN, HA HA!

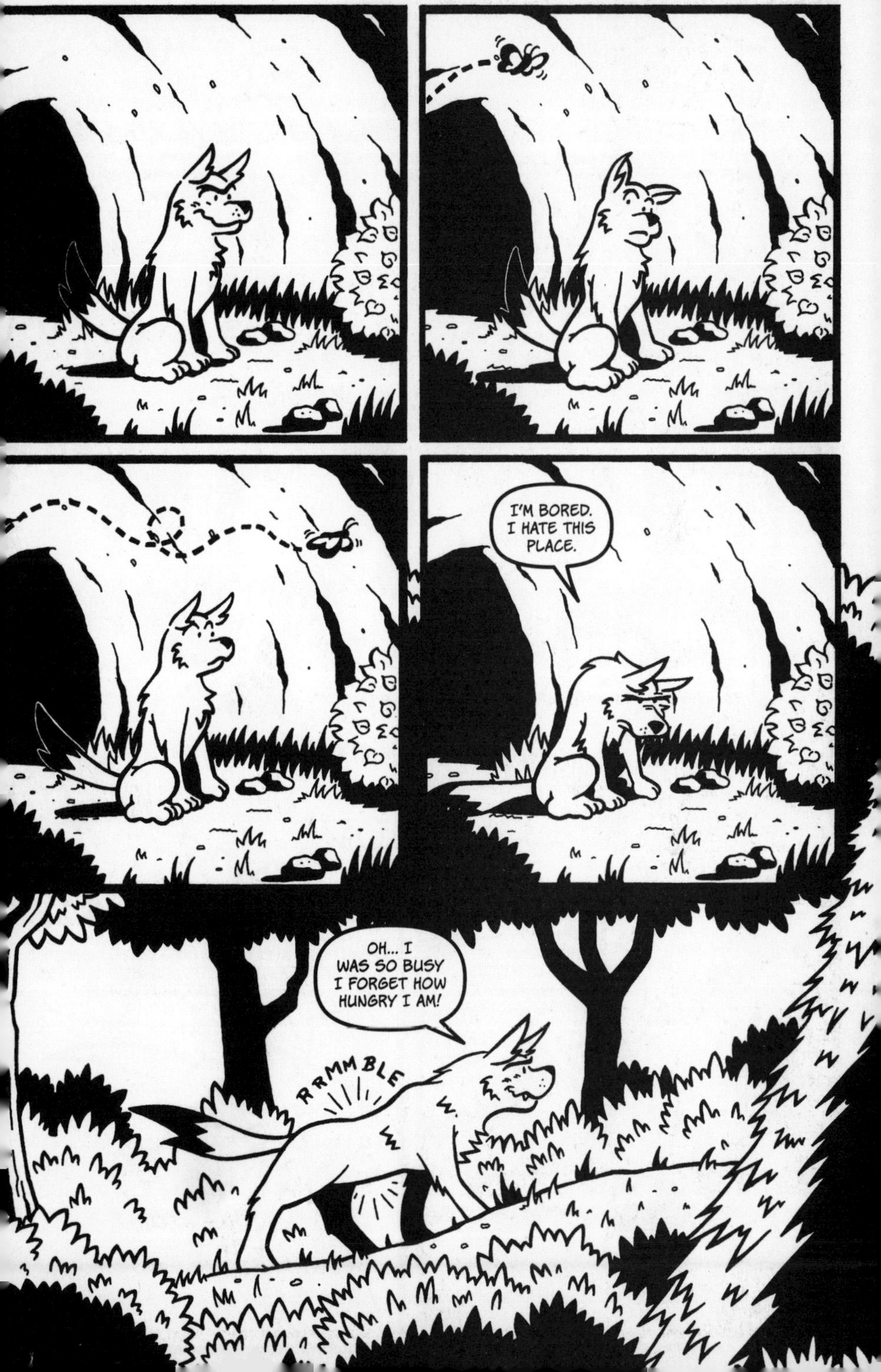
I'M BORED. I HATE THIS PLACE.
OH... I WAS SO BUSY I FORGET HOW HUNGRY I AM!
RRMMBLE

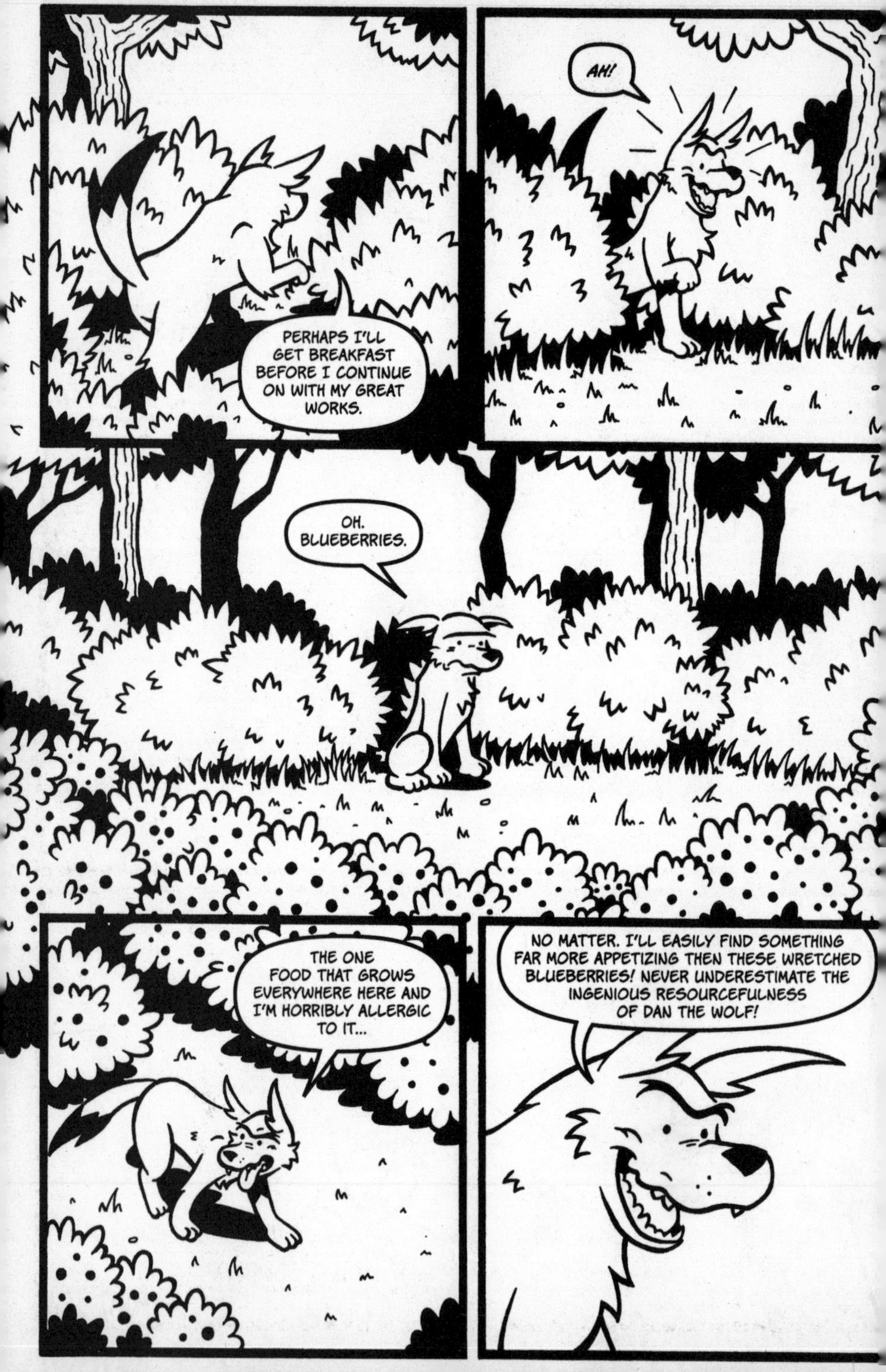
PERHAPS I'LL GET BREAKFAST BEFORE I CONTINUE ON WITH MY GREAT WORKS.
AH!
OH. BLUEBERRIES.
THE ONE FOOD THAT GROWS EVERYWHERE HERE AND I'M HORRIBLY ALLERGIC TO IT...
NO MATTER. I'LL EASILY FIND SOMETHING FAR MORE APPETIZING THEN THESE WRETCHED BLUEBERRIES! NEVER UNDERESTIMATE THE INGENIOUS RESOURCEFULNESS OF DAN THE WOLF!

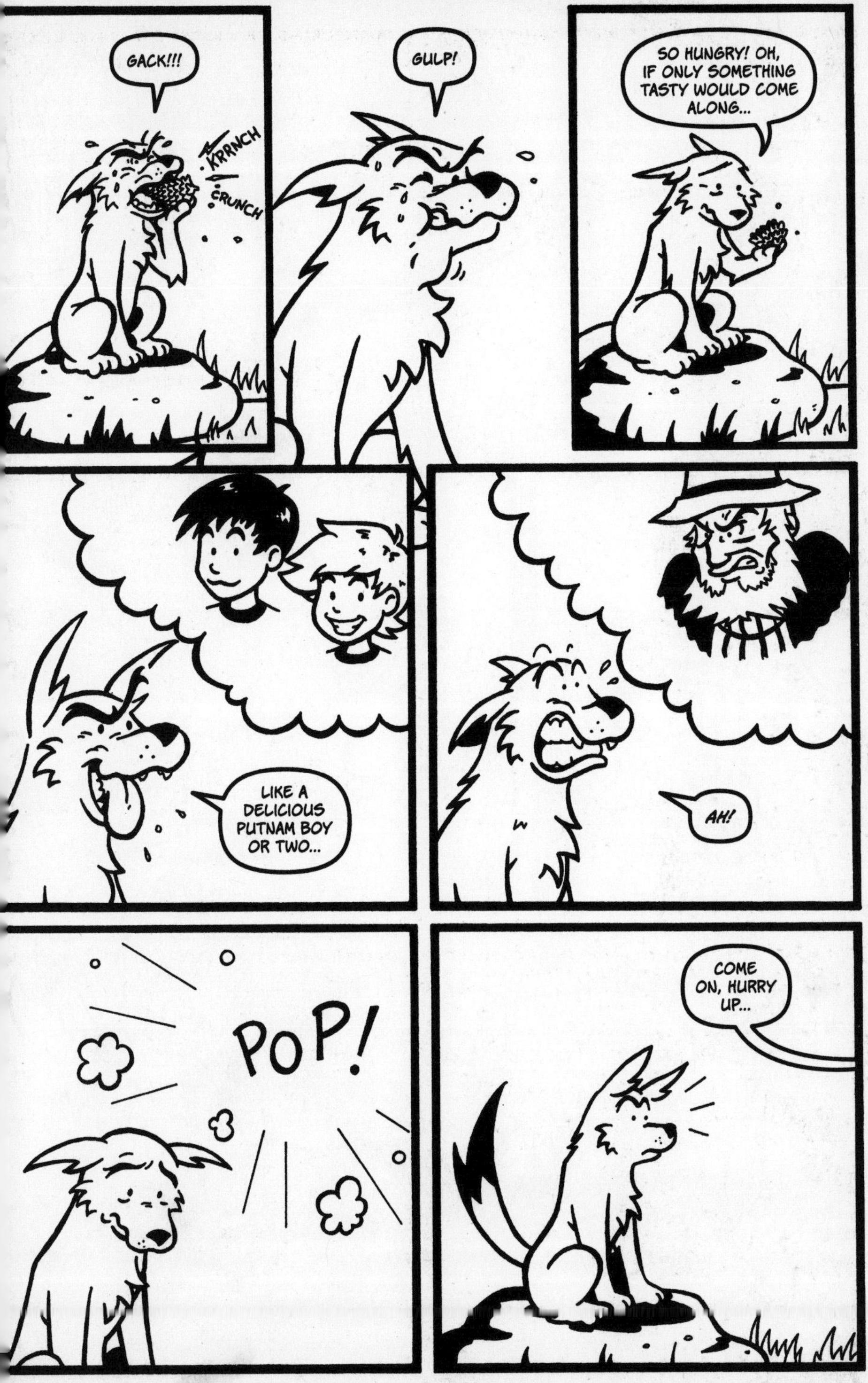
GACK!!!
KRRNCH
CRUNCH
GULP!
SO HUNGRY! OH, IF ONLY SOMETHING TASTY WOULD COME ALONG...
LIKE A DELICIOUS PUTNAM BOY OR TWO...
AH!
POP!
COME ON, HURRY UP...

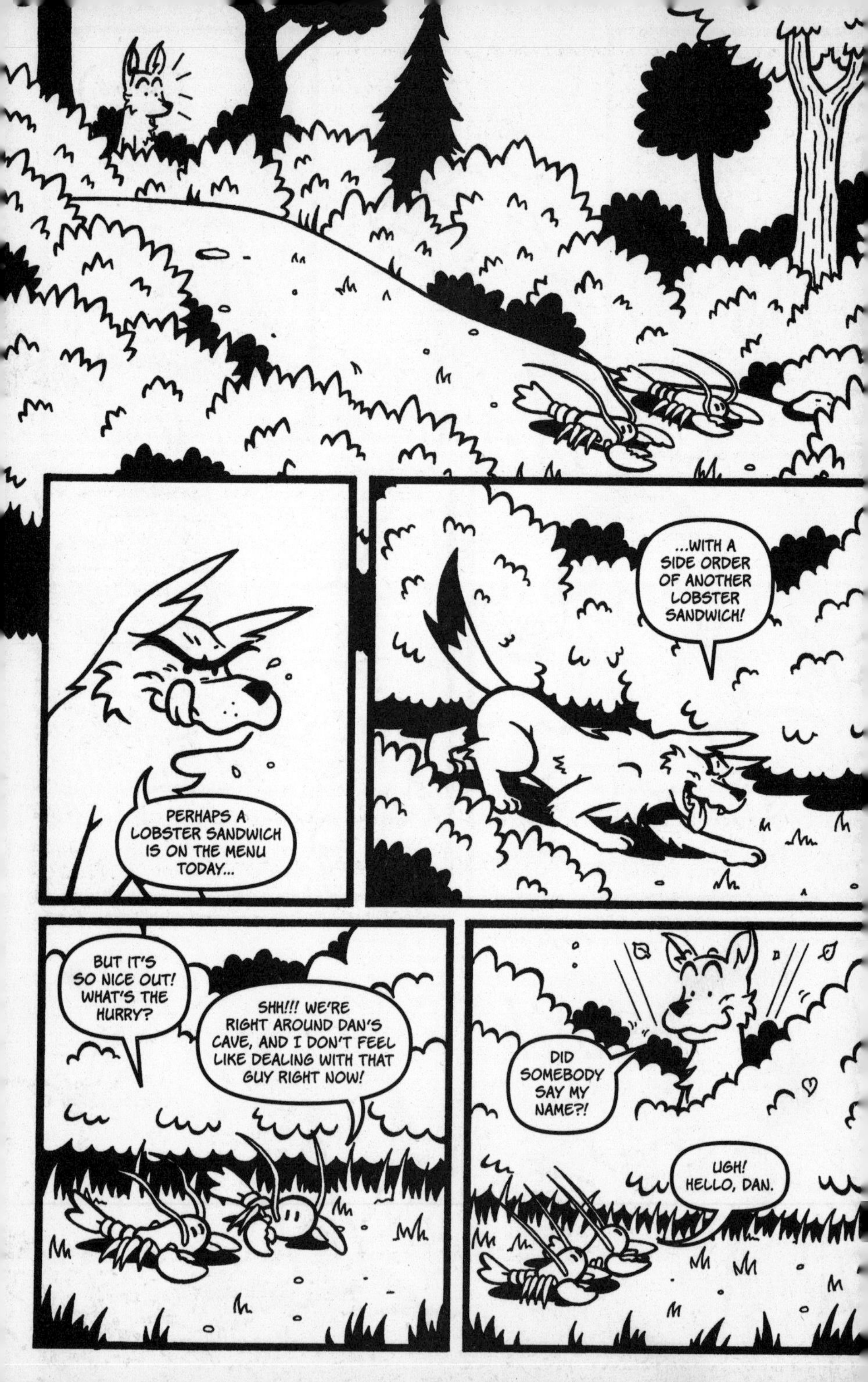
PERHAPS A LOBSTER SANDWICH IS ON THE MENU TODAY...
...WITH A SIDE ORDER OF ANOTHER LOBSTER SANDWICH!
BUT IT'S SO NICE OUT! WHAT'S THE HURRY?
SHH!!! WE'RE RIGHT AROUND DAN'S CAVE, AND I DON'T FEEL LIKE DEALING WITH THAT GUY RIGHT NOW!
DID SOMEBODY SAY MY NAME?!
UGH! HELLO, DAN.

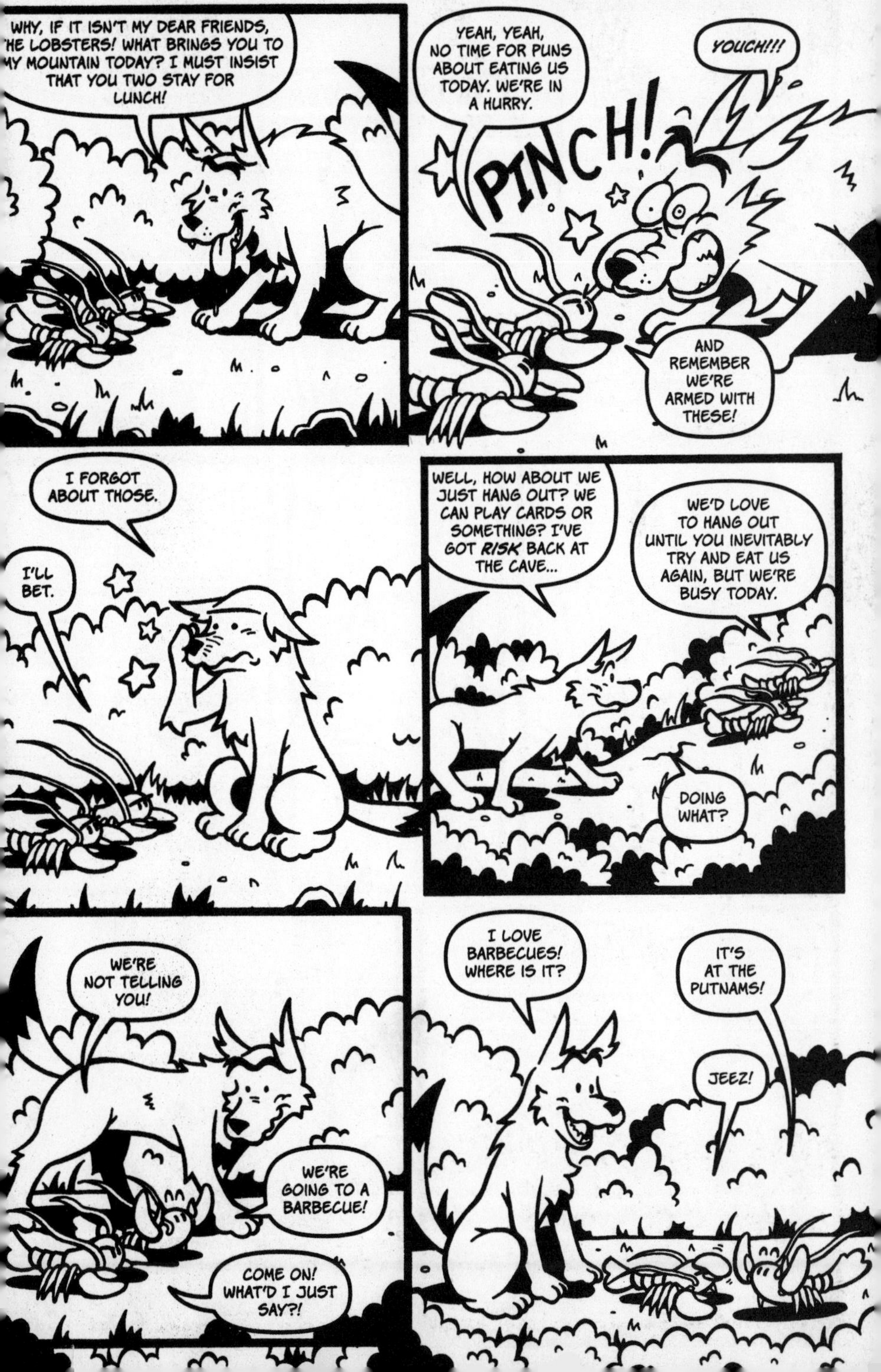
WHY, IF IT ISN'T MY DEAR FRIENDS, THE LOBSTERS! WHAT BRINGS YOU TO MY MOUNTAIN TODAY? I MUST INSIST THAT YOU TWO STAY FOR LUNCH!
YEAH, YEAH, NO TIME FOR PUNS ABOUT EATING US TODAY. WE'RE IN A HURRY.
PINCH!
YOUCH!!!
AND REMEMBER WE'RE ARMED WITH THESE!
I FORGOT ABOUT THOSE.
I'LL BET.
WELL, HOW ABOUT WE JUST HANG OUT? WE CAN PLAY CARDS OR SOMETHING? I'VE GOT RISK BACK AT THE CAVE...
WE'D LOVE TO HANG OUT UNTIL YOU INEVITABLY TRY AND EAT US AGAIN, BUT WE'RE BUSY TODAY.
DOING WHAT?
WE'RE NOT TELLING YOU!
WE'RE GOING TO A BARBECUE!
COME ON! WHAT'D I JUST SAY?!
I LOVE BARBECUES! WHERE IS IT?
IT'S AT THE PUTNAMS!
JEEZ!

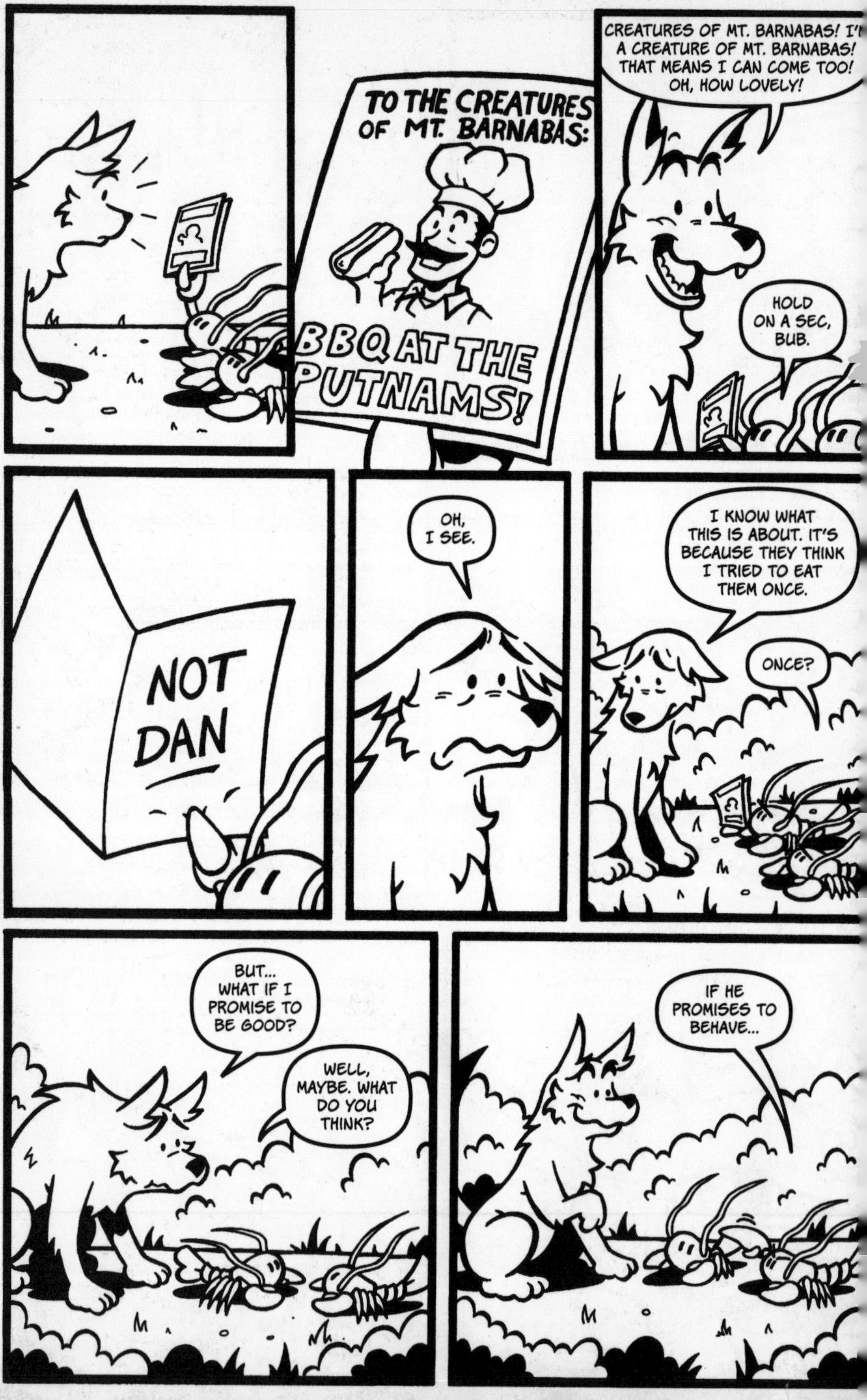
TO THE CREATURES OF MT. BARNABAS:
BBQ AT THE PUTNAMS!
CREATURES OF MT. BARNABAS! I'M A CREATURE OF MT. BARNABAS! THAT MEANS I CAN COME TOO! OH, HOW LOVELY!
HOLD ON A SEC, BUB.
NOT DAN
OH, I SEE.
I KNOW WHAT THIS IS ABOUT. IT'S BECAUSE THEY THINK I TRIED TO EAT THEM ONCE.
ONCE?
BUT... WHAT IF I PROMISE TO BE GOOD?
WELL, MAYBE. WHAT DO YOU THINK?
IF HE PROMISES TO BEHAVE...

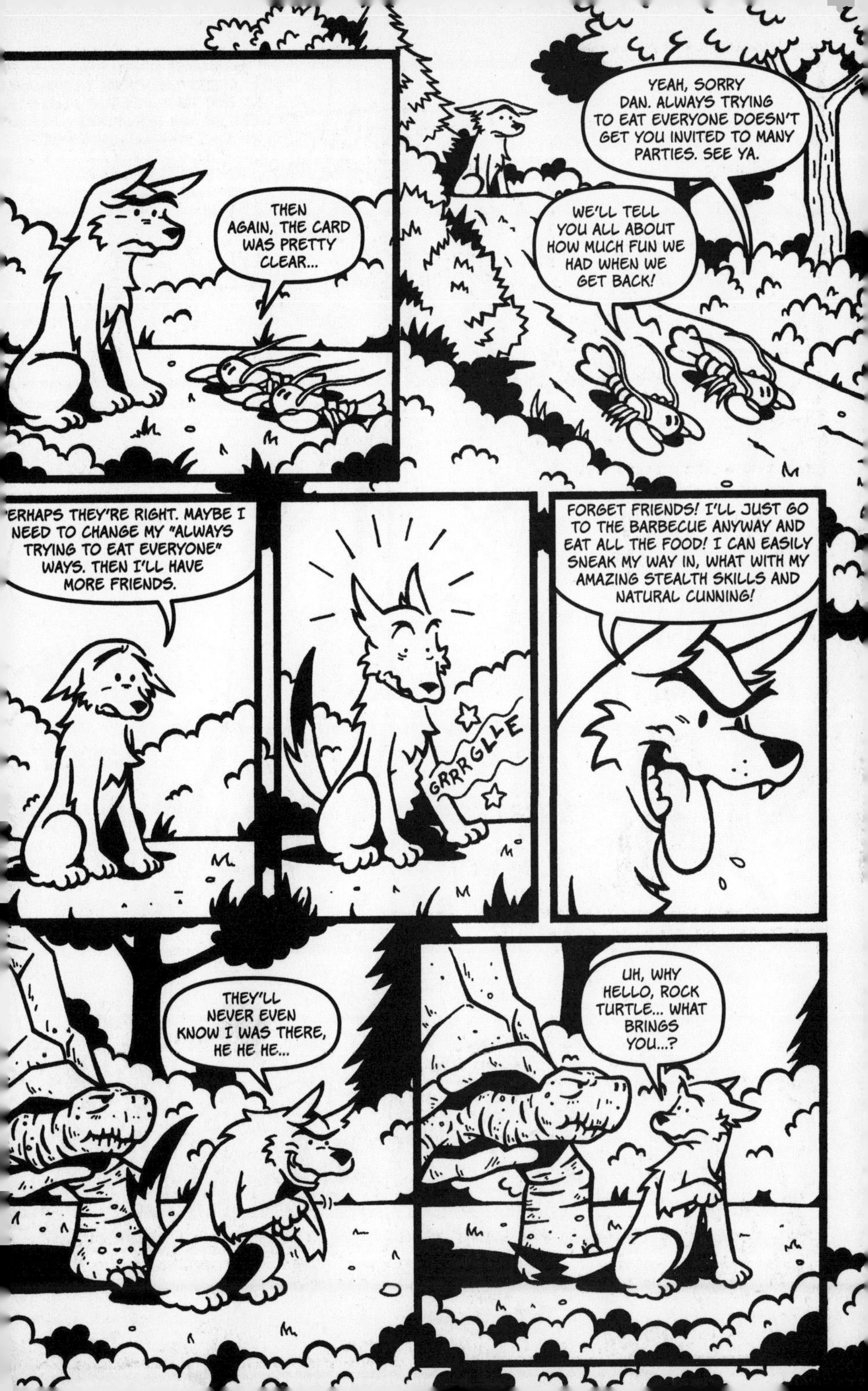
THEN AGAIN, THE CARD WAS PRETTY CLEAR...
YEAH, SORRY DAN. ALWAYS TRYING TO EAT EVERYONE DOESN'T GET YOU INVITED TO MANY PARTIES. SEE YA.
WE'LL TELL YOU ALL ABOUT HOW MUCH FUN WE HAD WHEN WE GET BACK!
ERHAPS THEY'RE RIGHT. MAYBE I NEED TO CHANGE MY "ALWAYS TRYING TO EAT EVERYONE" WAYS. THEN I'LL HAVE MORE FRIENDS.
GRRRGLLE
FORGET FRIENDS! I'LL JUST GO TO THE BARBECUE ANYWAY AND EAT ALL THE FOOD! I CAN EASILY SNEAK MY WAY IN, WHAT WITH MY AMAZING STEALTH SKILLS AND NATURAL CUNNING!
THEY'LL NEVER EVEN KNOW I WAS THERE, HE HE HE...
UH, WHY HELLO, ROCK TURTLE... WHAT BRINGS YOU...?

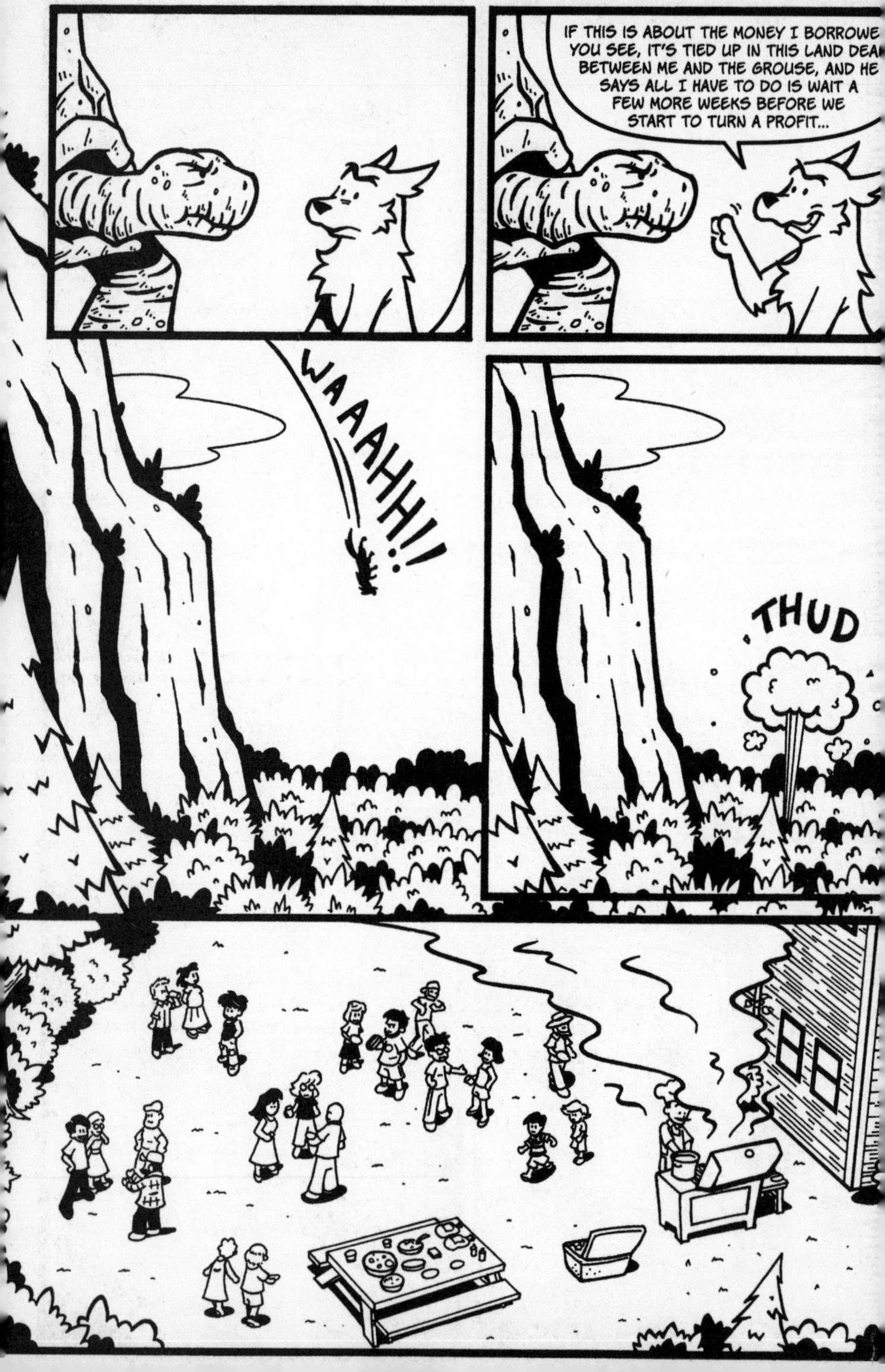
IF THIS IS ABOUT THE MONEY I BORROWE
YOU SEE, IT'S TIED UP IN THIS LAND DEA
BETWEEN ME AND THE GROUSE, AND HE SAYS ALL I HAVE TO DO IS WAIT A FEW MORE WEEKS BEFORE WE START TO TURN A PROFIT...
WAAAHH!!!
THUD

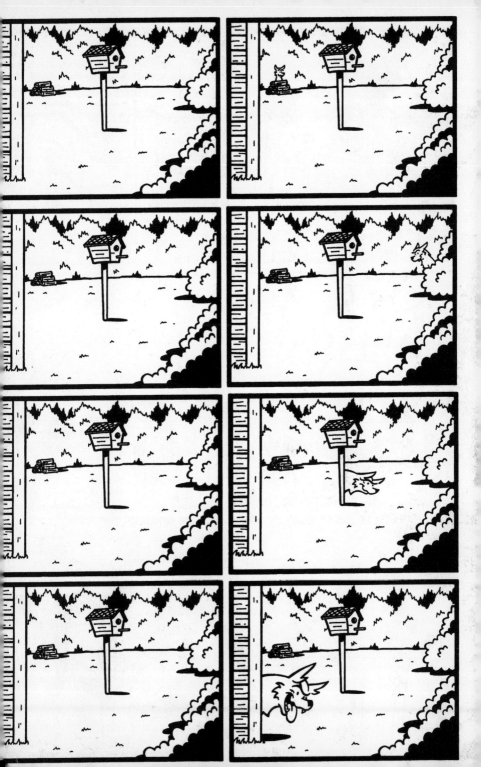

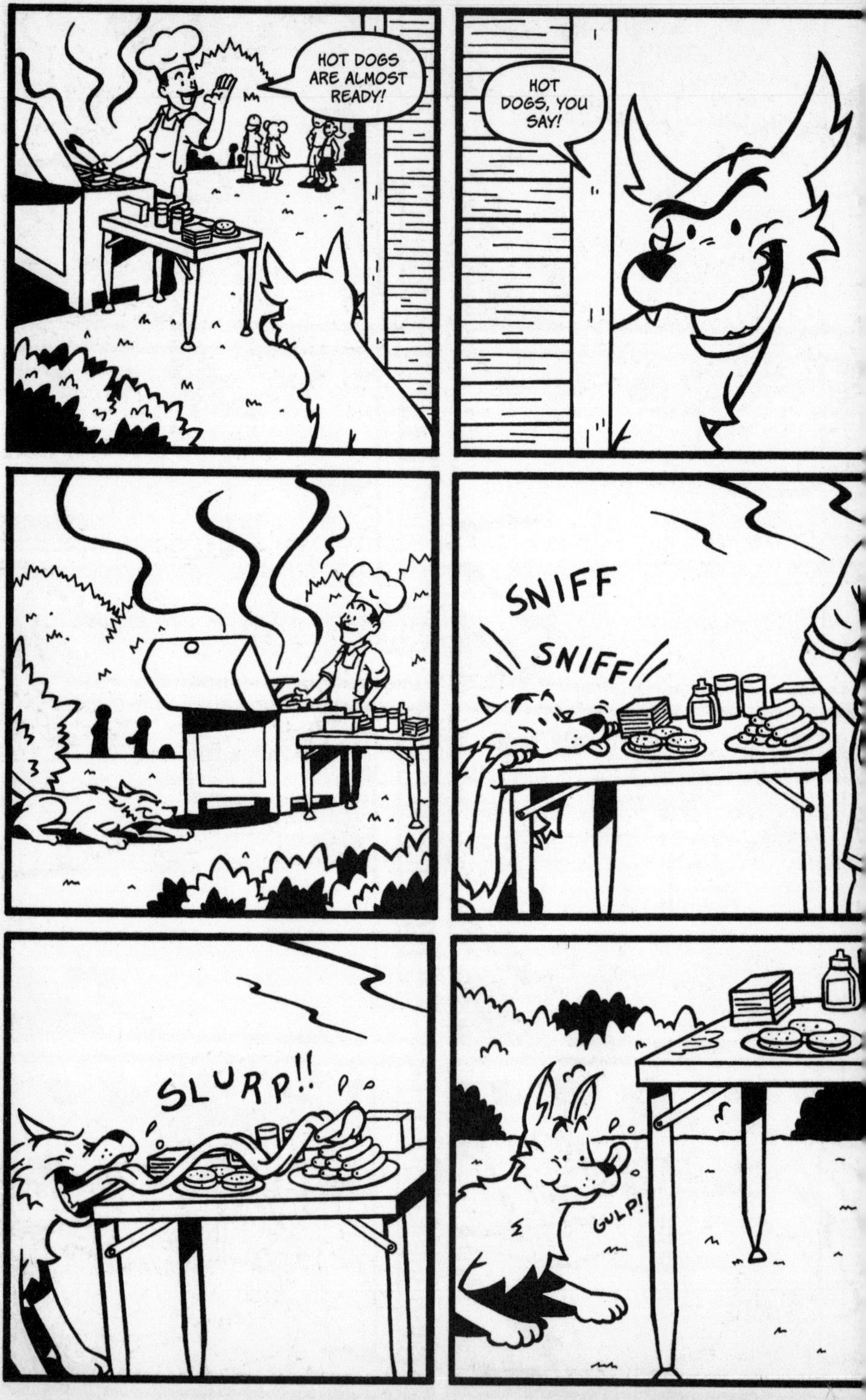
HOT DOGS ARE ALMOST READY!
HOT DOGS, YOU SAY!
SNIFF
SNIFF
SLURP!!
GULP!

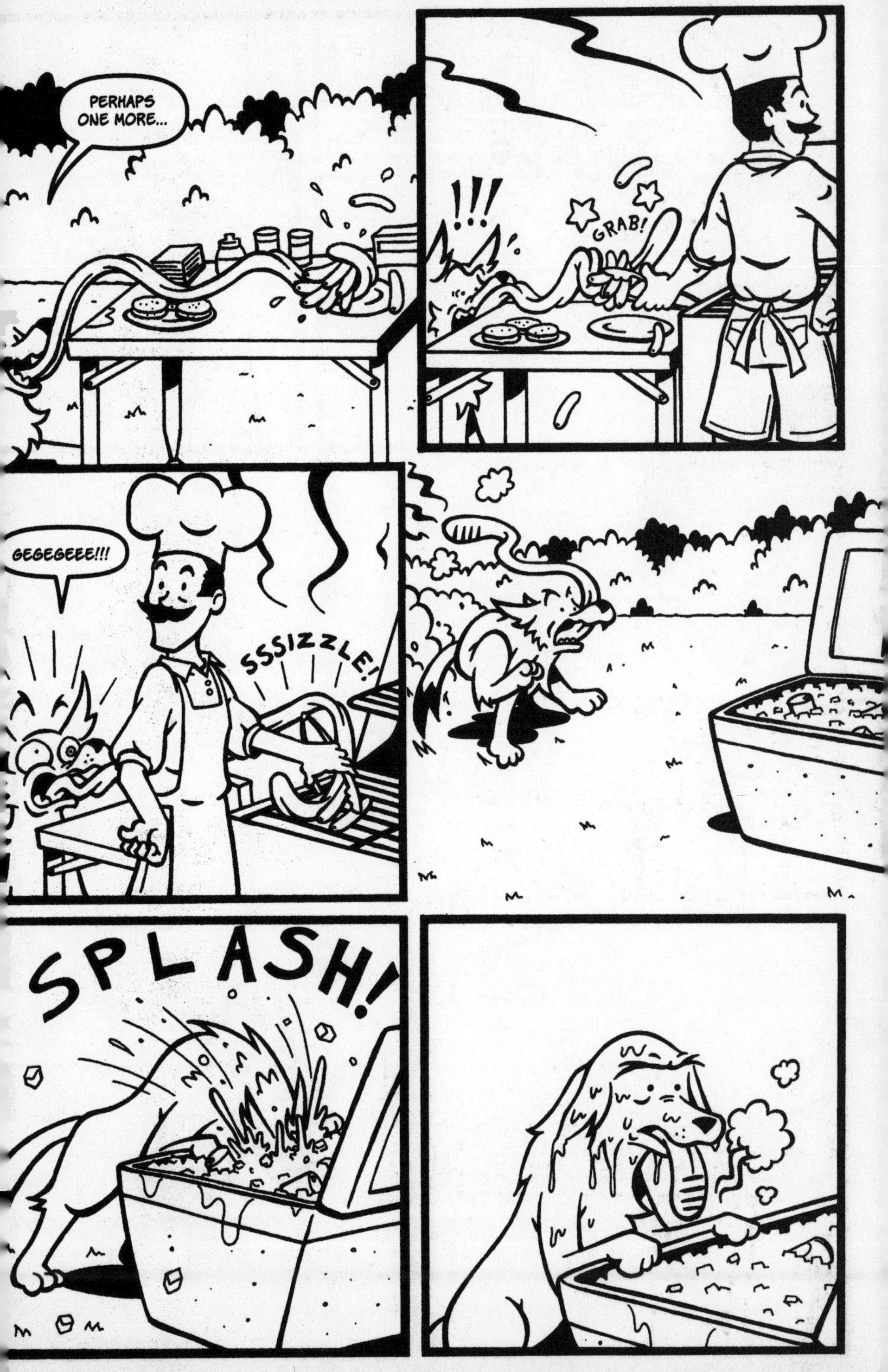
PERHAPS ONE MORE...
!!!
GRAB!
GEGEGEEE!!!
SSSIZZLE!
SPLASH!

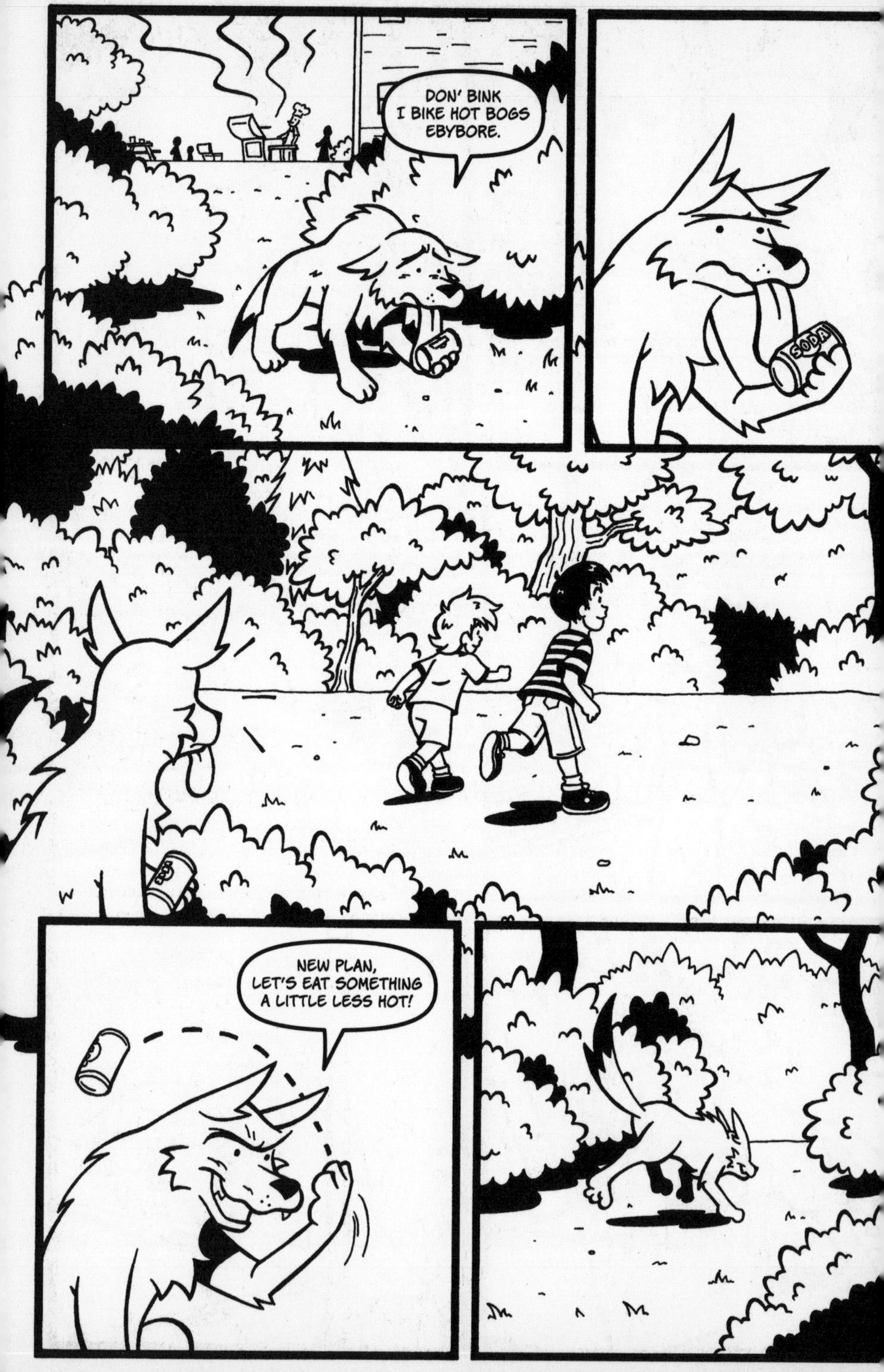
DON' BINK I BIKE HOT BOGS EBYBORE.
SODA
NEW PLAN, LET'S EAT SOMETHING A LITTLE LESS HOT!

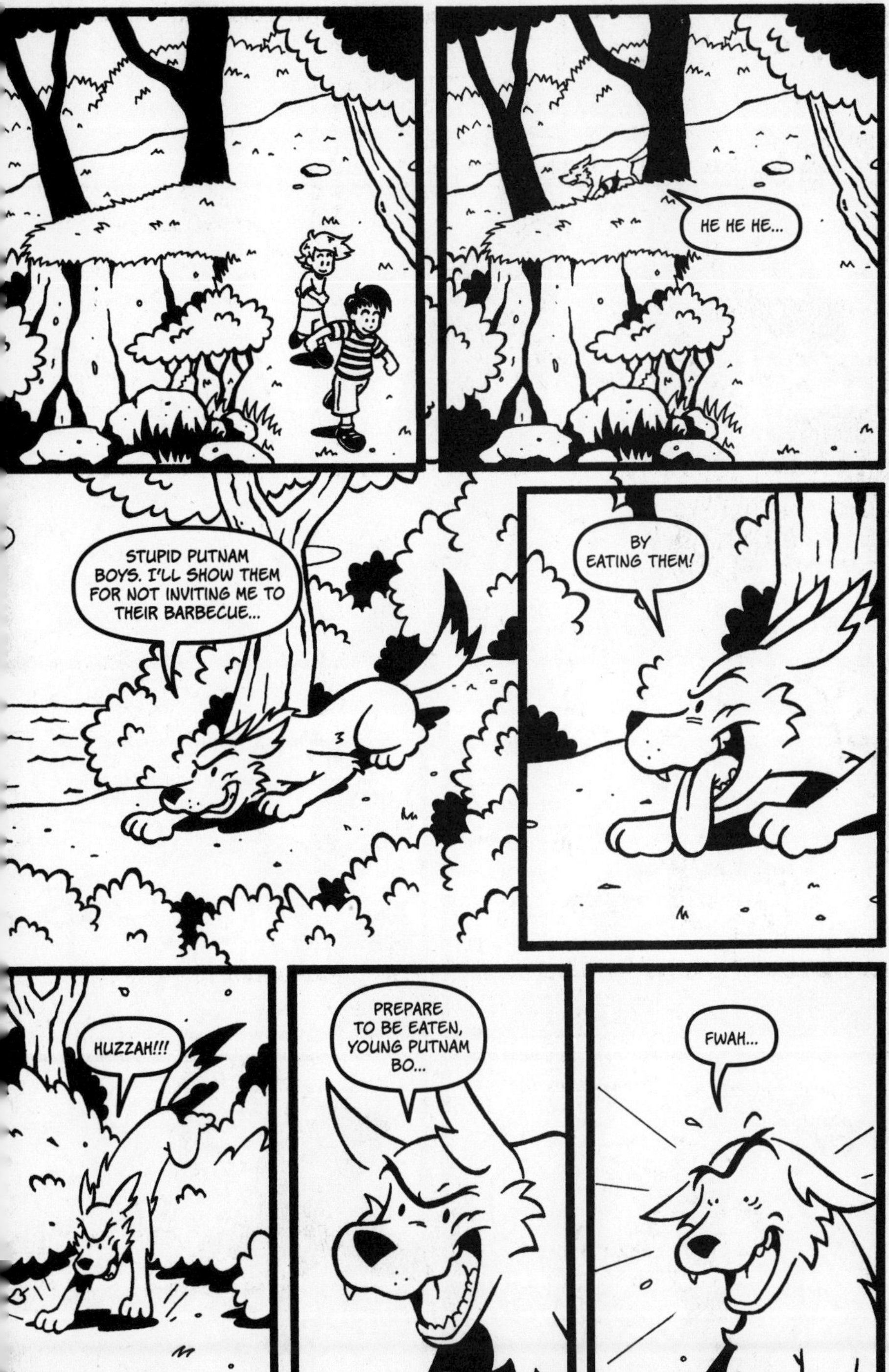
HE HE HE...
STUPID PUTNAM BOYS. I'LL SHOW THEM FOR NOT INVITING ME TO THEIR BARBECUE...
BY EATING THEM!
HUZZAH!!!
PREPARE TO BE EATEN, YOUNG PUTNAM BO...
FWAH...

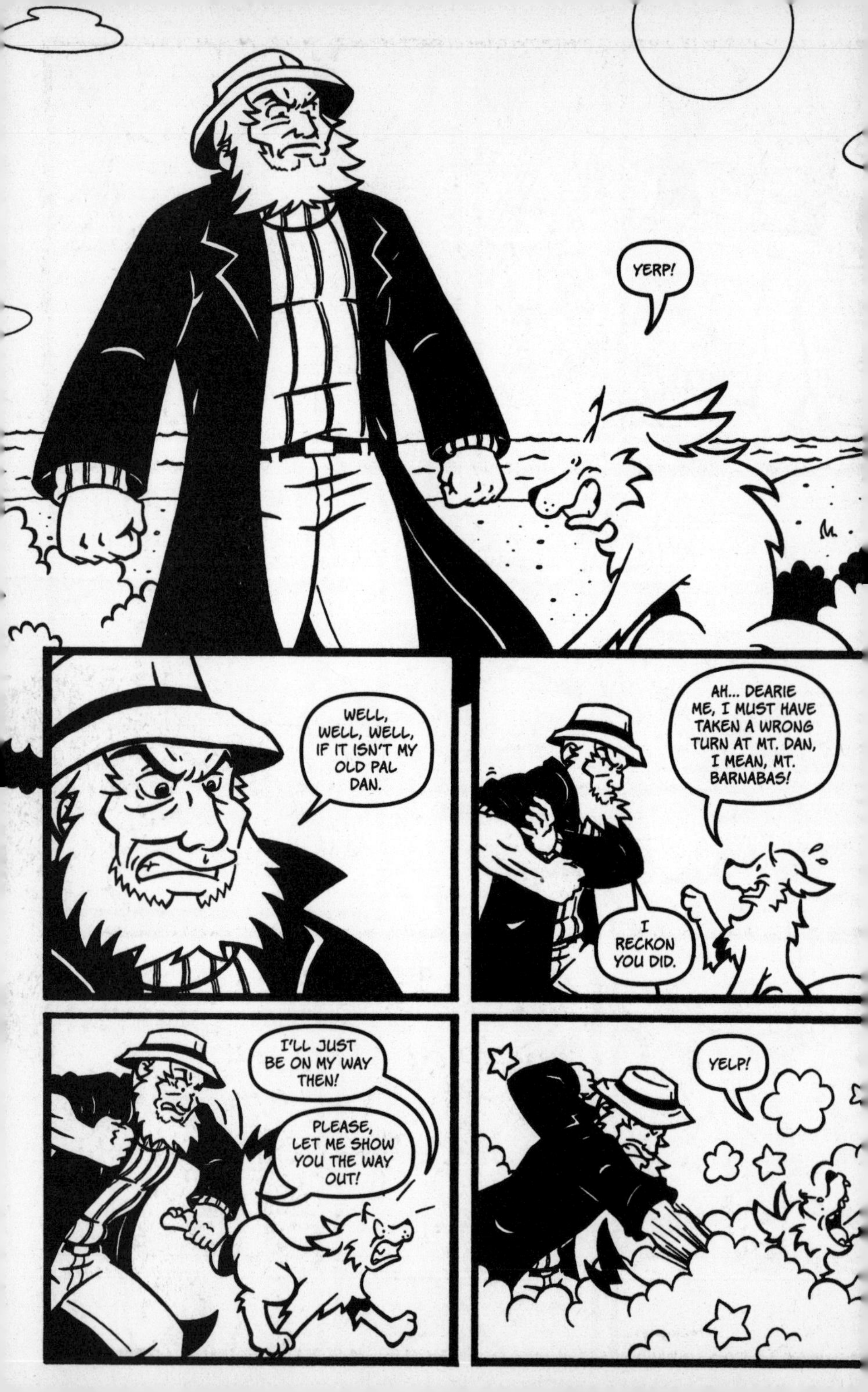
YERP!
WELL, WELL, WELL, IF IT ISN'T MY OLD PAL DAN.
AH... DEARIE ME, I MUST HAVE TAKEN A WRONG TURN AT MT. DAN, I MEAN, MT. BARNABAS!
I RECKON YOU DID.
I'LL JUST BE ON MY WAY THEN!
PLEASE, LET ME SHOW YOU THE WAY OUT!
YELP!

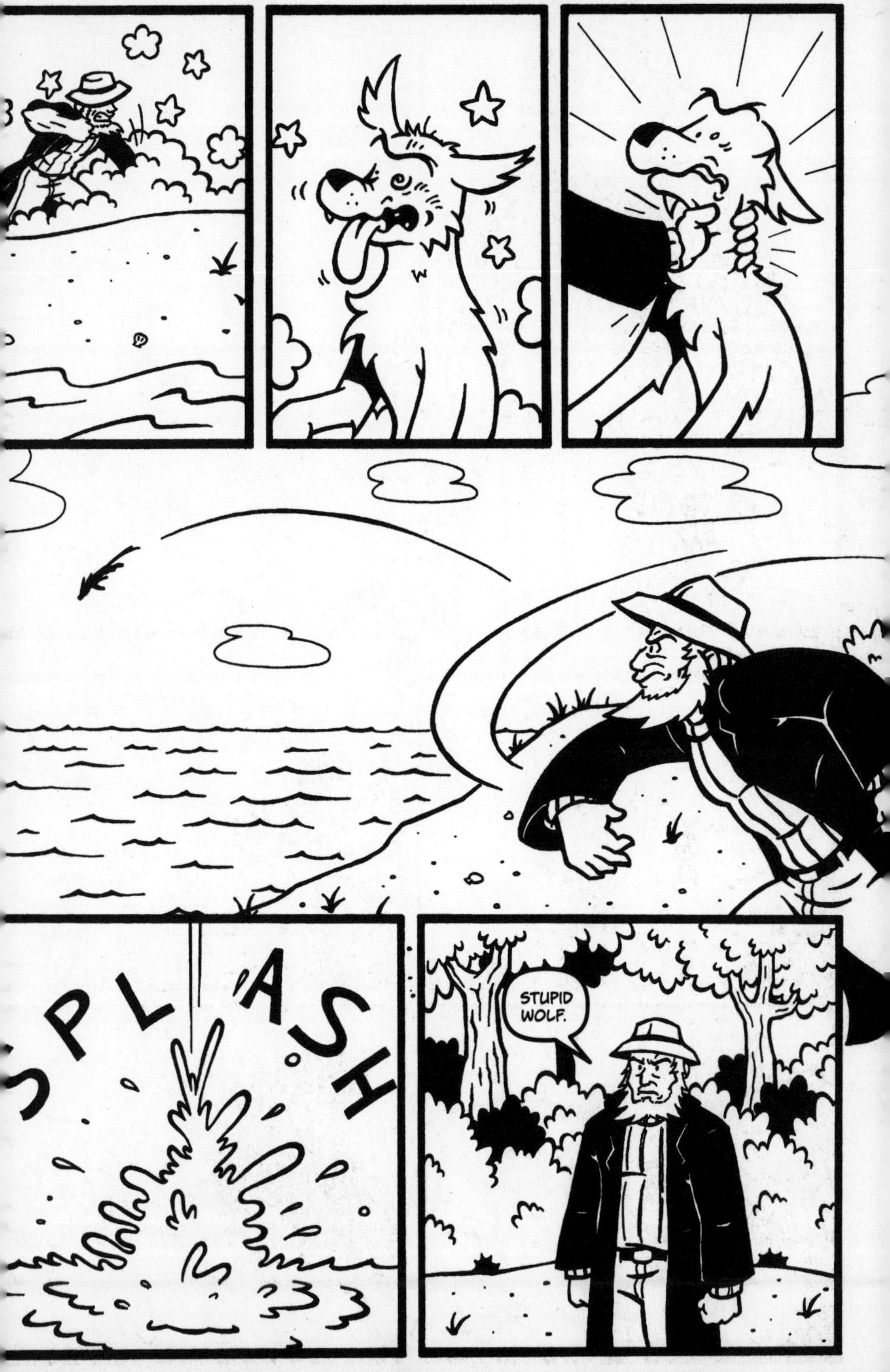
SPLASH
STUPID WOLF.

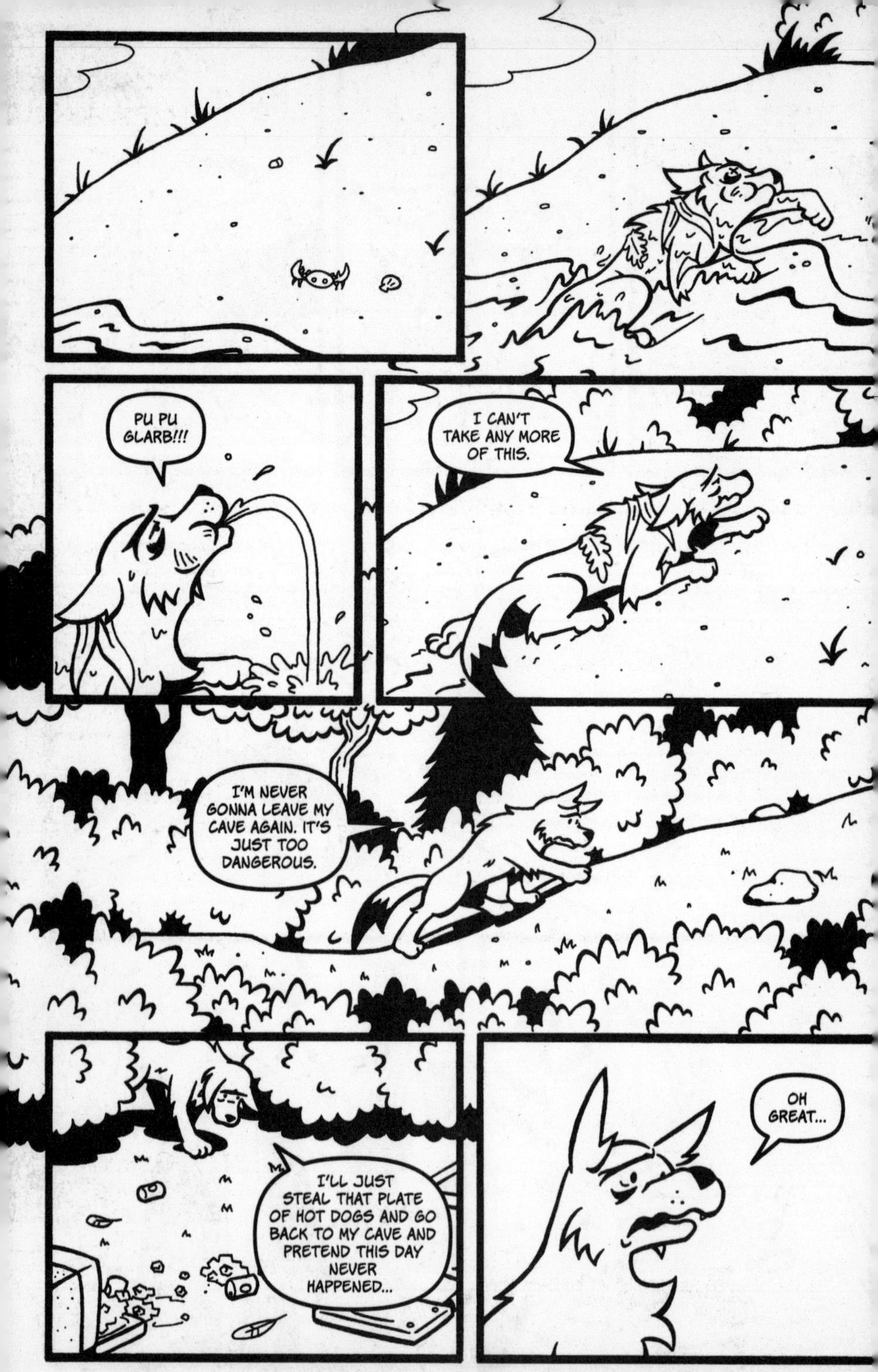
PU PU GLARB!!!
I CAN'T TAKE ANY MORE OF THIS.
I'M NEVER GONNA LEAVE MY CAVE AGAIN. IT'S JUST TOO DANGEROUS.
I'LL JUST STEAL THAT PLATE OF HOT DOGS AND GO BACK TO MY CAVE AND PRETEND THIS DAY NEVER HAPPENED...
OH GREAT...

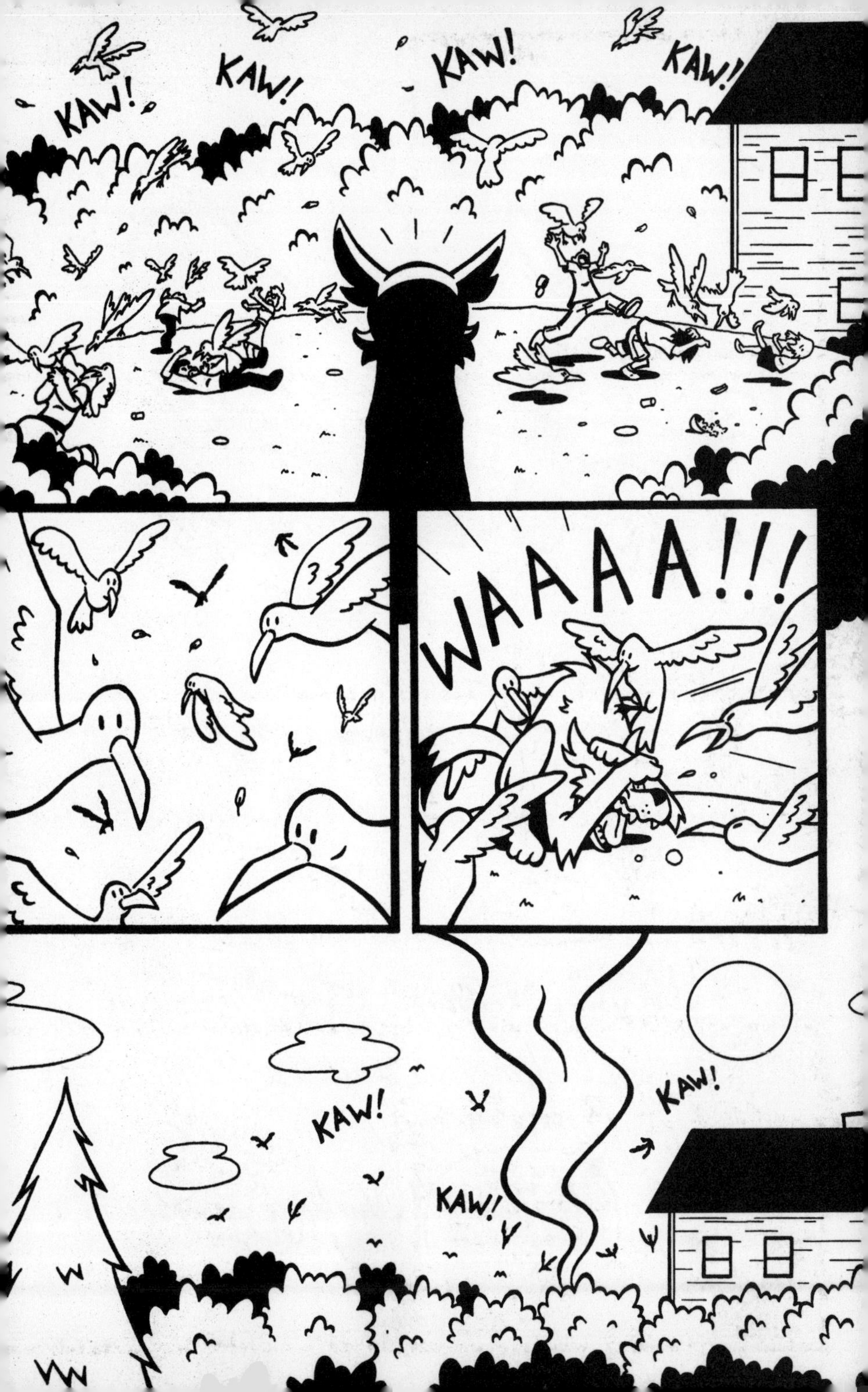
KAW!
KAW!
KAW!
KAW!
WAAAAA!!!
KAW!
KAW!
KAW!

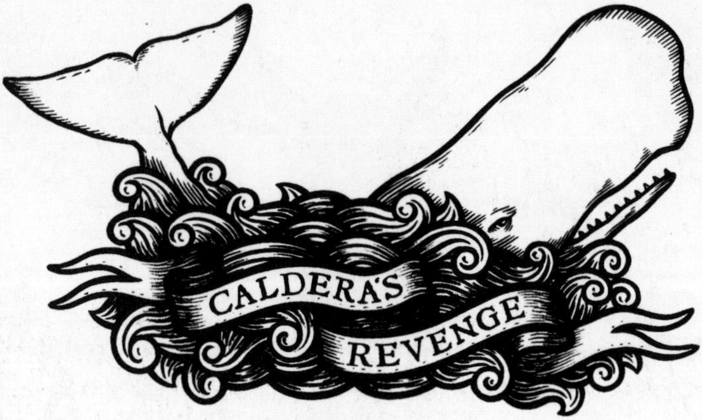
CALDERA'S REVENGE

PART 1

Special thanks to

Abby Denson and Brian Stone

and the resources of

Mystic Seaport: The Museum of America and the Sea

and the

New Bedford Whaling Museum

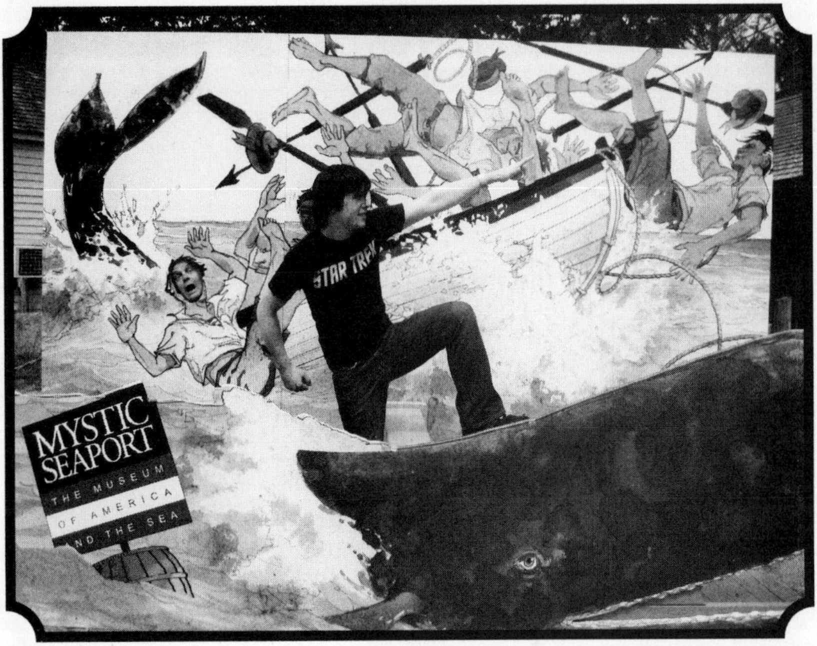
STAR TREK
MYSTIC SEAPORT
THE MUSEUM OF AMERICA AND THE SEA

Matthew Loux was born in Norwich, Connecticut and graduated from the School of Visual Arts, NYC, in 2001. He went on a whale watch as a kid where he got to see a humpback whale up close, and like many, is mildly preoccupied by the squid and whale diorama at the American Museum of Natural History (though his favorite is the T-Rex and Giant Ground Sloth skeleton). Matthew created the comic series SALT WATER TAFFY which was inspired by his youth spent in the New England countryside as well as vacationing in and around Maine with his family. In addition to the SALT WATER TAFFY series, Matthew also created the graphic novel SIDESCROLLERS, illustrated the graphic novel F-STOP, and illustrated the board comic GOOD NIGHT GABBALAND based on the popular TV program YO GABBA GABBA! Matthew was also the inker of the comic, STAR WARS ADVENTURES, HAN SOLO AND THE HOLLOW MOON OF KHORYA published by Dark Horse comics. Matthew resides in Brooklyn, NY.

OTHER BOOKS FROM MATTHEW LOUX...

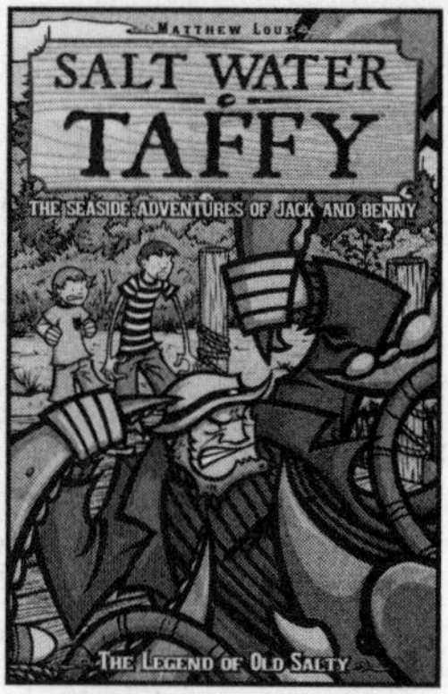
Matthew Loux
SALT WATER TAFFY
THE SEASIDE ADVENTURES OF JACK AND BENNY
The Legend of Old Salty

SALT WATER TAFFY, VOL. 1 - THE LEGEND OF OLD SALTY
By Matthew Loux
96 pages, digest, black & white
$5.99 US
ISBN: 978-1-932664-94-2

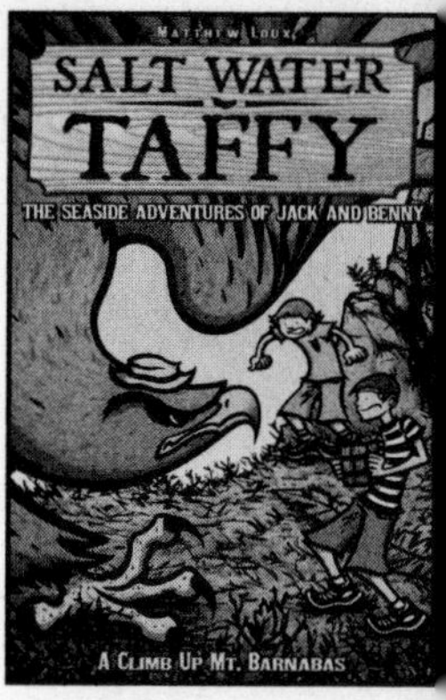
Matthew Loux
SALT WATER TAFFY
THE SEASIDE ADVENTURES OF JACK AND BENNY
A Climb Up Mt. Barnabas

SALT WATER TAFFY, VOL. 2 - A CLIMB UP MT. BARNABAS
By Matthew Loux
96 pages, digest, black & white
$5.99 US
ISBN: 978-1-934964-03-3

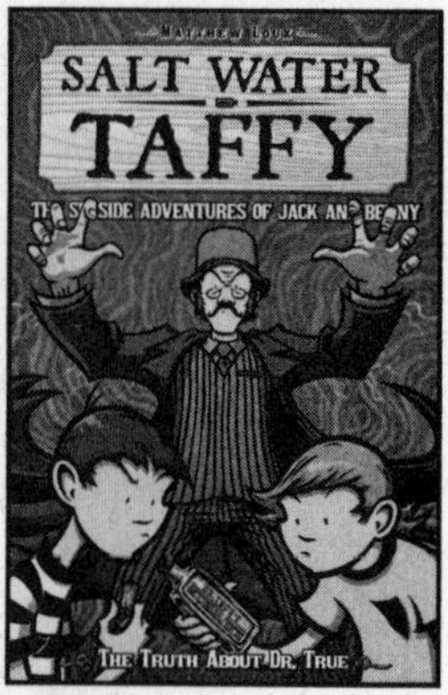
Matthew Loux
SALT WATER TAFFY
The Truth About Dr. True

SALT WATER TAFFY, VOL. 3 – THE TRUTH ABOUT DR. TRUE
By Matthew Loux
96 pages, digest, black & white
$5.99 US
ISBN 978-1-934964-04-0

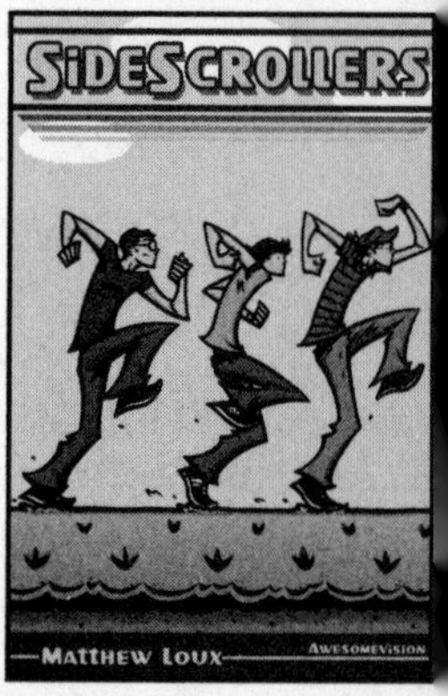
SIDESCROLLERS
Matthew Loux
Awesomevision

SIDESCROLLERS
By Matthew Loux
216 pages, digest, black & white
$11.95 US
ISBN 978-1-932664-50-8

Available at finer comics shops everywhere. For a comics store near you, call 1-888-COMIC-BOOK or visit www.comicshops.us.
For more Oni Press titles and information visit www.onipress.com.

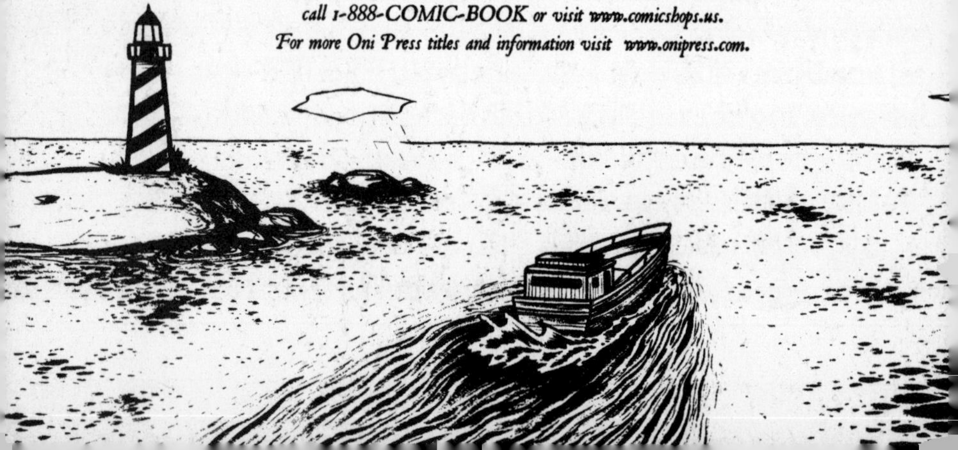